RURAL AND AGRARIAN SOCIAL STRUCTURE OF NEPAL

Rural and Agrarian Social Structure of Nepal

SOHAN R. YADAV

Commonwealth

Rural and Agrarian Social Structure of Nepal

ISBN : 81-7169-174-9

Edition : 2018

Published by :
COMMONWEALTH PUBLISHERS (P) LTD.
4831/24, Govind Lane,
Ansari Road, Darya Ganj,
New Delhi - 110002
Ph. : 23272541, 23242541
e-mail : commonwealthpublishers2016@gmail.com

Distributed by :
ARJUN PUBLISHING HOUSE
4831/24, Govind Lane,
Ansari Road, Darya Ganj,
New Delhi - 110002
Ph. : 23272541, 23242541
e-mail : arjunbooks2001@gmail.com

Laser Typesetting by :
Dimple Computers
Delhi

Printed at :
Balaji Digital
Delhi

Dedicated to

Shri Chandrajit Yadav (Member of Parliament) and Chairman, Centre for Social Justice for debts words cannot tell

Acknowledgements

Ever since I joined as Research Scientist 'B' in Sociology in the Department of Sociology, Banaras Hindu University, Varanasi, in 1986, I have been encouraged and inspired by a number of individuals and organisations. I acknowledge my thanks to the University Grants Commission for providing me this award which helped me carry on research work on the project: "Rural and Agrarian Social Structure of Nepal." I am thankful to the Librarian and other officials of the Central Library, Tribhuvan University, Kathmandu; Librarian, APROSC[1] Library, Kathmandu, and the functionaries of CEDA,[2] CNAS,[3] ADB/N[4] and Agriculture and Marketing Service Centre, Kathmandu. Most of the geographical data tables have been taken from Ram Kumar Panday, *Altitude Geography of Nepal* (Lalitpur: Centre for Altitude Geography, 1987). I am very grateful for the assistance provided by Prof. S.K. Srivastava, Prof. G.S. Kushwaha, Prof. R.R. Tripathi, Prof. Sharan, the successive Directors of the Centre for the Study of Nepal, Banaras Hindu University. To Shri Chandrajit Yadav, Member of Parliament, I owe special gratitude for being a continuous source of inspiration. My thanks are also due to Mr. P.N. Singh and his son Dr. Charu Sheel Singh (Research Scientist 'B' in English, Kashi Vidyapith) for

1. Agricultural Projects Service Centre.
2. Centre for Economic Development and Administration.
3. Centre for Nepal and Asian Studies.
4. Agriculture Development Bank of Nepal.

providing me practical help in the formulation and carrying out the work undertaken here. I owe a lifelong gratitude to Prof. S. Tripathi, Head, Dept. of Sociology, B.H.U., Varanasi, who has always been kind, resourcefully supportive and magnanimous. The supervisor of my Ph.D. doctoral research, Dr. H. C. Srivastava, Prof. of Sociology, B.H.U., has very kindly been inspiring and advising me and I owe so much to him. Dr. Umesh Chandra Rai's friendly help during the course of the progress of my work is duly acknowledged. Finally, I wish to express the inexpressible—my eternal debt to my wife Sushila Yadav, son Manaswi Kumar and daughter Namṛta, for their affection, fortitude and for seeing the work through to many an agonising moment.

SOHAN R. YADAV

Preface

Nepal is a country characterised both by inter-regional and international migration. It is situated just north of India and is one of the neighbouring nation like Pakistan in West, Bangladesh in East and Sri Lanka in South. All these countries were sometimes part of the great Indian peninsula. They possess a common culture. India's relations, however, with all these neighbours are of different nature. Pakistan is an Islamic country having fundamentalist approach to religion, while India is a secular country and has respect for all religions. So, relations with Pakistan have always been a constraint. The relations with Bangladesh and Sri Lanka too are different in nature and they follow only the path privileged to them. But Nepal is the Kingdom, a country, a nation, and at best a neighbour India can justifiably be proud of.

Nepal has never been subjected to foreign rule. Before unification, in the time of Prithvi Narayan Shah, it was ruled by various local principalities. It is also a Hindu Nation. Indian and Nepalese people enjoy the same ethics of religion and make free and frequent visits of each other's temples and Pagodas. There is no barricading on the border. Right through the ancient past, both countries have been practising a common culture. Their religious books, caste system and manners of practising religious and social customs are identical.

The southern part of Nepal called Tarai is very common in nature with India's Gangetic plains. The topography, climate, agriculture, man and his social attitude towards life and religion, is so common that it is impossible to distinguish the people of Tarai from those of the Gangetic plain if they stand at one place. Nepal Tarai has only been inhabited for the last two to three hundred years or so. Most of the inhabitants are Indians migrated to this land due to various reasons discussed in the chapter on migration. It is the Tarai region which has made both countries to have access to courtyards of each other's houses. Affinity and emotional tie is very strong. Since Nepal is a totally land-locked country, her passage to the outside world is only through India. This factor cemented our friendship.

The present work is more or less a groundwork to understand the Tarai of Nepal. This is supposed to supplement my research project on the Rural and Agrarian Social Structure of Nepal.

How a particular type of rural social structure did emerge and how it is transformed? What are the emerging rural attitudes today? What is the mode of economic and social developments during the past hundred years? How the Indian ethnic groups enjoy the socio-political status in Nepal? These are the theoretical issues which have been analysed in this research study.

I have given a brief account of Asian diplomacy and Nepal's part played in Indian diplomacy with East India Company prior to independence. Ancient and Eastern monarchs who were either ruling in Eastern Tarai or were living on the land very close to Tarai have also influenced the making of the past economically active, politically alive, with the day-to-day problems. On many occasions, I have made references of accounts available in the books and notes of British historians, thinkers, and administrators.

Tarai land was sometimes called 'Kala Banjar' as it was very densely forested and it was difficult for a sun-ray to penetrate through trees and shrubs. It was a land of Malaria. Nobody could muster courage to enter this land. Any one who dared was attacked by malarial fever and he could not recover again. As such this vast belt of Nepal remained a virgin land and is called 'Death valley'. It was really a defence wall for both countries—Nepal and India. No infiltration could be possible from either side.

However, in the advent of Muslim invasions in India, some Rajput principalities along with Brahmins fled from India and entered Tarai either from Pithoragarh side or from Eastern side. They settled here permanently. It was not only a simple case of migration from India but it was actually the beginning of an era or stream which played a giant role in carrying out the history of Tarai and Nepal both.

Through this Tarai region an important phenomena is to be observed that religion and Indian culture travelled upward right up to Tibet and China. Mansarovar is the remotest point of importance to Indian people both geographically and religiously. Mukti Nath a Hindu Shrine is near the border of Tibet. Kathmandu valley has many sacred places of Hindus as well as Buddhists. Pashupatinath, Gyoheshwari, Teleju, Surji Vinayaka Ganesh, Changu Narayan are Hindu temples. In the same manner Swayambhu Nath, Buddha Nath, Mahabuddha etc. are Buddhist temples. Here in Nepal Hindus and Buddhists practise their religion without any interference. The followers of both religions live with perfect harmony and brotherhood. No dispute could be traced in the pages of history between these two religious followers.

The other important point is that Chinese and Tibetan Scholars entered India through Nepal. They wrote much about India. It is their writings which have given a chronological clue to the history of the Indian people.

There are other examples in the world which are identical with Nepal, like Switzerland and Afghanistan. Both are mountainous countries. Both have borrowed their language and culture from neighbouring countries. Switzerland is socially and linguistically divided into Teutonic and Latin languages (including French and Italian groups). So also Afghanistan has Turkish population in the North speaking Turkoman dialect and Aryan population in the West speaking Persian, while Indo-Aryans in the rest of the country speak Pushto.

Similarly Nepal is the meeting point of Tibetan and

Indian languages and races. Here we find that mass immigration which changes the racial and linguistic composition takes places from higher altitudes to lower altitudes or from colder places to warmer ones, whereas culture and religion have travelled upward. For example Tibetan immigrants have brought influence of mongoloid languages but the religion and people that travelled upward to Tibet and China are Buddhist, and along with them travelled Sanskrit and Pali languages, and of course, Indian culture.

The other main influences of Indian civilization, Indian culture, religion and language, have been seen very much in the Tarai people. In the rural development of Tarai, Indian ways of agriculture, social manners, putting of cottage industries, making of passable routes for approaching markets etc. are the other factors which cannot be ignored.

The Geography of Tarai has been separately added to appreciate the method of this study. Agricultural factors and Indian ethnic groups living in Tarai have been put into intensive study. What is the contribution of this group in the social and economical order of Nepal? What is the thinking of Indian ethnic groups for national integration? How far they have assimilated themselves in the society of other Nepali citizens? What contribution they have made in socio-political conditions of Nepal? How they are being regarded as citizens of Nepal or as outsiders? How the "Kala Banjar" virgin land area having population vacuum was filled by Indian origin people and other migrants? All these factors have been studied in detail in different chapters. For up-to-date information many statistical data have been produced. A separate chapter to depict the overall activities of agriculture and holdings and average production has been added to present economic activity behaviour of Tarai people in particular.

Since Nepal is a land-locked country, it is the moral duty of India to look after the interest or transit of Nepal. Our relations with Nepal have always been cordial. Leaving aside all the political situations, Nepalese and Indian people have the same religion and culture; therefore they cannot remain isolated for long. Many Nepali citizens are members of our defence forces and many are serving in different capacities all over India without the challenge of law of citizenship. Likewise Indian people too visit Nepal either for religious pilgrimage, for temporary or casual work or for business without any visa on either side. The tie of brotherhood between the two countries is very firm. This study reveals the facts not known to Indian people so far. This study contains varied problems which are found in any nation. But Nepal as a country with varied topography, climate, land formation, has many such elements which are not traceable in other nations. Therefore, I have made the study knowledgable by giving all the details in chapters needed for the general appreciation.

Geography, border problems, migration-factors, agriculture, horticulture of both Nepal and Tarai region have been discussed. A vast study of Indian origin people living in Tarai has been done to apprise as to what way these ethnic groups are treated in Nepal? The socio-political, linguistic, economical and hierarchical ranking of Indian ethnic people, economic development through these people—all such factors have been discussed in different chapters. This study, therefore, may not be exhaustive but it attempts to impart a lot of information with reference to Nepal and Tarai.

SOHAN R. YADAV

Contents

1

Brief History of Nepal and Her Relations with India

Sources

Nepal's history before sixteenth century was surrounded in mist. The sources were examined many times, but nothing could come out definite as level of education and interest of finding historical events were both absent from the minds of Nepali people. However, the process of foreign people coming to Nepal and interacting with the people, generally commenced in the 19th century. Sylvian Levi in his book 'Documents on Nepal' did a great job. He tried to collect sources and evidence through various means. In 'Documents on Nepal' he has categorised these sources into four main bases namely Chinese, Tibetans, European and indigenous. As he was a great exponent of different languages he also tried to find the chronology of Nepal's history from the records (written) of Chinese and Tibetans.

After Levi no serious efforts were made for revealing the problems of Nepal's history. Sri K. P. Jayaswal, Basak and Majumdar of India did pay their attention towards the history of Nepal. For early history study had to be made on inscriptions, coins and writings of Chinese and Tibetan Buddhist travellers.

The second important source is *Vanshavali.* It is presumed that it is the most authentic document regarding National History of Nepal. It provides the names of different princes of the different dynasties, but this document lacks the time factor for historical certainties. Like *Puranas* of India *Vanshavali* consists of many questionable elements. It reveals that some princes rule for thousand years and some for hundred years. Sometimes only names of rulers and dynastic heads have been mentioned. As such, this confusing state makes one to infer that no correct system and time could be evolved to depict the chronology. On many occasions it is evident that two or more authorities were ruling at the same time. This makes the matter quite confusing.

However, *Vanshavali* is the most important document to find out the link of Nepalese history after 15th century. This document gives us substantially the reliable and accurate account of the Malla Kings of the Valley of Bagmati and Gorakha Kings of Sahi dynasty.[1]

The indigenous description accounted for in the *Vanshavali* is quite elaborate for the period before Prithvi Narayan repeated conquests. Thereafter, Father Giuseppe, who had himself been involved to witness many incidents, had given descriptions of events in his book[2] written on Nepal in volume II of *Asiatic Researches*, 1769. By reading these two accounts, *Vanshavali* and Father Giuseppe's book, we get a fairly accurate picture of the events leading to the establishment of Gorakha dynasty in Nepal.

Enough material is also available through the books and accounts recorded in the history of East India Company. Whenever acute problems cropped up between Presidency of Bengal and Nepal the records were maintained for political events and secret orders in a progressive way. In these documents a lot of information is available as to how transfer of boundary dispute arose with East India Company which

1. Wright, Danial, History of Nepal, Cambridge, 1877, translated by S.S. Singh and Gunanand.
2. Father Giuseppe, 'Description of Kingdom of Nepal', in Asiatic Researches, Vol. II, 1769.

ultimately led to war in 1814. These documents also reveal the policies of Lord Hastings, his strategy for the war of Nepal. After 1816 it is seen that Nepal could not draw good attention from British writers. However, random record regarding intrigues in Kathmandu Darbar for dispatches of the residents is available in reference to Gardener 1816-1829, Hodgson 1829-31, 1833-43 and Major H. Lawerence from 1843-46.

On diplomatic side enough details are available from the 'Treatise, Engagements and Sanads' of Aitchison, but unfortunately we know such documents were not maintained in Kathmandu Darbar. David Ochterlong's account in Ludhiana papers gives a good account of the part played by Amar Singh Thapa in negotiating the proceedings of Nepal war. So when Nepal was in continuous communication with East India Company many residents lived in Kathmandu and have written stray accounts. Brian Hodgson had only stayed in Nepal for about 20 years first as assistant and later as British resident in the court of Kathmandu. He is the only writer who tried to pen down conditions of Nepal subjects their natural history, geographical situation, social order, languages and religions of Nepal and customs. Unfortunately he did not write a comprehensive book on Nepal, it may be due to his engagements otherwise.

Ample information is, however, available from the number of accounts written by British residents and surgeons who had chance of posting in Kathmandu Darbar. For example, the exhaustive and detailed accounts can be read regarding the prime ministers of Nepal in the two volumes kept in London's library.

In brief, the main sources for getting the information regarding Nepal's history which can be relied upon are the following :

1. Sanskrit books—Epics, Kalidas' *Meghdoot* and *Puranas*
2. Chinese memoirs of travellers
3. Europeans' documents
4. East India Company's records

5. Coins and inscriptions of different times
6. Secondary books of History, written by Historians of India, Britain and other countries.
7. Reference books like Census Reports, Gazetteers, Pamphlets, Journals, also give a floodlight for infering History of Nepal.

List of reference books and reports/records needed in briefing the history is appended in the end. The purpose for brief description is that the object of this thesis is not history, but history has relevance in drawing out social conclusions.

Ancient History of Nepal

The knowledge of early history of Nepalis is available through the book edited by Daniel Wright, a resident surgeon who lived in Kathmandu from 1863 to 1876. This book was translated by Munshi Shiv Shanker Singh and Pandit Guranand. The knowledge is supplemented by the descriptions of Chinese Buddhist pilgrims, who visited the sacred places of their religion in Nepal and India through Nepal.

This indigenous record is just similar to the Sanskrit, Pali and Prakrat literature of India. The tune of *Puranas* is identical here too. In the very first sentence it reveals the rhythm of old fashioned writings on India. For example, "The valley on the southern side of snowy range, which is within Sumeru (The Himalayas) was created by *Ishwar* (who emanated from the great *Ishwar*, the first Buddha...) was formerly known as Naghrad i.e., the tank of the serpent God."[1] Here who was the serpent God ? The idea may be indicative of Lord Shiva, the legendary God associated with serpents, whose abode is still believed to be the great Himalayas.

It is, therefore, inferred that the valley of Nepal was a big lake in about 2000-1500 B. C. At that period the valley must have been infested by Himalayan water-snakes. This lake was visited by Indian and Chinese sages from time to time as is being done in the present case of Mansarovar. There

1. Danial Wright, *History of Nepal*, p. 77.

should have been enchanting beauty in this Naghrid lake to attract wandering sages from South and North. An area of roughly 500 square metres where this lake is supposed to be situated at high altitude must have been heart-ennobling with charmic beauty par excellence. Indian philosophers and religious *yogis*, *sadhaks* found this lake not conducive for their spiritual practices.

The parbatiya History records that in very early times a sage named Bipaswi came to the lake from the city, known as Bandhumati and resided there in the mountains which he called as 'Jat Matrochcha' (Nagarjun).[1] Later a Sikhi Buddha came and resided for some time and called the mountain as Dhyanochcha (Champadevi) because of the meditation of Sadhana practised by this sage on this very mountain. The third sage Bishwabhu Buddha also came there from the same country called Anupam and stayed at the mountain which he called as Phulchok. It was about this time that the hillock on which Swaymbhunath temple is built first showed itself above the surface of the water and sage Bishwabhu pointed out to his disciples the place through which the water of Naghrid should be made to drain out.

The task of making way for draining out water by cutting mountain was done by another sage, named as Bodhisatwa Manjusri who came from Tibet. He managed to cut through hills between Champadevi and Phulchok at the place where Bagmati to this day passes out the valley. When water was drained out it left two hillocks or mounds Swayambhu and Guhjeshwari. Saint Manjusri also built a town called Manju Patan and the first king was installed there named Dharmaker. The sage then returned to Tibet.[2]

Nothing can be said with certainty as to when this event occurred, but it can be safely placed about 100 B. C. Manju Patan was visited by Krakuchhand Buddha, Kanakmuni etc. The valley was gradually developed and the land was reclaimed, step by step. In due course the entire valley was made a prosperous settlement with cultivation.

1. Ibid.
2. Danial Wright, *History of Nepal*, pp. 78-105.

Bond with India

The mythical history of Nepal relates that Pandit Dharm Sri Mitra visited the valley. He came from Varanasi. Subsequently, Rai Gunkamdeva from Gaur and Kirati Rajas also visited the valley. It is evident from the record that Raja Dharam Datta from Kanchi built the Pashupatinath temple and presented much wealth and valuable articles to this shrine. A chaitya to the north-west of the temple was also built by him. Rani Pingala from Marwar India also contributed adequately to the temple culture.[1]

Nepal's authentic and positive history can be traced in the fourth century A.D. The first known document which mentions this country is the inscription of the Emperor Samudra Gupta engraved on the pillar at Allahabad. This record reveals that the King of Nepal was one of those many who paid tribute to and obeyed the orders of the Imperial Gupta king. His name is also mentioned between the names of the Kings of Katrapura and Kamrupa. The name of the King of Kamrupa is frequently mentioned in literature. His country is said to be north-west Assam bordering independent Bhutan.

Early literature, whether Hindu or Buddhist, is vague as far as Nepal is concerned. Even epic poems of *Ramayana* and *Mahabharata* are silent on this land, though Himalayas, Kamrupa, Kiratas are commonly mentioned therein.

It was sometime during the early days of progress in the valley that the dynasty of patron Saint Ne Muni was first established at Bagmati and Vishnumati. From here he exponded his doctrine. He was regarded as an oracle of all things.

Gopala Dynasty

Ne Muni with the common consent selected a most pious cowherd known as Gopala to be the king of Nepal. There were eight kings in his dynasty. Thereafter, on the matter of

1. Danial Wright, *History of Nepal.*

grazing lands there arose a dispute and another person of the same Gopala clan became King. The later dynasty was known as of Ahirs, a race very common in India. Both these names are identical and mentioned in the history of Nepal. Both Gopala, Gwala and Ahirs are of the same clan. In Bengal such people are called Gwala while in Bihar they are called Ahirs and in the modern times they are known as Yadavas in India and Nepal both.

Kirantis

Nepal, however, could not enjoy peace for longer time and the barbaric race of Kirantis from neighbourhood attacked Gwala (Ahir) kings who by nature were very peace-loving. They won them over and established their own rule. Though Kiranti kings were reported to be barbarous but they had their Royal Geneology. The name of the first king is said to be Yalambar. He is supposed to be the first king of the Tibetan race who had his sojourn on the bank of river Yalung. It is mentioned that fourteenth king of this dynasty Stunko in 250-249 B. C. was the host of great Asoka, a king from Pataliputra—modern Patna. Asoka's daughter subsequently settled there and founded Devapatam near Pasupati. That time Asoka's dominion was comprised of whole Northern India including Kashmir. Asoka was a staunch Buddhist. He was revered all over due to his edicts engraved on rocks and pillars in various parts of India one of which is installed at Rummin-dei, the ancient Lumbani, to mark the birth place of Buddha. This place lies still within the boundaries of modern Nepal.

Kirantis too could not sustain longer like other previous Kings of Nepal. A Hindu King Numikha invaded Kirantis and after winning them over established his own Sombansa dynasty. There were five kings in this dynasty. The last one Bhaskera Varman was so powerful that his name is conventional and regarded with great respect. It is said that he conquered the whole of India. As this king had no son, so he appointed his successor, from Surajvansi clan. This dynasty lasted for thirty one generations. Except that Mahadeva, the twenty first king of the dynasty no other king could make a niche in the history of Nepal. The kingdom of Mahadeva extended outside the valley both to the east and to the west beyond the Gandak river and included fortresses of Mallas—another sect, which was quite prominent in later days. The last king of Surajvanshi dynasty, Vishwadeva Burman, since he had no son, married his daughter to Vishya Thakur of pure Rajput descent. Thereafter, a period of distress and internal trouble followed in the closing days of the dynasty.

Nepali historians have mentioned a famous ancestor which according to descriptions resembles king Vikramaditya of Ujjain in 57 B. C. The real conqueror of Nepal was an Indian king, named Sri Harsha, who forced the adoption of his era on to the Nepalese princes. Data of this era is in the year 606-607 A.D. It is generally believed that Sri Harsha returned to India after invading Nepal but he must have left some one to rule behind him and this ruler was Ansu Barman. The well-known Chinese traveller Hiuen Tsang, who is most reliable and best among foreign informers visited the country (Nepal) in A.D. 637 and he recorded that this king was enthroned in the first part of seventh century. Nepalese chronicles have given that Ansubarman belonged to Vaishya Thakur dynasty.

Thakurs

Ansu Burman, who founded the Thakur dynasty, was first among eighteen kings who followed him one after the other.

Ansu Burman is regarded as most vigorous and active. He was greatly applauded by both writers—Nepalese and Chinese. The first Sanskrit Grammar is said to be published during his regime. On one side the King of India, Harshavardhana was concentrating his power in making great empire from Gujrat to Bengal and on the other side one new power was emerging in the Himalayas. It is said that the country known as Tibet or Bod was inhabited with rough and untutored people. These people formed an army of 100,000 soldiers which threatened the peace of China and India both.

The first king of Tibet named Namri Srong Btsan was a man of energetic ways and of firm determination. He had received from China the elementary education of medicine and astrology. His rule extended to south-west up to the country of Brahmans i.e., India. The name and fame of this king, however, was put to the reverse gear by his son Srong Btsan Sgam Po. He died in 650 A.D., but he is the first king out of Tibet's barbaric race to acquire knowledge of arts. He sent a mission to India to study the secrets of arts. Consequently, an alphabet which was in use in northern India was adopted to suit the sounds of Tibetan language. He extended the frontiers of his empire and covered the whole of present Tibet. His ministers entered into relation with India in South and Nepal to the West. He even sent an emissary to the court of Nepal to seek the hand of a princess of that country.

Ansu Varman died in 640 A.D., but the seventh son of this dynasty Narendra Nath was linked with Guru Machhendra Nath, the patron saint of the valley. Although evidence through coins, inscriptions and documents is not available about Narendra Nath, his name comes repeatedly in the legends and in Nepal's history. From all the legends, hearsay that is available it is a fact he was a benign ruler and wise enough to earn applaud of his people. His son, Jay Deva describes him as: "He had an exalted idea of honour and all the kings prostrated themselves before him." It was in the time of Narendra Dev that the Chinese mission visited Nepal for the first time in 643 A.D. and second time in 647 A.D. But the second mission headed by Wang Hiuen Tse was subjected to torture by the militants guarding the mountain border states of Indian ruler. Throughout the reign of Narendra Dev Nepal was frequently visited by Chinese pilgrims. Chinese records show that in the reign of Narendra Dev there was great prosperity and advanced civilization. Nourished religious atmosphere whether Hindu or Buddhist, was equally prevalent. A judicious system of taxation was introduced in the year 650. As such, Nepal could be compared with the best administered state of India.

Visit of Shankeracharya

After the death of Narendra Dev and in the time of his successor, Vara Deva Shanker Acharya, a Brahman from India entered Nepal and criticised all those people who practised Buddhism. He destroyed their temples, their literature and massacred their priests. But Buddhism was very well rooted in Nepal so nothing could be done to uproot the religion completely. Vara Deva was, however, impressed for the ideals of Shanker Acharya and named his son as Shanker. Exact date of Shanker Acharya's visit is yet a point of debate. His son also followed the tenets of Shanker Acharya and he also persecuted Buddhist.

Anecdotes of Ancient History to Assess Approximate Periods

The following record may be of use in approximately locating the sequence of traditional and historical events in the early periods of Nepali history.

B.C.

563 Gautama or Sidhartha born at Rummindei, Nepal

520 Sakyamuni visits the valley.

360 Bhadrabahu, the Jain Teacher dies in valley.

250 Emperor Asoka visits Nigliva, Rummindei and the valley where he leaves princess Charumati.

150 Reference of Nepal in Indian Literature

340 Asoka pillar at Allahabad of Samudra Gupta gives first reference of Nepal

A.D.

406 Fa-Hsien visits Rummindei.

417 Vrsa Deva was born.

437 Saint Machhendra Nath visits the valley.

440 Shanker Dev was born.

460 Dharam Dev was born.

480 Man Dev was born and Vasubandhu visits the valley.

496 Man Dev succeeds. His mother Rajyavati was regent.

497 Rajyavati dies.

524 Man Dev dies, Mahi Dev succeeds.

539 Mahi Dev dies, Basant Dev succeeds.

540 Shiv Dev was born.

565 Anshuvarman was born.

585 Shiv Dev succeeds.

595 Anshuvarman jointly rules with Shiv Dev; married Shivdev's daughter.

635 Hslian Tsang visits Rummindei.

639 Princess Bri-btsun, daughter of Anshuvarman marries Srong-Tsan-Gambo, King of Tibet, introduces Buddhism into Tibet. Her huband founded Lhasa.

640 Anshuvarman dies, Srong-Tsan-Gambo becomes the King of Nepal.

641 Srong-Tsan-Gambo marries Wen-chieng, a Chinese Princess.

647 Visit of Wang Hiuen Tse, Tao Faung, Tao.

655 Chaung Hiwen I'ai, Matisimha, Hiuen-Hoei.

651 Narendra Deva sends a mission to China.

657 Second visit of Wang Hiuen Tse.

665 Wang Hiuen Tse writes his narratives.

Regarding the fifteenth King of Thakur Dynasty nothing is available in black and white. No inscription, no coins or icons of this king are traceable. However, he is a great source in the Nepal legends. By name of Guna Kam Deva he is famous for building a town named Kantipura at the confluence of river Bagmati and Bishnumati. This town in the modern time became Kathmandu. Another town Patan was also built at the same time. So Dev Patan and Kathmandu two twin towns were made hubs of economic growth.

Gradually trade with India flourished and Tibetan kingdom also offered new field of market. So the result was that cultivation started dwindling. People started patronising trade and industry. Newars getting scope developed their manual art, handicrafts and made living better. It was also a signal for improving the economy of people and more and more townships started growing. Skills progressed. Markets were enlarged, commercial prosperity was increased.

The death of Jayakama the last king of Thakur Dynasty brought another big change. As this king had no son, a new Raja was elected from among the Thakurs of Nawakot, a small town, about 30 kms west of Kathmandu. Thereafter Vama Deva, a descendent of Ansu Burman drove away the Thakurs of Nawakot and established his own rule and dynasty of another Thakur clan.

In the time of the 9th king of this dynasty Arideva the word Chhatri was first introduced though this word is quite prominent in Hindu system of division of labour. Chhatris in Hindu scripture are those who defend the state and fight when a case arises. These chhatris of Nepal were later known as Mallas. A legend goes to explain that once while Arideva was enjoying his favourite pastime of wrestling he got sweet news of the birth of a son. As he was doing the malla practices so he named the boy as Malla which means an athelete, a boxer or a wrestler. Many other legends are also in the mouths of Nepal people. The second such legend tells the story that once Nag Bamba, the king of Malebum was defeated by an invincible wrestler from Delhi, and so he put the title of Mall on him and his descendents became Mallas.

From the early days of Buddhist history Malla name has been prominent. In the vicinity of Vaishali a colony had been developed by Mallas. Traces are there in the pillar of Changu Narayan. In the east of the Nepal valley it is inscribed. Surajvanshi Man Deva had defeated Mallas of Mallapuri and rejoiced the occasion. Ancient history reveals that Mallas and Surajvanshi had identical craze for power and valour. They fought each other for coveting land. Subsequently, Surajvanshi occupied the Central Nepal called Valley. Thus Malla title was adopted even by Indian kings. It is really coincidence that one of the rulers of Conjeevaram was by the name of malla. Therefore, Nepali tradition has proclaimed it as the home of one of the first known Malla kings of Nepal, Dharmadatta.

There were many kings of this clan who have a special mention in the history of Nepal. Abhara Malla, successor of Arideva, Jaydeva ruler of Patan, and Anand Malla, founder of Bhatgaon are famous. He started Nepal Era also which corresponds to 1257 A.D. Thus, in the lineage of Malla kings there were about 10 kings who contributed historical, social and economic events for Nepal on the death of Shiv Singh, who repaired the temple of Shyambhu Nath. In 1594, his sons divided the kingdom in five parts. The Elder Laxmi retained Kathmandu while younger Harihara founded dynasty at Patan. As Bhatgaon was already there ruled by a king there were thus three separate states in the valley of Nepal.

Laxmi, elder one, though remained insane for sometimes but he built Kathmandu (Temple) in Kantipur. From then onward Kathmandu-Kantipur became Kathmandu. He had a very wise and intelligent minister in the name of Bhim Malla, who eventually made Lama of Tibet to conclude treaty of commerce with Nepal. Laxmi Malla, it is said also invaded Tibet. While his army was proceeding towards Taria village, a Tibetan Lama detached a large rock out of his spiritual power and rolled down it towards Nepal Army to crush them dead. But Bhim Malla alone held back the rock by raising his hands and thus a great blow upon Nepal was averted.

On succession Pratap Malla ruled for fifty years. He allowed each of his sons to reign in turn for a year. The eleventh king of this dynasty died childless. Ultimately the throne was given to Jaya Java a distant Malla. He once defeated Gorakha King, who invaded valley and came up to Nawakot.

Prithivi Narayan Shah

After dwindling of Malla Kings the declining effect was the seen in the valley as kingdom was divided into more than four states. Though Jaya Prakash Malla dispelled the two attacks of Gorakha king in 1736 and 1748, but third time a most powerful, intelligent Gorakha king, Prithvi Narayan invaded the valley in 1768 with a large army of Gorakhas. He was helped by many chiefs of Nepal, who were indifferent to

Malla King. Thereafter step by step Gurakha dynasty made its roots quite deep and became the most powerful kingdom of the valley.

As per *Vanshavali* the ruling house of Gorakhas is a brand of Rama family of Chitor. Gorakha family traces its origin from one Rishiraj Bhottarak, raja of Chitor—Rajputana India. When Muslim rulers attacked Rajput principalities, many of them could not resist. They were defeated and made subjects of Muslim empire. When Akbar attacked Chitor, the king of Chitor, Bhupati was killed with his son Fateh Singh, but Udai Brahma escaped and founded Udaipur. The youngest took refuse at Ujjain. Youngest Manmath had two sons—one Bhupal came to Nepal *Tarai* and settled at Palpa.

Bhopal was successful in marrying his two sons Kancha and Mincha with Rajput Raghuvanshi Kshatriya girls. These marriages were quite fruitful and proved very instrumental in conquest of the country of Magars, while Mincha established himself at Naukot. In the dynasty of these Rajputs no outstanding events happened. In 1716 Narbhupal Shah sat on throne, who was the 10th ruler of Gorakha clan from Drabya Shah. He was very ambitious. Realising that in the valley there were at least three main rulers at Bhatgaon, Kathmandu and Lalit Patan and that no affinity was available between these rulers, he invaded these principalities. However, in 1736 Nar Bhopal had to take defeat at the hands of Jaiprakash Malla of Kathmandu. He retreated to his own mountains territory and in 1742 he died leaving his heir Prathivi Narayan Shah a young lad of 12 years only.

Prithvi Narayan was a giant, a great administrator, an ardent warrior and star-monger. He had tremendous organising capacity. He was courageous and resolute. He realised the truth of difficulties. Out of his personal efforts he gathered around him the brave sardars who were not only brave in fighting but loyal to him also. His act of motivation resulted in collection of a well trained army of 4000 to 5000 soldiers, consisting of Magars, Gurangs, Thakurs and Khas. He is the first king who had no caste bias. Patronising every caste and changing of superficial customs he was able to recruit a good and loyal Militia.

In his very first pursuit in 1748 he attacked Navakot and marched up to Kirtipur successfully. But on going further he could not bear resistance of Jay Prakash Malla of Kathmandu and had to escape on palanquin to his native mountain region. Fortune was yet in his favour. Ranjit Malla of Bhatgaon was not in good terms with his brother of Kathmandu, so he extended his hand of friendship to Prithvi Narayan Shah who was very ambitious and wanted to inflate his boundaries of Kingdom. This was realised very late by Ranjit Malla. So in spite of the fact he went back to the fold of Malla Kings, he could not repair much.

Prithvi Narayan was successful in winning the cooperation of many mountain chiefs because he promised to restore their jagirs to them. So by their assistance he possessed all the mountainous principalities around the Kathmandu valley. He also built many forts upon the hillocks, in which he could keep has troops. So after concentrating more and more strength he attacked repeatedly on Malla Kings, but could not succeed. He adopted another trick of *Bheda* (Dissension). After giving enticing promises, he motivated nobility and people of higher echelons and created a great gulf between them and the King.

In 1767 he invaded Kirtipur and through the treachery of one of the nobles of Jay Prakash Malla he entered the town. Entire garrison was put to sword. Male inhabitants were punished. He further marched to Patan and fought on outskirts of the city. In the meantime after getting the information that Capt. Kinloch of East India Company already arrived in the valley he retreated to protect his southern border. In 1768 Gorakha found Capt. Kinloch had gone back, again attacked and Malla Kings surrendered to him. In 1769 he captured Bhatgaon also. Prithvi Narayn was a close friend of Bir Nar Singh, the only son of Ranjit Malla, who had died during the lifetime of his father. So, when Prithvi Narayan Shah appeared in Darbar, he requested Ranjit Malla to continue his rule as he was not to capture his kingdom. But as there remained no heir to Ranjit Malla, he made Prithvi Narayan the sole ruler and retired to Benares for penance.

Thus, in 1769 the two kingdoms, Gorakha and Nepal were united into one. Prithvi Narayan Shah further moved up to Dodh-Kosi river on east and subjected the rulers of Kirats and Limbus. But in 1772 in one fierce battle between Gorakha and Raja of Tambu the Gorakha army had to bear a great loss. It was reduced and discouraged, so they stopped further consolidation for another battle. In 1774 Prithvi Narayan Shah died leaving the throne to his eldest son, Singh Pratap Shah.

History of Post Prithvi Narayan Shah

The most important date in the history of Modern Nepal was 1768 when Prithvi Narayan Shah conquered Kathmandu and put to firm footing the process of Gorakha expansion in Nepal. But after Prithvi Narayan Shah Nepal's consolidation was again fragmented.

Around 1750 Nepal was divided into various loose federations of smaller principalities. The following groups were prominent:

(i) Baisi *raajas* whose Chief was raja of Jumla.

(ii) Chaubisi *rajas* of whom one was Gorakha King.

(iii) Baghmati Valley principalities.

(iv) Group of Kranti Chiefs under the King of Makwanpur.

(v) Limbus and Lepcha Chiefs under the King of Sikkim.

(vi) Various small *rajas* of *Tarai* under the suzerainty of *raja* of Butwal.

(a) Baisi *rajas* lived mainly in the valleys of Gogra and they were twenty two in Doti Gumla etc.

(b) *Chaubisis* were twenty four and included chiefs of Palpa, Gorakha, Nayakot, Piuthan etc. and were found in the valley of Gandak.

(c) Newar principalities included chiefs of Kathmandu, Patan, Bhatgaon, Kirtipur and Chomkot.

(d) Raja of Mackwanpur was *kranti* Rajput. He was most influential Rajput after Newar princes.

(e) Limbus and Lepcha Kings were concentrated in the far east. They pretended themselves as Rajputs and considered a Lepcha Raja of Sikkim as their superior head.

(f) *Tarai* Rajas of petty standing were paying tribute to hill *rajas* of interior so that mountaineer kings may not plunder their possessions.

These zamindars found it more economical to pay tribute to big *rajas* than to keep a big military for defending their borders. Other chieftains were *rajas* of Tulsipur, Tapa, Siwa and Argha etc.

Main polity of these small states reveals that those territories were not influenced at all by the events that happened outside Nepal country. Secondly, all the political changes that took place in those territories were determined and guided by Hindu ideas of statecraft.

Relations with India

Analysing the history of Nepal we find that Nepal was not influenced by the events taking place in India. They kept secure within their own mountain fortresses. In time when Mohammadens invaded India, established their kingdoms and Islamic culture was forced on people, they were converted to the tenets of Islam. Big towns like Delhi, Agra, Lucknow took to Persian culture. Nepal remained Hindu-cum-Buddhist. In spite of large influence of Islamic culture in India this neighbour country remained undisturbed. But it is also a fact that due to isolation Nepal was not able to play any part in the course of Indian History.

It is interesting to think that before British people were active Prithvi Narayan Shah could have tried to drink the Ganges water at Calcutta. The reason Nepalese did not like to influence Indian polity while other neighbours like Afghanistan and Punjab were quite instrumental. It is because Nepal was short of good horses. They only maintained ponies who could transport their arms and ammunition, luggage and provisions for soldiers. So in absence of good mounts Nepal did not venture to interfere in the history of India. In general, Nepalese are simple, peace loving and religious people. They lacked cavalries, so did not venture to attack India.

The second reason was that *Tarai* land separating Nepal with India remained a natural barrier. Neither Indian princes nor Nepalese ever tried to penetrate through the barren land heavily forested and infested by virulent Malaria fever. The passages were, however, made for communication adjacent to streams and rivers. The third reason seems to be that Nepal remained a separate historical unit. Though it had various number of small divisions, but its political unity remained intact under diversity.

The fourth point is that Nepal accepted the tenets of Brahmanical ethnics. People respected their king like God incarnate and kingship was taken to be hereditary and the child once born to the king possesses all the rights of royalty.

We find, then all the political changes in Nepal took place within the framework of customs and polity guided by Hindu Laws.

Conditions in Nepal After Gorakha Conquest

The main member of Gorakha Kingdom was Prithvi Narayan Shah, who was born in 1730 A.D., sat on throne at the age of twelve years and ruled over 31 years. He is thus the founder of modern Nepal. Being a good strategist, a soldier, a general, imbibed with military virtues he ventured for victory. He consolidated small fragments and established Gorakha reign as one solid power. He realised the importance of blockade as an instrument of war. His instruments were real propaganda and intelligences right application. He called for services of many Brahmins, created dissension among his enemy force and won them over one by one.

Hereditary kingship is the greatest weakness of despotic principalities. Without considering the weaknesses and virtues of the heir sometimes most unworthy sons were crowned on throne. In constitutions in time of vagaries the kingdom is controlled by the ministers of the Crown, who are responsible not only to authority, but also to convention and Brahmanical permissions of code.

After Prithvi Narayan Shah this dynasty did not produce any notable prince. Thereafter only two names, Bhimsen Thapa and Jang Bahadur Rana appear more prominent as they were prime ministers to Nepal Sahi Kings. Bhimsen Thapa established the convention of permanent prime ministership and civil and army services to the Thapa family. He guided the destiny of Nepal Kings in difficult times. So, Nepalese had will to conquer more and more territories. In the 19th century they conquered Kumaon, Garhwal Districts and went right up to Himachal Pradesh in the west and to the Sikkim in the east. They, however, could not succeed in Tibet where Chinese army gave great blow to them in 1792.

Jang Bahadur Rana's position was unique. He was the most courageous and ablest administrator. At times when Hindu princes were following the orthodox tenets of Hinduism this prime minister was courageous enough to take a voyage by ship to England and France. He had insight and could assess that even all the princes of India united could not defeat British Army—so powerful and fully-equipped with most modern war weapons which were not available with Indian princes.

The fundamental element which was injected in the people of Nepal by Bhimsen Thapa and Rana Jang Bahadur is *Gorakha Nationality*. Though Gorakhas were one of the social groups, but they were given more importance as the Nepal state was run by Gorakhas for the welfare of others. Gorakhas include only those groups which call themselves as Thakurs, Khas, Gurangs and Magars.

Nepal's Relations with East India Company

In a letter dated 20th April, 1767 T. Rumbold, the chief officer of the Company's Government at Patna sent to the president of the council at Calcutta, he indicated that

Gorakha King has besiezed Nepal and due to military activities started by Gorakhas it was difficult to continue trade in the valley. He also mentioned in this letter whether help to newer King be rendered as requested by him. In reply Rumbold was instructed to write to Gorakha King to take off sieze and use force also if need be. The letter authorised him to raise battalion of sepoys in case it was necessary. By this time two emmisaries came to Patna and requested immediate help for newer King. Company's Govt. thus sanctioned full powers to Rumbold. It transferred its responsibility on the soldiers of Rumbold.

Thus, with the guidance of Muktanand and Sadhu Ram Das Capt. Kinloch moved ahead though passage was through roads which were in bad shape. People were slow in bringing the provisions of soldiers. Captain was frustrated in his pursuit on such limitations. The committee at Calcutta, however, blamed Capt. Kinloch taking hasty steps.

Further Capt. Kinloch had to face court of enquiry even after fully explaining the circumstances by Rumbold. On one side Capt. Kinloch was facing enquiry and on other side he was planning for the second invasion. Many chieftains who were harassed by Prithvi Narayan Shah, were promising assistance and guidance through thick and dense jungles. At last considering many ifs and buts Capt. Kinloch was made to stay back and not to take second venture. Nepal was then put into oblivion by East India Company.

Gorakhas in the meantime invaded Tibet. Brief chronology is as under :

1774 Gorakhas attacked Sikkim.

1788 Gorakhas occupied Tibet territory near Nepal.

1789 Agreement was signed by Tibetans to pay Rs. 50,000 annually to Gorakhas.

1791 Yet another invasion on Tibet by Gorakhas

1792 Chinese army defeated Gorakhas and dictated peace. Gorakhas agreed to send a mission to Peking every five years.

Out of the war with Tibet and China East India Company continued its efforts to increase its trade and find out the way to have link with Kathmandu. Consequently, Col. Kirkpatrick made recourse to Kathmandu to make himself acquainted with the terrain and topography of Nepal and also to make on the spot knowledge of up-to-date development in the history of recent Nepal.

Knox Mission

Eight years after the return of Col. Kirpatrick from Nepal events developed in such a fashion that Raja Ram Bahadur Shah had to leave throne and to retire to Benares. Public and nobility all denounced him. At Kathmandu dissentions were mounting under such conditions, that the Company decided to reap out the advantage. So during the next four years the Company extracted one or the other advantage from Nepal. The Company sent Capt. W.O. Knox to meet Ram Bahadur at Benares. But Nepal deposed king was more smart so he wanted some financial assistance from Comany so that he could make himself powerful enough to retaliate Nepal Government. The bargaining earned Raja assistance of Rs. 6,000 per month. Thereafter, in September he requested Governor-General to loan him a Battalion of sepoys, one battalion of Europeans and artillery to accompany him back to Nepal. Britishers were clever and they felt the evil designs of Ram Bahadur. So they made their link with ruling party at Kathmandu. Raja was supposed as deceptive and was put under the surveillance. Gajraj Misra who had also come along with Ram Bahadur gave many promises to English people. English assured him to decorate with Raja title if their conditions were fulfilled. Capt. Knox Continued to assure Nepal that after fulfilling their agreement draft Britishers would withdraw from Nepal territories.

Nepali-Chinese War, 1791-93

Treaty signed in 1789 after the 1st Tibetan-Nepal war was not honoured as it was desired, so conflict between these two parties remained alive as cold war for sometime. On Aug. of 1791 about 4000 Nepali troops under the command of Damodar Pandey, Dev Datta Thapa and Ram Shah crossed the Tibetan border and seized trade centre of Kunti, further advanced and captured Tingri and further Tibetan trade centre. One after another trade centres were occupied by Gorakhas. Tibetans then requested China for assistance. On hearing the invasion, Emperor sent A.O. Hiu to Tibet to warn Nepalese that Chinese army would be coming to inflict good blow to Gorakha military if it did not go back. The circumstances so developed that China Government lost confidence over his officials in Tibet. China arranged to send his army under the command of Fu-Kang.

Meanwhile, Nepali Army started withdrawal on October 4, 1791 by a direct but difficult and rugged pass. This adventure was very adverse and proved disastrous to the army. After first 12 days of running battle Tibetan led force was defeated at Chainpur and Sidhipur in early 1792. Amar Singh Thapa fighting well came back to Kathmandu via Kerong Area and Muktishetra. China then wanted time lag and started preparing for other invasion on Nepal. In process she sent her diplomats to those Rajas who were captured by Gorakhas and also sought help from East India Company. In July 1792 letters to Governor-General were sent by Dalai Lama and Pancham Lama which were carried by the messenger Gosain Purangir. On the other hand, Nepal also sent its emmissary in February 1792 to Patna and treaty between Calcutta and Nepal was signed. After many circumstances in favour and against of both nations Chinese invaded Nepal and inflicted a considerable damage. So a treaty was signed on September 30, 1792 and withdrawal of Chinese force started a week later. Consequences of war made both countries to think twice before making an offence on each other. Due to topographical condition of the terrain it is not possible to cross borders at will. There was enough for repentance. Between 1792 and 1846 Nepal had followed policy of non-interventionist towards Tibet.

Relations with Company

On March 1, 1793 Col. Kirkpatrick entered Nepal and entered into a treaty with it acknowledging its independence and right. This treaty did not act satisfactorily. British Government negotiated terms of keeping her resident at Kathmandu but it could not be settled and Nepalese refused to accept treaty of closer binding upon them.

In the meantime when negotiating machinery was active and keeping link with British Government, brother of Damodar Pandey invaded Garhwal and inflicted a great blow defeating Garhwal King. With the conquest of Garhwal Gorakha Kingdom was extended from Bhutan to Kashmir and from High mountains of Tibet to Agra and Oudh borders of United Provinces. General Amar Singh Thapa, the father of Bhimsen turned his face towards west. After seizer of Garhwal he threatened Kangra in Punjab. Here he found an adversary Ranjit Singh, who was also engaged in conquest of Punjab, Kashmir, Kangra, he therefore could not proceed further.

After dissolution of 1804 alliance for the next 10 years relations between British Government and Nepal remained strained. Right from 1787 Nepalese were active in seizing villages and encroaching British borders. Continuous aggressive activity by Nepal and capturing of British territory of Ram Nagar and murder of some police officers near Batoli led to declaration of war in 1814 again.

Valour of Gorakha Soldiers

It is praiseworthy that Gorakha soldiers, consisting of 12,000 personnel face our army of 30,000 with 60 guns. In the operation they taught very well and gave a good blow to the British Army. General Gullespie was in command for British Army but Purana Gorakha unit of 500 men resisted well against the attacks of the General. In this fight a British Commander along with 31 officers and 750 men were killed and wounded.

General Martindell succeeded Gullespie and he passing through Nahan proceeded to attack Jythak but Col. Kehar Singh with 2000 Nepalese pickup soldiers had retired from Nahan. But Major Ludlow and Richards faced a stubborn resistance and held the Britishers at Nalapani. Further Major Ludlow had to retreat with the loss of 12 officers and 450 men killed and wounded. Such defeats of Britishers were not the last. In February 1815 they suffered another loss and defeat. Only 200 Gorakha soldiers defeated 2000 British Armymen. In the meanwhile, Cap. General Wood commanding the division of Gorakhpur advanced towards Batoli. He retired due to his incompetency without any achievement.

Many other sorties were made by British through Tarai but availed no success. Sporadic and stray wars were continued. A treaty was in offing but Gorakhas never wished to surrender on conditions of Britishers. In February 1816 Gen. Ochterlony advanced direct to Kathmandu by main route but he was checked at Bichia Khoh Pass. Finding the positions unpregnable he gave up further idea of advance. Luckily a secret path, unknown to Nepalese, was searched out and through this pass he reached Hariharpur and fought well in jungles.

On Feb. 28 Gorakhas attacked Sekha Khattri but strong garrison of British did not yield. Later on reinforcement reached to help Gorkha army and the brave soldiers were able to beat off British army thereby killing and wounding about 800 men.

On March 1, Gorakhas, however, lost at Hariharpur due to the attack by machine guns. By the loss of these two points Sekha Khattri and Hariharpur Gorakhas lost the courage as well as they surrendered to well-equipped British Army without any qualified condition. Thus second war with British ended herewith.

On March 4, 1816, Treaty of Sugauli was signed. By the terms settled, Nepal lost Sikkim, Kumaon, Garhwal and all the west territory of Gandak river. Thus, the area of Nepal was reduced to the present space i.e., between river Mechi in east and Kali in the west, but the Treaty was further modified by Lord Hastings on the wish of Nepal and some portion of Tarai as directed by Nepal was restored to them.

Thereafter, though Nepal throne was decorated by many princes, but nothing outstanding happened with India and a perfect peace was maintained between the two countries. Internal squibbles with Darbar were always brewing and Nepal's stability was intact. Thus Nepal had continuous link with India from 200 B.C. to date. There is common cause in both the countries which if happens in one country reflects its rays on other also. Dynasty of Kings of Nepal is given below :

Dynasty of Kings of Nepal

1. Drabya Shah	1559-1570
2. Puromder Shah	1570-1605
3. Chhatra Shah	1605-1606
4. Rama Shah	1606-1633
5. Dambar Shan	1633-1642
6. Krishna Shah	1642-1658
7. Rudra Shah	1658-1669
8. Prithvi Pati Shah	1669-1716
9. Birbhadra Shah	1716-1742
10. Narbhupal Shah	17 -17
11. Prithvi Narayan	17 -17
12. Singh Pratap Shah	1774-1777
13. Rama Bahadur Shah	1777-1799
14. Girvan Yudha Vikram Shah	1799-1816
15. Rajendra Bir Vikram Shah	1816-1841
16. Surendra Bir Vikram Shah	1847-1881 (17.5.81)
17. Trilokya Bir Vikram Shah	1847-
18. Prithvi Vir Vikram Shah	1875-1881-1911
19. Tribhuwan Bir Vikram Shah	1911-1955
20. Mahendra Vir Vikıam Shah	March 1956-
21. Birendra Bir Vikram Shah	Continues

REFERENCES

Giuseppe, Father, 'Description of the Kingdom of Nepal', *Asiatic Researches*, Vol. II.

Ballantine, Henry, On India's Frontier or Nepal the Gorkhas' Mysterious Land, New York, 1895.

Bendall, C., 'Outline Report on a Tour in Northern India in the Winter' 1898-99 in Proceedings of Asiatic Society of Bengal, Feb. 1899.

Bendall, C. 'History of Nepal and surrounding Kingdoms' (1000-1600 A.D.)

Written as a Historical Introduction to Pt. Harprasad Shastri's 'Catalogue of the Nepal Durbar Library', J.A.S.B. (1903) pp. 1-32.

Mukerji, P.C., Report on a Tour of exploration of the Antiquities in the Tarai, Nepal (1901).

Basak, R.C., History of Nepal Eastern India (C.A.D. 320-760). Calcutta.

Bruce, Major, C.J., *Twenty-three years in the Himalayas*, London, 1910.

Hamilton, Francis, An Account of the Kingdom of Nepal, Edinburgh, 1819.

Hodgson, B.H., et al, *Miscellaneous Essays Relating to Indian Subjects*, 2 Vols., London, 1880.

Levi, S., Le Nepal, 3 Vols., Paris, 1905-08.

Kirkpatrick. W.J., *An Account of the Kingdom of Nepal*, London, 1811.

Landon, P., Nepal, London, 1928.

Northey (Major) W.B. and (Captain) C.J. Morris: *The Gurkhas*, Cosmo Publications, Delhi, 1974.

Oldfied, H.A., *Sketches from Nepal*, Cosmo Publications, Delhi, 1974.

Wheeler, A short history of India and the Frontier State of Afghanistan, Nepal and Burmah, London, 1880.

Wright, D., M.D., History of Nepal (translation of a Parbatiya uamsavalu of Shew Shanker Singh and Pandit Shri Gunanand). Cambridge, 1877.

Atchinson's Gazetteer of the Himalayan Districts.

Treaties, Engagements and Sanads of Atchison.

The Gazetteers of Garhwal. Almora, Naini Tal, Darjeeling, Gorakhpur.

The Imperial Gazetteer of India, Vol. XIX (for Nepal).

Papers Respecting the Nepal War, London 1824.

Journals of the Royal Asiatic Society of Bengal.

2

Geographical Structure of Tarai in Nepal

Nepal is situated in the heart of Asia and landlocked between two neighbours, India in the South and China in the North. It is shaped like a rectangle with an average length of 800 Kms. (East-west) and about 200 Kms. breadth (South-north). Nepal is located between Longitudes 80°-4 and 18°-12 East and Latitude 26°-22 to 30°-27 North. It is a land of diverse landscape of the largest Himalayan kingdom. It exhibits high mountains and their peaks, making a small plateau here and there, terracing slopes, smaller hills and then low lying area of Tarai. Like diversifying foothills, its people also have diversified customs with many colours of gaiety.

Topography : The outstanding geographical feature of Nepal is its land formation. The structure is composed of high mountains with nearly 50 peaks ranging from 23000 ft. and above and highest ranges of the world. Such land formation is on the north side of the country adjoining China border. So a gigantic staircase with rugged topography is sloped down gradually towards South. There are many villages, rivers and their basins kneeling down slowly and slowly making life possible for creatures. River valleys and the perennial flow of great rivers have formed a big *Tarai* land which is a level formation and is best suited for human residence. The land is fertile and the soil is alluvial. There are many special features which can be said to be attracting the knowledge of the whole world.

The world's highest peak Sagarmatha (Mt. Everest) is located in Nepal along with Nepal-Tibet border. It is 8,848 metres high and reported to be rising 1/2 inch per year.

In the central Nepal Dana is the deepest gorge in the world which is 1200 metres deep on Kaligandaki River, Kalidanki River flows 6,967 mtrs. above its flanking summits of Annapurna (8091 mt.) and Dhaulagiri (8167 mt.) between the valley of 35 Kms. apart. The depth of Dana Gorge from Dhaulagiri is 6,967 mts.

Tilicho of 4919 mtrs. is the highest great glacial lake located at Morang; it is 1107 mtrs. higher than the Lago Titicaca 3812 mtr. in Peru and Bolivia in South America.

In the eastern Nepal Arun valley stands deepest in the world. It is 457 mtrs. high from sea level and is situated between Sagarmatha 8,848 m. in the West and Kanchenjunga (8546 m.) in the East. Their flanking summits lie 125 Kms. apart. The point of attention is that the valley is 8391 mtrs. deepest from the highest points of the earth. 3613 m above sea level Suligad waterfall with 167 mtrs. height coming out of the Phoksundo lake in Dolpa district is the highest one.

The Range of largest number of Highest Peak: Himalaya is the greatest land mountain and is youngest in mountain system. Though every continent has its highest peak but none of them is more than 7000 m. high. The highest one other than Himalaya is mount Aconcagua 6961 m.) Argentina in the Andes range. In Nepal, there are more than 11 peaks above 8000 m. high. About 144 peaks range above 7000 m., 1166 peaks above 6000 m. and a dozen successive peaks high with a total of 1311 in Nepal exceed 6000 m. height.

Mahalangur range in Himalaya has concentrated ranges of 10 peaks at one place. Therefore, the altitude of Himalaya is a special feature in the Geography of Nepal.

Arun river is the biggest river of Nepal located in the highest source region of the world. It is the river which flows from Tibet to India crossing Nepal. In Tibet it is Phung Chu which has many tributaries. One is Menchu flowing from Gosaithan at 8012 m. high point. Nepal has the highest passes over 6000 m. high, to cross between South Asia and Central Asia.

Passes Thanna, Jhinsand are over 6000 m. high while Lugu la 6723 m. is highest in the world situated in Nepal.

Altitude Effects on Physical Aspect

It is seen from the topography of Nepal that altitude has a great part in the formation of Nepal. It has played its part and is quite significant in deciding the physical divisions, drainage systems, climatic conditions, vegetal variations, land formations, land use patterns, environmental differences and strategic contingencies.

It has three dimensions of land surface. About 77% is high Himalayas with rolling hills. The flat land area is about 23%. The variations of land formation can be seen from the following table :

Table 2.1

Land as per Elevations

Elevation (in metres).	*% of area*
1. Below 300	20.00
2. 300-1000	22.30
3. 1000-3000	32.80
4. 3000-5000	18.90
5. above 5000	5.90

Source : Atlas of Economic Development, HMG/1980.

The cultivable land is, therefore, very scarce. But every part has its own economic value which is explained in the following chapters.

General Features of Nepal's Land

The land in Nepal has mountainous areas with ground beauty and exotic landscapes. Most of the land lies on the southern slope of high Himalaya. Himalayan ranges are extended from mount Nanga Parbat of Kashmir (8126 m.) in the west of Namcha Barwa (7756 m.) to the big bend of Yarling Zamgho Jing (Brahmaputra River) in the east and is extended about 2400 Kilometres. The terminal high peak on the Indian side is Nanga Parbat and on Brahmputra side Namcha Barwa. The breadth varies from 150 to 400 Kms. Thus Himalaya embraces an area of 5,00,000 Sq. Kms. and consists vast snow fields of about 4,0000 Sq. Kms. The region 885 Km. alone lies within Nepal. Average height of western wing is 2000 metres while in the eastern wing it is about 1500 m. and in mid Himalayan region average is 6000 m.

Natural Staircases

Owing to the successive slopes from the North to the South, altitude of land varies tremendously and form a natural Staircase. The higer Himalayas of North slope down to the flat land in the South. The different terrains are situated between the two peaks; for example Dana Gorge of Kaligandaki lies between Annapurna and Dhaulagiri. It is less than 50 Kms. but the elevational difference is 7344 m. The distance between Pokhara plain and Mallerhorn Machhapuche is 25 Kms. but altitude change is 819 m. to 7039 m. In the South Himalchuli the difference in altitude is very pronouncing between 8000 m. and 3700 m. Morangadi river has eroded its basement down to 1400 mtrs. but deepest bed cuttings are found along the gorges of Kali Gandaki and Arun rivers. The highest Himalayan ranges with deep cut valleys are mostly concentrated in Nepal Himalaya.

Geological Condition of Himalayan Region

Geologically Himalayan region is unstable. It is evident that the heights of Himalayan peaks are changing at a rate of

0.33 cms. per year (Geography of China 1983, p. 38). This is the youngest range among the would's mountain system. The orogenesis of Himalaya is responsible in creating the variation altitude and changes in physical features.

Himalayan mountain contains stone and earth both, therefore, it is very unstable. Landslides are frequent. A small stream of water can slide the large chunk of range within minutes. So it is not convenient to make home without considering the deceptive altitude of this mountain.

Geophysical Features of Nepal

There are three distinct geophysical divisions of Nepal which have their own variations of altitude. On account of gradients Nepal is divided into three regions.

1. Himalayan region.
2. Hill region.
3. Tarai region.

All of these are unique topographical units. From the following table it can be inferred as to how these regions are spread.

Table 2.2

Division	*Area%*	*Sq. Km.*	*Altitude (M) range*	*Kms. North South*
1. Himalayan region	15	22,077	5,000 (4877-8848)	25-50
2. Hill region	68	1,00,000	3,000(305-4877)	75-125
3. Tarai region	17	25,021	200 (60-305)	25-30

Himalayan Region

The altitude of Nepal Himalaya have the magnificent crissrcross system of this youngest and highest mountain. Nepal is a model country for the study of geographical patterns of Himalayan system. It presents its totality in

Nepal. According to altitude Himalaya can be put into three specific divisions.

(a) The timber zone (4000 m. tree-line)
(b) The alpine zone above the timber-line to the snow-line (5000 m.)
(c) Snowy zone above the snow-line.

Actually alpine zone is here taken in the global context. It is a low altitude zone.

Snow-Line

The higher Himalayas have contributed to the creation of different geographical aspect. Due to the height factor even the region lying at 27°—40′—58″ north has become snow-line being above 3650 m. Though in normal course it should not have been. But the static snow line ranges from 4000 m. to 5000 m. from west to east Nepal. In the winter season even the Mahabharat region of Nepal becomes snowy. The population in the east is more than in the west.

The snow condition is affected by the slope aspect also. In north the snow remains longer whereas in the south it melts down faster due to warmer temperature. In the northern part of Nepal the highest chain of gigantic mountain can be classified as :

(i) Border Himalaya
(ii) Inner Himalaya
(iii) Greater Himalaya

These sub-divisions can be accounted for as under :

(i) Border Himalaya

Just in the South of Tibet plateau (Xizang over 4,000 m. above sea level) Nepal possesses a chain of Himalaya mountains extending along the northern edge of Nepal. The height is lesser than the main ranges. The slope is also gentle. This

Table 2.3
Sub-Division of Himalaya Region

Sub-division	*Altitude in Mtrs.*
(i) The border of Himalaya	6,000 (6,000-7,000)
(ii) The inner Himalaya	4,000 (2,500-5,000)
(iii) The greater Himalaya	5,000 (5,000-8,848)

marginal chain forms the border of northern Nepal. Actually, it would be appropriate to say that Nepal does not possess any regions of the so-called 'roof of the world', but this country possesses the roof-top of the world.

(ii) Inner Himalaya

In the south of the border Himalaya and north of greater Himalaya there lies some 'Silver Bowl' valley. These elevated Bhot Valleys of Tibetan landscape are surrounded by ice-clad high mountains where glaciers and moraines are spread up to the valley floors. There are also east-west valleys. The popular chains of these valleys can be known as under:

Table 2.4

Region	*Valleys*	*Altitude (M)*	*Location*
Eastern	Walangchung Gola	3,200	Taplejung
	Ghunsa	3,810	Taplejung
	Khumbu	3,880	Solukhumbu
Central	Langtung	C. 3,323	Rasuwa
Western	Manang	3,505	Manang
	Thakkhola (Jomsom)	2,612	Mustang
Mid-western	Tarakot	2,744	Dolpa
	Mugu	3,811	Mugu

The geater Himalaya is not actually the northern part of the country as it may seem so, but it is an extension of Nepalese terrain in the north from where one can observe high peaks in the south from within the Nepalese land. The typical feature of the high Himalayan valley in most cases is locally known as Bhot. This is the rain shadow area of Nepal. This is also the driest as well as a low productive land.

(iii) Greater Himalaya

The ranges of Himalaya having 6000 m above peaks in Nepal are given below :

1. East of Sunkosi —Kanchenjunga (8,586m)
Kumbakarna-Makalu (8,463m)
Mahalangur-Sugarmatha (8,848m)
2. Kali-Gandaki to Sunkosi —Langtang-Shisa Pangma (8,012m)
Manasiri-Manasalu (8,163m)
Annurana-I (8,091m)
3. West of Kali-gandaki —Dhawalagiri-I (8,167m)

This region is composed of super high mountains with crystal clear snow-capped panoramic peaks. Mahalangur has 10 peaks above 8,000 m, 47 peaks above 7,000 m and 156 above 6,000 m. It is quite typical in Nepal that 1,310 peaks are above 6,000 m but only 20% of them i.e., 272 peaks have their names. Most of the names are of Tibetan, English and Nepali origins. The lower peaks have no names at all.

Glaciers

The Nepal Himalaya contains huge glaciers. They are of two types. The former is lower in elevation but longer in length than the Tibetan type. Nepal glaciers are longer in the east than on the west. So one cannot find glaciers above 15 km. in the western part of Langtang region. Eastern Nepal has the biggest and longest moving glaciers than in the west.

Symposium—Tibet 1980, 220.

Khumbu glacier is longest and 32 km. long (200m thick) which moves 50m per year (April-August). The biggest Langtang glacier is about 18 km. long. I give herewith the particulars of glaciers which are of 15 km. length and above.

Table 2.5

		Elevation (m)	
Glaciers	*Length (km)*	*Highest*	*Lowest*
Kanchenjunga-Lumbasumba			
Lanchenjunga	19	7,000	4,240
Yalung	20	7,500	4,240
Khumbu-Rolwaling			
Langshung	18	8,000	4,500
Lower Barun	15	6,500	4,200
Rongbuk	16	7,000	5,150
Khumbu	16.4	7,500	4,900
Ngojumba	20	7,000	4,500
Tolambau	20	6,200	4,500
*Langtan**			
Langtang	18	6,500	3,900

*C.K., *River System of Nepal*, 1977, pp. 48-50.

Glaciers gave big rivers and beautiful lakes around Himalayan Region. But the huge amount of water under it is a risk in changing the ecology of the country. This slow but forceful agent has a prominent role in shaping the topography with glaciofluvial actions of water and materials and the speed of the movement does play its part. In my study in the next chapters I will show as to how Nepal and its Tarai were contributed by glaciers and its rivers.

The Hill Region

Between the north of Tarai and the south of Himalayan region there is the chain of massive mountains running from west to east, full of rolling hills, hillocks, sadles and peaks, wide and narrow Bensi and maize of valleys of different sizes and tars as well as foothills, terraced slopes and spurs. This chain of middle order consists of metamorphic and sedimentary rocks. More than 42% of the total land area of Nepal is under this hill section. The region has 600 m. to 3,000 m. elevation. In this region only southern most ranges of Himalayan system are found. Mahabharat Lekh and Siwalik are two parallel ranges.

These ranges of mountain have actually worked as defensive wall to the southern portion. They protected arts, culture and crafts of the country. The cloud enveloped peaks enclose some depressed basins and form river valleys, tars and low lying areas. The extensive highlands in the western side and deep valleys with high ridges in the eastern side have diverse and unique landscapes in Nepal.

Table 2.6

Sub-Division of the Hill Region

Sl. No.	*Region*	*Altitude (m)*	*Breadth N South (km)*
1.	Inner Hills	600-1,500	25-50
2.	Mahabharat Lekh	1,500-3,000	50-100
3.	Siwalik	600-1,800	15-30

Inner Hill

It is extended from Mahabharat Lekh in the south and high Himalayan in the north. This part also has rolling hills 900 m. to 1500 m. high. This region provides wide possibilities of agriculture, livestock breeding and crop varieties.

Valleys and Bensi of Inner Hill Region

The valleys of big rivers are enriching the settlement in enormous variations in altitude. Arun is the deepest valley on the earth. Rivers like Kosi, Gandaki, Trisuli, Sunkosi, Arun and Tamour have carved out vast valleys. The eastern Nepal has narrower valleys with slopes.

The tectonic valleys like Kathmandu, Pokhara, Banepa and Spure are extensively cultivateed. In the terraced manner agriculture is done right up to deeply cut rivers. While saddles and passes provide routes to enter in inner portion of the midland region, the valleys of various sizes are surrounded by the Mahabharat mountain chain, Bhojpur, Okhaldhunga, Kathmandu, Gorakha, Pokhara Dailekh, Silgadhi, Bajhang and Baitadi are located in the midland of Nepal.

Contribution of Rivers

The rivers have created enriched settlement and enormous variations in altitude. The flat uplands are called tars along the river confluence and add economic value to Nepal. About 5% of the river flat area is from river terraces. Agricultural and trade potentials have been increased by these rivers. Some valleys, Bensi and tars are given in Table 2.7.

Mahabharat Lekh

A chain of ranges with lesser heights in the south of inner Himalayas runs west to east with several sadles (low passes) and steep relief features. It is about 80 km. downward from the main Himalaya range. In this region also Lekali, Bensi, valleys and tars are seen with typical geographic features due to elevational differences.

Kaligandaki, Trisuli and Karnali have carved this region to give entrance to Tarai. Tansen and Dhankuta are the examples of commercial passes to enter hills.

The height of the folded Mahabharat lekh runs mostly in the ranges between 1,500 m. to 3,000 m. continuously from west to east. It is also considered as lesser Himalaya. Slopes on southern side are steeper than in the northern. Where gentler slopes are available they are utilised for terrace cultivation. Higher and steeper ranges are yet occupied by dense forests.

Table 2.7

Valleys and Bensi of Inner Hill Region			*Important tars (Table land) of Nepal*		
Valleys	*Location*	*Altitude*	*Tar Name*	*Altitude*	*Location*
Kathmandu	Kathmandu	1,337	Suke tar	1824	Taplejung
Trisuli	Nuwakot	579	Tumling tar	457	Sankhuwasava
Pokhara valley	Kaski	819	Rumja tar	350	Okhal Dhunga
Panchkhal	Kavre Patanchok	871	Sangu tar	878	Ramechhap
Banepa	—do—	1,554	Jarayo tar	760	Sindhupalchok
Madi Valley	Palpa	518	Mangal tar	609	Kaverepalanchok
Khimtibensi	Ramechhap	1,180	Bat tar	518	Nuwakot
Patan Valley	Baitadi	1,534	Sallyan tar	488	Dhading
Dhunnibensi	Dhading	850	Gajuri tar	671	Dhading
Chutrabensi	Araghakhanchi	915	Palung tar	457	Gorakha
Serabensi	Lamjung	800	Chepe tar	1,220	Gorakha
Bensi sahar	Lamjung	686	Khaireni tar	550	Tanahu
			Chapokot tar	366	Shyanja
			Karpu tar	442	Kamjung
			Chaurjahari tar	755	Rukum
			Ramput	182	Ghitwan
			Bel tar	200	Udaipur

Table 2.8

Popular Lekh (Upland) of Nepal

Name	*Altitude (m)*	*Location*
Sailung	3,159	Dolakha
Tyamke	3,005	Bhojpur
Jathak	2,858	Salyan
Phulchoki	2,765	Lalitpur
Siwapuri	2,732	Kathmandu
Kafle	2,720	Udaipur
Chimkeswari	2,591	Tanahu
Kumakh	2,439	Salyam
Chandragiri	2,534	Kathmandu
Swargadwari	1,907	Pyuthan
Daman	2,318	Makwanpur
Kaude	1,043	Palpa
Khoche	1,670	Baitadi
Sakin Danda	1,497	Dadeldhura

The Siwalik

It is a long mountain range spread right from Baluchistan to the east of Nepal. It is named differently in different regions like Mekaran in Baluchistan, Salt range in Punjab, Manchar in Sindhu and Siwalik in the east of Punjab. In the western part of Nepal it is called Dunduwa, and in the west of Bagmati it is called Bhawanchure. In Nawalparsi it is Daunne danda. Siwalik means Saiwal, moss and tress. Chure is derived from the Sanskrit word Chuda meaning Shikhare (peak). This is the southernmost, youngest and lowest range of Himalayan mountain system. It is just parallel to the Mahabharat range upto Kosi river. In the east of Kosi chure is isolated and it is difficult to identify it.

Siwalik ranges are full of hogback landscape, steepy towards the south and gentle towards the north. It consists of hard and soft strata of coarse rocks composing sandstone, pebbles, clay, conglomerates, quartz and sand-like materials. They are very loosely consolidated in Siwalik hills. Due to porous structure deep rooted natural vegetation is found where altitude has decreasing tendency from west to east.

Siwalik zone has enclosed wide Tarai like valleys which is known as inner Tarai. Little land is available for settlement and cultivation. The hill portion, higher than 2000m. is sparsely populated. This region has 37%of national cultivation and nearly 50% population and the livestock is found in this area.

Tarai Region

Tarai is situated in the southernmost part of Nepal and is about 200 m. above the sea level. It is also called Duwars in Bhutan. This is the northern portion of Indo-Gangetic alluvial plain situated like southern courtyard of Himalaya. The narrow strip of flat field of fertile soil has high water-table also. The width north-south is not even and about 65 kms east of Naraini river. Plain land, a part of Gangetic plain is absent due to mountains. This region is quite flat, formed of sediments and silts deposited due to alluvial deposition. The soil deposited thus is estimated to be 2400m. deep. Topography presents a part of Indo-Gangetic plain. It is divided into three parts—(1) Inner Tarai, (2) Bhabar Belt and (3) Plain Tarai of Gangetic extension.

Table 2.9

Sub-division of Tarai Region

Sub-division (area %)		*Altitude (m)*	*Length E-W (km)*	*Breadth N-S (km)*
The Inner Tarai	(8)	600	25-100	15-30
The Bhabar	(4)	300	125-400	10-15
The Plain Tarai	(15)	200	125-400	25-30

The Inner Tarai

The sloping terrain enclosed by two separate ranges is called Doon Valley i.e., Plain land between two hills. So this region is plain land between Mahabharat and Chura. Breadth varies according to size. Rapti and Dang are called *Bhitari* (Inner) *Madesh* of Nepal. Altitude varies from 110-665 m. In India it is called Dwar while in West Nepal it is named as Danduwa. The narrow river valleys are called *khonch.* Trijuga (Udaipur) and Kamala (Sindhuli) *khonch* are two having small low lying valleys.

The Bhabar Belt

In the south of Chure there is a loosely consolidated, rugged and sandy strip in the upper part of Tarai plains. It is porous and consists of big boulders, pebbles, gravels and sandy soils. It is covered by forest and grass and is called Bhabar Belt. The name Bhabar means heat rash. Altitude of this belt is 300 m. and rises up to 381 m. in Bahundangi of Jhapa. Slope falls 18 m. to 30 m per two kms. The water percolates in this porous region and appears again in Tarai plain in the form of springs.

The small rivers, revulets and streams are not visible here. Only big rivers like Mahakali, Karnali, Rapti, Banganga, Narayani, Tinau, Bagmati, Kamala, Trijuga, Kosi and Kanki etc. are crossing this belt. This is actual filter portion where waste material brought by rivers is deposited. The Region covers about 9095 Sq. Km. This belt contains the fine forest known as *Char Kosh Jhadi* or a belt of 13 Km. long forest.

Tarai Plain

The broad belt of low and level land is lying on the southernmost part of Nepal. The slope is very gentle and falls only 3 m per km from north to south. For about 65 km this belt is interrupted by Chure range, east of Narayani river and Dang Deokhuri respectively. The Himalayan rivers have deposited fertile alluvial soil which is one of the most economical aspect and prospect of Nepal country. The soil is much more fertile. The eastern Tarai is wetter than the western on the northern side.

The water level in the region is very high. Therefore, temperature and water together provide good opportunity to grow vegetation. About two-third of the agro-production is found in this region alone. Tarai region is a broken strip in Nepal side. There are three distinct divisions—(a) eastern Tarai extends from Parsa to Jhapa. It is more extensive, wide and productive than others. It produces cash crops; (b) Central Tarai is from Shivraj to the Gandaki; and (c) western one is from Banke to Mahakali. It is irregular, narrow and drier.

Physiographically Tarai can be divided into three parts

(i) Banger—higher parts of old alluvium (Tand)

(ii) Khader—(Dhap Pradesh) Flood Area of newer Alluvium.

(iii) Deltas are found along the confluences of rivers. They possess both new and old alluvium

Drainage System

For all practical purposes it is undoubtedly known that rivers are the life line of Nepal. The passage, if at all possible from and to Nepal was through these rivers. Old civilization and new culture are developed on the banks of rivers of Nepal. Rivers were regarded as Devi or Goddesses like in India. Their names in Sanskrit literature are put with most reverence like Ganges of India. Rivers were treated like the sacred mother. Though there is different vocabulary in present Nepal language but their old names indicate as to how such men have been obliged by rivers. Some of the terms for water streams are as under :

Nadi	—River
Khola or Nala	—Small stream or rivulet
Kholsa or Khahare	—Seasonal brook—torrents etc.

Kulo or Kulya —small stream.

Gad and Kosi are widely used terms.

Every river has its own mythological origin in Sanskrit literature.

Tibetan words also appear for these rivers like Cu—Ko, Kha Khu etc. Upon these words many valleys were named like Nwa-Khu, Balakhu, Kot-Khu, Dor-Khu, Chan-Khu etc. It is a popular term for rivers in Kathamandu valley. In the process of change even local names were Sanskritized and Tibetan, Chinese, local and Sanskrit all names are prevalent in the present system of naming rivers.

Sanskrit names of rivers can be seen herewith

Prabhawati	Na—Khu
Ikshumata	Tu—Khu—Cha
Manimati	Sa—Khu
Dhanavati	La—Khu
Rudramati	Nija—Khu—Dhobi—Khola
Ratnavati	Bal—Khu
Bhadramati	Bhacha—Khu
Karamnasa	Ku—Khu—mati

Mati and vati are popular suffix of Sanskrit. In the same manner there are same parallel names.

Sapta Kosi	Kaushiki
Sapt Gandaki	Salagrami
Mahaprava Shivaduti	Arun
Dukhagni Barahi	Tamor
Shuvasrawa Durga	Sun Kosi—Swaran Kaushika
Swetbahini	Indirayani
Papagni Narayani	Tamakosi
Bhadramati Chandi	Dudhkosi
Barada Chamunda	Barun
Dharmavati Maheshwari	Trisuli
Yoshodhara Bramayani	Burhi Gandaki

Vishwodhara Narsinha	Marsyangdi
Sitprabha Ganga	Seti
Ratnaprava Kumari	Kali
Krishnaprabha	Mahakali

All these names are the terms of Sanskrit and are identical in India also. Terminology and naming of rivers show how people respected and worshipped rivers giving them names according to the quality they possessed.

Main Features of Nepal Rivers

Nepal rivers cross the ranges of different altitude and cut deep gorges and valleys. The water velocity is very high, that is why they are able to cut deep gorges. Even when they start from lower altitudinal region of the border Himalaya and cross the greater Himalaya and flow down to Gangetic plains, they fall down from a height of 6000 m. The geological history of the Himalayas reveals that Nepal rivers are older than Himalaya itself. It is evident from Kali and Arun rivers. The gorges of these rivers are very deep. River Kali has 7000 m deep gorge which is the deepest in the world. It proves that rivers were already in current while Himalayan ranges started rising up. These rivers, though very swift, narrow and strong in the Himalayan portion, when come out to plains they become wide, slow and sluggish in the Tarai region.

Nepal has about 6000 rivers and rivulets. Total length they attain is about 45,000 km. About 100 rivers are more than 160km long, 1000 are 11 km long, others are still shorter. Big river systems are there. They each cross Mahabharat lekh to only one destination that is plains of Gangetic lands. It is only Nepal which contributes 75% water to Ganga by her rivers through the melting of snow.

The three major river basins with a drainage area of about 36,000 sq. km have 45,000 sq. km catchment area in Tarai. The two rivers Mechi in the east and Mahakali in the west demarcate the east-west border of Nepal. Mahakali 223 km long takes off from Api Himal and joins Karnali in

Table 2.10

Details of Major River Basins

Sl. No.	Name	Drainage Area (Sq. Km.)	Length (km)	Mean Discharge (Cu. m./Sec.)
1.	Mechi	579	26	—
2.	Kankai	1440	108	—
3.	Kosi	30000	720	5564
4.	Baghmati	3523	163	161.6 (2810 max)
5	Gandaki	40000	338	10000 (7,00,000 max)
6.	Rapti	5049	157	—
7.	Babai	1440	108	—
8.	Karnali	50000	507	1317
9.	Mahakali	15300 (Nep. 4652)	223	—

the Indian Territory where it is known as Sharda. As per river system Nepal can be divided into three regions. They are Saptkosi in the East, Sapta Gandaki in Central and Karnali in Western region.

The water resources of Nepal are, therefore, golden for hydro-power and irrigation. In each sector of Nepal 7 more rivers are running in full with direction from north to south.

Kosi Basin

The spheres influenced by this river are Kanchenjunga in the east and Langtang in the west. Phung Chu starting from Tibet becomes Arun after crossing the Himalaya. Eastern Nepal area of about 33,000 sq. km. is drained by Saptkosi system. Its total length is about 750 km. It is the biggest and longest river of Nepal.

Gandaki Basin

Sapt Gandaki means system of 7 rivers which drains the central Nepal. Gandaki covers an area of drainage about

26,000 sq. km. in central Nepal. This river is 338 km long. Its average flow is 1700 cu m/sec while in rains it is increased to 7,00,000 cu m/sec. This river is also known as Narayani at the confluence where other tributaries join Gandaki. In India this river joins Ganges at Hazipur.

Karnali Basin

This is the longest river flowing inside the territory of Nepal. Its length is 547 km in U Bend (Acham), is about 30 km in length, flow is 1300 cu. m/sec. It also has seven tributaries and many other sub-tributaries. It drains 4900 sq. km in western Nepal. The river is called Ghagra in India. Melting of snow and high altitude glaciers are the perennial source of water to these rivers.

I wish to reproduce more details of these three river systems and their basins. Table 2.11 depicts the position.

Apart from the rivers there are third grade rivers also which are rainfed, small, short and sluggish for local irrigation work only.

Climate of Nepal

Though Nepal lies a little north of the tropic of Cancer in the northern temperate zone her two factors are her altitudinal and rainy conditions. All types of climates of world zones are available here. It is full of tropical jungles in Tarai land, arctic desert waste lands in high altitude and the arid zone of Tibetan Plateau.

The temperature distribution in the country is not equal. Altitude has played a great part in making it so. On higher places cooler climate prevails. Low lying lands like Tarai and inner Tarai parts are warmer while midlands are a little less warmer. Hilly and Himalayan regions are cooler. Cold is more on increase in January while hottest months are June-July. The trend of temperature is that it rises from March to June-July and decreases from October to January. In Tarai region there is variation of temperature on the eastern

Table 2.11

1. Gandaki (Sapt) River System

Name of river	*Source region*	*Length (km)*	*Catchment area (sq. km.)*	*Fall (m)*	*Confluence*
Trisuli	Tibet	362	4,000	1,500	Kali (Deoghat)
Burhi Gandaki	Tibet	117	3,700	5,000	Trisuli (Benighat)
Daraundi	Gorakha	53	900	3,500	Marsyangadi (Tanahu)
Marshyangdi	Damodar H.	153	4,600	6,000	Trisuli (Mugling)
Madi (Madri)	Annapurna H., Kaski	74	1,100	5,100	Seti (Damauli)
Seti	Annapurna H.	125	2,7′0	4,800	Trisuli (Kandrang)
Kali (Krishna)	Mustang	316	9,3C0	4,100	Trisuli (Deoghat)

2. Kosi (Sapt) River System

Name of river	*Source region*	*Length (km)*	*Catchment area (sq. km.)*	*Fall (m)*	*Confluence*
Tamor	Janak H., Taplejung	198	5,800	5,400	Arun (Barachhetra)
Arun	Tibet	720	36,500	8,200	Tamor
Dudhkosi	Mahalangui H., Solukhumbu	113	4,100	7,000	Sunkosi (Kurule)
Likhu	Rowaling H., Ramechhap	23	800	4,000	Sunkosi (Kilajor)
Tamakosi	Tibet	90	2,600	2,800	Sunkosi (Bangighat)

Sunkosi	Tibet	256	14,100	1,600	Arun (Pangma)
Indravati	Langtang H., Sindhupalchok	68	1,200	3,500	Sunkosi (Dolaghat)

3. Karnali Watershed System

Sanibheri	Rukum	98	2,300	4,100	Karnali (Kuneghat)
Thuli Bheri	Dolpa	136	3,300	4,600	Sanibheri (Jajarkot)
Tila	Jumla	99	3,400	4,500	Karnali (Kalikot)
Mugu Karnali	Mugu	384	6,100	4,900	Humla (Galwa)
Karnali	Tibet	507	10,100	5,000	—
Humla Karnali	Tibet	528	6,100	5,000	Mugu Karnali (Galwa)
Burhi Ganga	Bajura	84	1,700	4,700	Seti (Bajura)
Seti	Bajhang	202	7,500	5,100	Karnali (Doti)

and western parts. On hills it depends upon the height of the hill. Higher and higher the place, cooler and cooler the temperature.

Climatic changes are prominent within short distances due to altitude. In the valley and bensi bottoms below 600 m. climate is tropical with hot and moist atmosphere. At 2000 m. height, it is cool temperate and above 3000 m. it is ice cold and still above it is arctic cold like that of poles. Rise in altitude means fall in temperature. The following table presents the trend.

Tabie 2.12

Trend of Temperature at Various Places
Temperature Extremes (in Degree Celcious)

Region	*Altitude (m)*	*Max. Rise*	*Min. Drop*
Birat Nagar	72	34.0 (April)	9.1 (Jan.)
Janakpur	73	34.8 (April-May)	8.0 (Jan.)
Bhairahawa	106	36.6 (May)	8.0 (Jan,)
Nepalganj	152	39.2 (May)	9.1 (Jan.)
Tulsipur	663	34.5 (May)	6.9 (Jan.)
Dhangadhi	171	37.5 (May)	6.2 (Jan.)
Illam	1208	25.3 (August)	8.7 (Jan.)
Dhankuta	1158	25.8 (August)	7.2 (Jan.)
Bhojpur	1585	23.8 (August)	5.0 (Jan.)
Okhaldunga	1849	23.7 (August)	5.4 (Jan.)
Kathmandu	1337	27.7 (June)	1.9 (Jan.)
Gorakha	1522	28.7 (May)	8.1 (Jan.)
Tansen	1310	28.3 (May)	8.1 (Jan.)
Pokhara	819	29.6 (April)	6.9 (Jan.)
Dailekh	1448	28.3 (May)	6.7 (Jan.)
Dadeldhura	1891	26.1 (May)	5.0 (Jan.)
Namche Bazar	3880	16.1 (July-August)	8.0 (Jan.)
Jumala	2344	25.1 (May-June)	4.9 (Jan.)

Source: Deptt. of Irrigation, Hydrology and Meteorology.

Rainfall

Rainfall varies due to the topographical diversions in Nepal. As the South-east monsoon winds approach in summer the rainfall is heavier in Churiya range. It is more prominent on the windward side and decreasing on the leeward. Pokhara Hill region experiences the heaviest rainfall. The eastern part of Nepal receives more rain than the western. Rains are also prolonged in that Eastern part.

The average annual rainfall is 750 mm. The trend in different localities and regions is shown in Table 2.13.

According to the rainfall and cycle of seasons the climate of Nepal can be divided like this:

(i) Hot and dry pre-monsoon weather between March and May.

(ii) Hot and rainy summer season—April to September.

(iii) Hot wet summer weather in June to September.

(iv) Cold and dry winter season—October to February.

(v) Cool-wet post-monsoon weather in October.

(vi) Cool dry winter weather—November to February.

Climatic Classification

(1) *Sub-Tropical Climate* (*Up to 1200 m*): It is in Tarai, Bhaber, inner Tarai, Tar, Bensi, Khonch and in deep valleys in the middle mountain of Nepal.

(2) *Warm-Temperate Climate* (*1200-2100 m*): The climate in the upper part of Chure and midland Mahabharat region is mild and moderately hot on higher altitudes and on hill top it is cooler.

(3) *Cool-Temperate Climate* (*2100-3300 m*). Extreme altitude of Nepal have influenced the weather and climate, summer is 15°C to 20°C while winter is below 0° C.

(4) *Alpine Lekali Climate* (*3300-5000 m*). In the north and down the Snow-line region and in Himalayan Valley and most of the parts of Alpine area, the temperature is 10° to 15°C in summer and falls below 0°C in winter.

Table 2.13

Mean Precipitation of Important Places

Locality/Station	*Altitude (m)*	*Min. mm per month*	*Max. mm per month*	*Annual (mm)*
Dharan	428	5 (Dec.)	59 (July)	2292
Birat Nagar	72	0 (Nov.-Dec.)	448 (July)	1703
Birganj	88	2 (Nov.)	375 (July)	1103
Nepalganj	152	0 (Nov.)	376 (July)	933
Tulsipur	663	7 (Nov.)	476 (July)	1706
Dhangadi	171	7 (Jan.-Dec.)	418 (July)	1485
Illam	1208	8 (Dec.)	440 (July)	1553
Dhankuta	1158	10 (Dec.)	256 (July)	1014
Bhojpur	1585	9 (Feb.)	316 (July)	1352
Okhaldhunga	1849	8 (Nov.)	438 (July)	1731
Sindhuli	1417	13 (Dec.)	685 (July)	2883
Ramechhap	1428	8 (Dec.)	232 (July)	862
Kathmandu	1337	5 (Nov.)	371 (July)	1399
Syamgja	852	11 (Dec.)	756 (July)	3153
Dailekh	1448	10 (Dec.)	476 (July)	1689
Dadeldhura	1891	6 (Dec.)	312 (July)	1297
Num	1508	15 (Jan.)	947 (June)	4783
Shyangboche	3833	1 (Dec.)	265 (June)	988
Dhunche/Rasuwa	1962	38 (Dec.)	453 (Aug.)	1955
Manang	2592	11 (Nov.)	202 (July)	908
Jomsom	2612	3 (Dec.)	43 (July)	248
Jumla	2344	16 (Nov.)	218 (Aug.)	935
Mugu	2043	3 (Nov.)	168 (Aug.)	583
Dharchula	915	12 (Nov.)	650 (July)	2129

Source: Department of Irrigation, Hydrology and Meteorology.

(5) *Himalayan Desert Climate (above 5000 m)*: Snow remains freezed above snow-line. Snow-clad Himalaya is also the rainshadow area. The temperature remains below 0°C.

Vegetation of Nepal

As Nepal has various types of climates, various altitudes and adequate water resources, vegetation is boundless. There are different floral names in different ethnic areas, altogether 1445 Nepali names have been collected by natural history museum in Nepal. Regarding the spatial distribution of the forests, they are dense in Hill areas while they gradually decrease towards North and South. The western parts are eovered more than any other part.

As per Hindu mythology a number of trees have been termed as sacred and so they are protected religiously. Pipal, Bar, Bel, Amla, Nim, Tulsi, Kuss etc. and some flowers, Fruits, Leaves and Woods are considered religiously important.

Types of Natural Vegetation

Nepal Himalayas not only cover the central Himalaya variety of flora and fauna but also represent eastern and western varieties of Himalayan range. According to the different varieties of vegetation Nepal can be placed in three divisions.

1. *Sub-Tropical Evergreen (Up to 1200 m.)*

These types of forests are available mostly in the Northern part of Tarai, Bhaber, Inner Tarai, Siwalik Range, river Basins and deep valleys of Mahabharat region. In the Bhaber zone and inner Tarai tropical deciduous forests consisting of Khair and Shisham are seen in the riverside valleys. Evergreen forests are to be seen in the high rainfall region of 1000-1600 m ın the foothills of Nepal. Simla, Zamun and many shrubs are popular. In Bhaber Charkose Jhadi (13 km long) the forest is famous for wild animals due to very dense forests; trees like Sal, Sakhuwa, Agrath and Oak are very popular in the Tarai Jungle.

2. *Temperate Deciduous (1200-2100 m)*

Deciduous and mixed forests are available in hilly region. Sub-tropical variety goes up to 1000-2100. In western Nepal Chirpine Khote Salla and in the eastern and central Nepal Chilaune, Dhalne, Katus, are found along with wet ravines and gullies also. In the lower part Sal and in higher places Salla pine trees are the basic character of deciduous distribution. Bambu variety is found in Arun valley, Sigame, Nigalo, Malingo or rato Nigale, Chitre, Choyabans, Bhalu Bans are local names of Bans found within 1800-2100 m elevation.

3. *Temperate Coniferous Forests (2100-3300 m)*

Evergreen needle-shaped trees are found in coniferous forest belt within 2100-3300 m. Above 3000 to 3500 m in the higher part of Mahabharat range and lower parts of Himalaya such forests are found. In about 2400-2800 m. mountains are covered with coniferous forests of soft wood. Varieties of juniper, spruce, deodar, birch, magnolya, fir, larches, cedars etc. are abundant in this region. Above 2500-4000 m rhododendrons are prominent. In the eastern parts trunk of trees are covered with moss.

4. *Alpine Grass Land (3300-5000 m)*

In the cold climate and low rainfall varieties of grass, bushes, flowering plants, creepers are quite prominent. Below snow-line (4,700 m) the grass is very dominating along with medicinal plants and herbs of many species.

5. *Himalayan Desert Vegetation (above 5000 m)*

The cold and dry desert (Tundra type) climate is found above 5000 m. This region is always absent of trees, shrubs of general nature. But some parts are laden with mosses, lichens (leu) at 6000 m in Himalaya. Fungi and Yeast are found up to 8000 m. North and South vegetation differs in

Table 2.14

Altitudinal Limits of Major Crops

Region	*Crops*	*Altitude (m)*	*Location*
1	*2*	*3*	*4*
Himalaya (Highland)	Buckwheat/Mithe and Tite Phapar (Fagopyrum asculentum, Moench and Tataricum gearth)	Up to 43000	Inner Himalaya
	Naked barley/Uwa (Hordeum valgare)		
	Foxtailmillet/Kagume (Setaria italica)		
	Barley/Jau (Hordeum vulgare)	1800-3700	Upper limit 4,470 m.
	Potato/Alu (Salanum tuberosum)	2400-4200	Central Nepal 4300 m, Western Nepal 3000 m.
	Horse chest-nut/Karu (Panicum miliaceum)		Upper limit 4690 m.
Hill (Midland)	Rice/Dhan (Oryza sativa)	Up to 2500	Lowlands Central Nepal 2000, western Nepal 2100
	Wheat/Gahun (Triticum aestivum)	Up to 3000 lekh	Central Nepal 3000 m, western Nepal

(*Contd.*)

1	2	3	4
	Maize/Makai (Zea may:)	Up to 2800	Hills—Central Nepal 3000 western 2400 m.
	Millet/Kodo (Eleusine coracana)	Up to 3000	Upper limit is higher than rice Hills and Tarai.
	Barley/Jau (Hordeum vulgars)	Up to 3600	Hills
Tarai (Lowland)	Rice/Dhan (Oryza sativa)		Tarai
	Wheat/Gahun (Triticum Aestivum)		
	Oilseeds/Tori (Brassica campestres)		Tarai
	Philinge (Guizotia abyssinica)		

Table 2.15

Fruits in Geographic Regions

Region	*Fruit Varieties*	*Altitude (m)*
High land	Apple/Syau (Malus sytrestris)	
	Apricot/Khurpani (Prunus armonicca)	
Mid land	Citron/Mimiro (Citrus medica)	
	Grapes/Dakh (Vitisacida champ)	
	Guava/Amma (Psidium guajava)	
	Junar organge/Junar (Citrus sinensis obbeck)	
	Lemon/Kagati (Citrus aurantefolia)	
	Orange/Suntara (Citrus reticulata)	
	Peach/Aru (Prunus persica)	1200-2100 m
	Pear Naspati (Pyrus communis)	
	Persimmon/Haluwabed (Diospyros)	
	Plum/Alubakhara (Prunus domestica)	1500-2100 m
	Pomegranate/Anar (Punica grantum)	
	Pommelo/Bhogate (Citrus grandis)	
	Rough lemon/Jyamir-Kali and Katha (Citrus junos and Citrus jambbiri)	
Low land	Banana or Plantain/Dera (Musa paradisica)	
	Black plum/Jamun (Eugenia jambolana)	
	Pomegranate/Anar or Darim (Punica granatum)	
	Jack fruit/Rukh Katahar (Artocarpus integra)	
	Pineapple/Bhuli Katahar (Ananas comosus)	
	Litchi/Lichi (Nephelium litche)	
	Mango/Amp (Mangigera indica)	Upper limit 1500 m
	Paw or Papita/Mewa (Carica papaya)	
	Custard apple/Saripha (Annona squamosa)	

the presence of dense undergrowth. While Northern high altitude forests contain bushes and thickets, bushy rhododendron, birch and juniper can only survive in upper Himalayas.

The timber line is up to 4000 m only. In the valleys primeval forests are also seen. One can see the merging of vegetation both in vertical and horizontal scales.

Geography of Tarai

Physically and geologically Nepal is divided into three main regions, running right from the west to the east. They are:

(a) Mountainous northern part.

(b) Hilly central part.

(c) Tarai (Plain southern part).

Tarai region extends from west to east along the southern side of the country. It is an extension of Gangetic plain of India and forms a low flat land. It includes most of the fertile land and dense forest area of the country. Forty per cent of its land is under cultivation. Water resources are good and land with alluvial soil is fit for varieties of crops like paddy, maize, wheat, sugarcane, vegetables and tobacco etc.

Altitudinal diversities in Nepal are found at every step. Within short span of about 180 km there is mountain Sagarmatha 8848 m. high in the north and the lowest is Budhha Nagar, 60 m. above the sea level in Morang district of Tarai. Tarai area is about 17 per cent of the whole area of Nepal measuring 25021 sq. kms. and with varying topography from 60 m. to 200 m. above the sea level. Overall average width of Tarai is 25 to 30 kms. Tarai is also called Duwars in Bhutan. The narrow strip of the flat field between Indo-Gangetic plain and low hills of Nepal is very fertile. The soil has waterable width, though it is not even everywhere. In the east of Narayani river for about 65 kms. it is fully isolated from Gangetic plain area. The rest of the flat plain is formed with alluvial soil, sediments and silts of sub-recent deposition. The Tarai alluvials deposited are estimated to the tune of 2400 metres deep. Tarai, as per soil, can be divided into (I) Inner Tarai, (II) Bhabar belt and (III) Tarai plain of Gangetic extension.

Table 2.16

Sub-Divisions of Tarai Region

Sub-Divisions	*Area %*	*Altitude m.*	*Length East-West*	*Breadth North side—kms.*
The Inner Tarai	8	600	25-100	15-30
The Bhabar	4	300	125-400	10-15
The Plain Tarai	15	200	125-400	25-30

The upper portion of Tarai is comprised of Bhabar and Chaure (low hills) respectively.

Formation of Top Crust: The altitude of Tarai belt has a sloping tendency from north to south ranging from 200 m and coming down to 60 m only. However, western Tarai is 100 m. higher than eastern Tarai. The gradient is from west to east i.e., from the western side it slopes down gradually. The maximum height at one point is 305 m. and out of total Tarai land this higher altitude accounts for about 23 per cent.

Inner Tarai: It is a portion above the plain land. The Siwalik Hills of India called Chaure range in Nepal enclose many terrains which are called Doors. In Nepal Doon land is between Mahabharat and Chaure Hills. The breadth varies as per plain land available between the two ranges. Rapti (Chitwan) and Dang are Doons or Bhitri Madesh (inner province). Altitude of these spindle shaped doon valleys varies from 110 m. to 665 m. Narrow river valleys in Tarai are called *Khonch* like Trijuga Khonch (Udaypur), Kamla Khonch (Sindhauli).

Inner Tarai's north side is barricaded by Mahabharat range and on the south it is bound by Chaure range. Chitwan and Deukhuri valleys are enclosed by a contour of 300 m.

Longitudinal Doon Valleys of Inner Tarai

The regionwise altitude and area of some important

places of Inner Tarai are given in the following table:

Table 2.17

Altitude and Area of Some Important Places of Inner Tarai

Region	*Inner Tarai*	*Altitude m.*	*Area sq. km.*
Eastern	Udaypur	360	4273
Central	Sindhulimadi	276-516	
Western	Nawalparasi	111-500	
	Chitwanpur (Rapti)	149-500	
	Makwanpur	466	1604
Midwestern	Dang	663	
	Deukhuri	213-244	1126
	Surkhet	664	41
Far Western	Dipayal (Doti)	549	
	Jogibuda		
	Dundeldhara	381	

The Bhabar Belt

There is one rugged and sandy strip between Chure range and plain Tarai. Porous soil with big boulders, pebbles, gravels and sand covered forest and grass is called Bhabar belt. The altitude of this belt is from 360 m. to 381 m. and the slope is 18 to 30 m. per two kms. Water percolates in this porous region and reappears in the form of springs in plain Tarai. So most of the rivers are invisible while crossing this belt, only big rivers like Mahakali, Karnali, Rapti, Banganga, Narayani, Tinau, Bagmati, Kamala, Trijuga, Kosi, Kanki etc. are crossing the belt in physical appearance. In this belt-course, material brought by rivers is deposited. The region covers about 9065 sq. kms. Bhabar belt is famous for containing finest forests called 'Char Kos Jhari' of 13 km. long belt. It is full of Sal trees. But deforestation has begun here too.

Plain Tarai

Located in the southernmost side of Nepal it is a broad belt. Slope from north to south is very gentle and is roughly 3 m. per 2 km. Tarai is extended from the foothills of Chure range and gently merged into the Gangetic plain in south. As referred to earlier there is a patch of about 65 to 80 km. in Tarai which is interrupted by Chure range, east of Narayani river and Dong-Deokhuri respectively. Indian border extends right up to Siwalik range.

All Himalayan rivers have deposited fertile alluvium which is one of the important economic and prospective factors of Tarai and for Nepal as a whole. The soil is much more a fine ingredient, fertile right from east to west and from north to south. In the modern narrow strip due to excessive moist and seepage, it is marshy and suitable for jungles. South Tarai is most suited to agriculture. Another advantage of the area is water table which is very high. So due to the temperature added with water abundance, the area is suitable for vegetation. The warm and moist climate condition in Tarai has made it very fertile, cultivable and most productive.

Divisions of Southern (Plain) Tarai

In Nepal the Tarai strip is broken and there are distinct divisions:

(a) *Eastern Tarai* : It extends from district Parsa to Jhapa. It is more extensive, wide and productive than any other region. Agriculture and cash crops are produced in this section.

(b) Central Tarai is from Shivraj to Gandiki.

(c) Western Tarai is from Mahakali to Banke. It is irregular, narrow and drier.

The whole Tarai is managed by divisions into 20 districts. All these districts are grouped into 5 regions. Eastern Region consists of 5 districts, Central region has 7 districts and western has 3 districts. Apart from the above 15 districts there are two regions namely mid-western region which has three districts and the Far Western region comprises of two districts only.

The following table will represent the typical relief features of each district with its headquarter.

Table 2.18

Area, Headquarter and Altitude of Tarai Districts

Region	*District*	*Area in Sq. Km.*	*Headquarters*	*Altitude m.*
Eastern	Jhapa	1606	Bhadrapur	75
	Morang	1855	Birat Nagar	72
	Sunsari	1257	Inaruwa	83
	Saptari	1363	Rajbiraj	78
	Siraha	1188	Sirha	76
Central	Dhunusha	1180	Janakpur	73
	Mohottari	1002	Jaleswar	61
	Sarlahi	1259	Malangiva	83
	Rautahat	1126	Gaur	76
	Bara	1190	Kalaiya	99
	Parsa	1353	Birganj	88
	Chitwan	1217	Bharatpur	191
Western	Nawalparsi	2162	Parsi	111
	Rupandehi	1360	Bhairahawa	106
	Kapilvastu	1738	Taulihawa	103
Mid-western	Dang-Deokhuri	2955	Ghorahi	663
	Banke	2337	Nepalganj	152
	Bardiya	2025	Gulariya	149
Far-western	Kailali	3235	Dhangadhi	171
	Kanchanpur	1610	Mahendra Nagar	116
Total	20 Districts	34019 Sq. Km.		

The following graph indicates that topography of all the twenty districts of Tarai is identical. Eleven districts are lesser

TREND OF ALTITUDINAL HEIGHT OF ALL THE 20 DISTRICT HEADQUARTERS OF TARAI

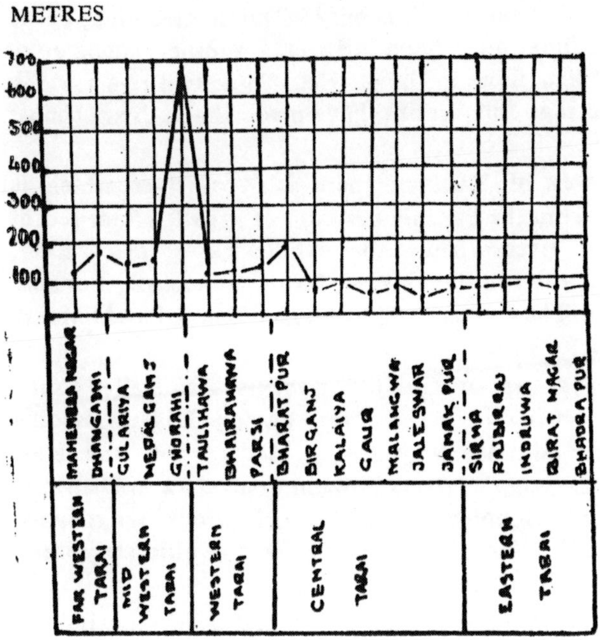

than 100 m. while eight are around 200 mt. and only one is abnormally high above 600 mt. Therefore, Tarai land is just flat land and a part of Gangetic plain; the climate is warm and the earth is alluvial, most fertile for agriculture and vegetation.

Rivers of Tarai

Nepal rivers flow from north to south. They take ice-melting water and cross the hill ranges in different altitudes and cutting deep gorges and valleys. These rivers fall from about 6000 m. and sloping down, meet Ganges in the plains. In Hills these rivers are very swift but when they enter Tarai plains they become sluggish and broad. Nepal's rivers contribute about 75 per cent water to Ganges and Gangotri plain of Uttar Pradesh and Bihar.

Starting from Eastern Tarai the rivers can be enumerated as under:

Easternmost river which makes boundary between Nepal and India is Mechhi which is only 26 kilometres long, but is very swift. It runs into Jhapa district. Another small river Kankahi 108 Km. flows in the district. These two rivers along with small springs and brooks, have made Jhapa district most fertile.

To the west of Kankahi there is Kosi river which is famous right from the Puranic period. It is called Sapt Koshi because seven rivers from the whole basin meet Kosi. They are Tamor, Arun, Dudhikosi, Jikhu, Tamakosi, Sunkosi and Indravati. These rivers make Morang, Sunsari and Saptari districts fertile.

Another group of Gandiki river is also called Sapt Gandiki comprising of seven rivers namely Trishuli, Budhicandiki, Daraundi, Marshayangadi, Madri, Seti and Kali (Krishan). This group of rivers flows in Central Tarai Districts. This group has high potential of Hydro-Electric power roughly 22 million KW. Narayani river and Gandak ultimately meet Ganges near Hajipur in Bihar.

Karnali Basin : Karnali is the longest river flowing in Nepal for 507 km. This river also has seven tributaries and many subtributaries. Sapt Karnali system is comprising of Sani Bhori, Thuli, Bheri, Tila Mugu Karnali, Humia Karnali, Burhi Ganga and Seti rivers. This system drains an area of about 49,000 sq. km. in western Nepal. When this river enters India it is called Ghaghara. The power potential of Karnali basin is 10 Billion KW (U.N. Survey, 1961). This river covers 22 principalities.

Second Grade Rivers: There are some second grade rivers like Mechhi 25 km. in East Kankahi 108 km., Trijuga 55 km., Kamala 117 km., Bagmati 163 km., Tinau, Rapti 155 km., Banganga 72 km., Babai 190 km. Apart from the above there are monsoon rivers which flow in rainy season.

Third Grade Rivers: They are smaller ones and they take off from Chure range and serve the purpose of local irrigation only.

Contribution of Rivers in the Formation of Tarai Land

These rivers are very effective in soil erosion and deposition of debris. From hills whatever sediments are brought by these river systems they are deposited in the Tarai, thus making Tarai rich with alluvium soil. Sometimes these rivers deposit so much debris on earth that they are forced for diversion by these islands or basin. Such island cases have been witnessed in case of Kosi river. Such island has been an apple of discord between Nepal and India.

To summarise the benefits of these river systems of Nepal it can be safely concluded that these rivers have given following advantages to Nepal:

(i) These rivers have made opening of passages.

(ii) Have turned Tarai land as the most fertile land of granary in Nepal.

(iii) Rivers have very high potential of Hydro-Power which is yet to be harnessed.

Apart from these benefits to Nepal these rivers are a boon to India also. Most of the Northern Part of India is benefited by these rivers. Though on many occasions they create havoc by flood and devastate many areas of Bihar, yet due to bunds and barrages built along the rivers the fury has been controlled to great extent.

Climate of Tarai : In all the twenty districts of Tarai the climate is quite tropical like that of Gangetic plain. As Nepal is very diversified in altitude from south to north so the climate is also varied. It is a land where all types of climate is experienced, from the icy-cold of Tundra to the tropical of the plains.

Temperature : The low lands of Tarai and Inner Tarai are warmer and hilly and Himalayan regions are cooler. Temperature remains constant like Gangetic plains. It touches 5°C in winter and 33.5°C in summer. In eastern Tarai, however, mercury goes up to 40°C in June. Below 600 m. the climate is tropical with hot and moist atmosphere. In the winter season Tarai experiences maximum of 23C° and minimum 7°C climate and temperature both are soothing for working, cultivation and living in Tarai. This fact has been instrumental in the rapid growth of population in Tarai.

Rainfall: Tarai receives moisture-laden clouds from south in Monsoon days. It therefore rains heavily in the whole Himalayan region. The eastern part of Tarai is more rainy due to Assam being near and prolonged rains are felt there. As we go to west it becomes drier and drier. In the low land of Tarai annual precipitation is 933 mm and 2292 mm. April has dry days with bright sun and clear nights in Tarai.

Winds : Before the arrival of Monsoon season the low-land in north feels isolated highly and so local winds start flowing swiftly. Sometime thunder storms with hail do occur. Furious flow of air is felt in Butwal. In Jumla also, each afternoon feels heavy blows of wind. In premonsoon season, winds blow from south-west and go towards north-east. Monsoon arrives from south-west with ample rains. The barren fields of Tarai are watered after a hot spell. People are seen merry-making. Agricultural activities start with great gusto.

Seasons : In Tarai just like in upper India the seasons are identical. It is hot in Summer between March and June, rainy between June 15 to September 15. The south-most part remains sunny, dusty and windy in March-June. Spring comes in April-May. Rains in July-August-September and autumn in October-November. The climate belts in Nepal can be classified as under :

Table 2.19
Climate Belts in Nepal

(i) Sub-Tropical	Below 1200 m.	Tarai and Inner Tarai
(ii) Warm-Temperate	1200-2100 m.	Midland Upper Chure
(iii) Cold Temperate	2100-3300 m.	Mahabharat & Himalaya
(iv) Lekhali (Alpine)	3300-5000 m.	Snow line Himalayan Valley
(v) Himalayan Desert	Above 5000 m.	Up of snow line

There are chances of variation when either cloud bursts or melting of ice is excessive. But such climate variations are temporary for few days only.

Vegetation : As discussed earlier there are many factors which have carved the Nepal Tarai as benediction of God Pashupatinath. On the one hand Hills and Hills-steep topography, barren lands, marshy terrains and deep gorges have left nothing to help Nepali people to earn their livelihood, on the other a boonland in the name of Tarai has been created by the Lord. Scarcity of provisions in the hills has been turned into abundance in Tarai.

Agricultural Encroachment: The productivity in the forest region of Tarai is mostly very high. So people from hills and Himalayas have been attracted to Tarai to own land and produce grains. This resulted in the heavy shifting of population which in turn to acquire cultivable land started deforestation. Agricultural activities and resettlement programmes of Nepal Government during the last 40 years have changed the shape of the landscape of Tarai Region.

Commercial Exploitation of Jungles of Tarai ; From the time British India had approached Tarai its forests have been cut down. Timber has been exported to India and Britain for use as sleepers in railways. After the independence of India, Tarai became more hazardous and everyone entered Tarai and made his living there. It is not only timber but also firewood and herbs of medicinal plants that were sent out in large number and large quantity. Since 1967 there was some check applied in deforestation. The quality of forest remaining is quite degraded.

Population Pressure : People not only from Hills migrated to Tarai but also outsiders mostly from India came in and settled here. So forests have been overused and actually misused. It became a victim of day-to-day needs of faggots and fodders. Over-grazing of animals have also deteriorated the position of firewood. So much scarcity was felt that people either had to walk miles away to jungles or cook their food with the help of cow dung. Deforestation is converting green land into desert, yet the remarkable shrubs found in most part of Nepal are called Bammara. It is a forest destroying species. It is one to five metre tall at different places. Bush can survive in dry alpine zones as well as in tropical ones.

Sub-Tropical Evergreen (up to 1200 m.) forests are found in the northern Tarai, Bhabar Belt, Inner Tarai, Siwalik belt, river valleys and deep valleys of Mahabharat region, Khatri-Siso trees can be seen in abundance. Evergreen tropical forests grow mostly below 1000 m. Deciduous forests consist of Simal Jamun. High temperature and moisturous soil and adequate supply of water have contributed for healthy shrubs and trees. Sal trees are very useful. Shorea robust grows tall up to 45 m. Below 1000 m. cheaper jungles and marshy vegetation is found. Trees like Sakhuwa or agrath and oak are very popular in Tarai. Sal grows 300 m in eastern Tarai and up to 900 m in western Tarai. Simal, Srish, Siso (Shisham), Khair (Katha), Katus, lamkuri are very popular in Tarai. Tall elephant grass *dhaddi* and thick shrub jungles are found where water is not very high. The shrubs mostly coil up big trees standing by their side.

Soil Condition of Tarai

The varied altitudes and steep slopes have contributed this mountainous country of Nepal a great potential of power and paradise. Landslides, glaciation, soil erosion and gravitational forces all create environmental energy which can turn Nepal into a land of paradise. Temperature rises in the plains while gradually it decreases as we go to north altitudes.

Soil condition in Nepal changes vertically in different geographical regions. (I) Tarai has alluvial soil, (II) Hilly region has sandy soil, (III) and Himalayan region is glacial. Though sixteen mapping units have been selected to represent the soil conditions of whole Nepal in different regions but here I have presented the condition of Tarai only. There are six divisions of soil groups in Tarai. Each group is presented with texture i.e. character of particles and reactions.

In the Tarai region the rivers flowing from northern highland bring alluvium and deposit it into Tarai plains. This makes the top layer very fertile. The undulating parts of Tarai have recent and sub-recent soils. The older soil is found in upper banger land and newer soil has been deposited in lower parts. Alluvial soil is found both in Tarai region as well as in river banks and valleys.

Table 2.20

Soil Distribution in Tarai

Region Altitude m.	*Soil Group*	*Texture Particle Character*	*Reaction*
1	*2*	*3*	*4*
Tarai			
60 m Recent and sub-recent alluvial sediments	1. Heptaquents Entrochrepts	Sandy loam Clay loam Silty loam	Moderately Acid to neutral
Intensive Agriculture deciduous forests	2. Heptaquents	Silt Loam	
Tropical Sub-Tropical	Entrochrepts Haptaquents	Silty clay loam Silty clay	Neutral to moderately Alkaline
Major Crops Rice, maize, wheat, oil seeds	Calcarious materials	Sandy loam Loam	
Cash crops Sugarcane Tobacco	3. Heptaquents Psammaquents Ustorthents	Loamy sand Sandy Loam Silt Loam	Slighlty acid to neutral
	4. Hapludolls Ustochrepts Entrochrepts	Sandy Loam Silt Loam Loamy sand	Slightly to mildly alkaline

(*Contd.*)

1	*2*	*3*	*4*
Inner Tarai			
150-800 m. Recent and Sub-recent alluvial sediments	5. Undorthents Ustorthents Heptaquents	Sandy loam Loam Salt loam Loamy sand	Moderately acid to neutral
Intensive Agriculture rice, maize, mustard, sugarcane	6. Dystrochrepts Entrochrepts Orgiudolls	Sandy loam Loam Salt loam Loam	Strongly Acid to neutral

Source : Division of Soil Sciences and Agricultural Chemistry, Deptt. of Agriculture, HMG., 1978.

The above soil chemistry has been given intentionally to indicate as to how the whole belt of the Tarai land was formed. The same chemistry is existing in the plains of Ganges in U.P. and Bihar Provinces. Therefore, vegetations, agriculture, forests, fodder and trees of both countries are similar except in case of Inner Tarai with an altitude above 200 m to 800 m. All crops which are produced in Gangetic plains are grown in Tarai also. The variation may be in the forms of cultivation. While India switched to more mechanical ways Nepal Tarai is yet to develop this technique on a large scale.

Minerals

Tarai has absolutely no minerals whether metallic or non-metallic. Fossil fuel of low quality of coal has been traced in Morang district and Narayangadh region. Though there is great potential of minerals in Nepal but geographical complexities and lack of transportation facilities have compelled Nepal to stay back. These are stumbling blocks which create difficulties in the development of mineral resources. The present digging method is crude and not conducive to the modern sciences.

Influence of Altitude on Economic Aspects of Nepal and Tarai

The uneven topography of Nepal has greatly affected the economic aspects of the country. The habitants of Himalayan regions are mostly engage in animal husbandry and cattle breeding. Horticulture and fruits are common in lesser heights and hill area. Tarai plain land is suitable for agricultural and cash crops. These major occupational sources have affected trade and industry also. Higher you go lesser the occupational opportuuities available. In fact ecological regions have restricted economic activities and means of subsistence. Agriculture, small scale industry and agriculture associated trade are main ways of man's occupation in Tarai.

Above the Tarai region ways and means change according to altitude. In Siwalik range forestry, cattle breeding, herb-picking like small jobs are done. But in Kathmandu Valley agriculture and other trade techniques are abundantly followed. Then on hill slopes sheep breeding, wool-carving is done with its trade in down country and with Tibet also; academically it can be said that contour lines of Nepal are fate lines of people regarding their labour and life ways.

Means of Transportation and Mode

Geo-topographical position of Nepal is such that circulation of men and animals is very much restricted. Altitude has totally controlled the movement and free resources Northernmost high peaks of Himalaya laden with snow and ice can seldom be passed.

Network of roads cannot be put on treacherous and uneven terrains. Contacts between two settlements is not easy. Even houses are apart and to each house one cannot reach easily. Means of transport in the Himalayan region is with the help of yak, mules, ponies and horses only. On many routes carvan of mules are run. One such example is a route between Pokhara and Jomson. Man himself serves the purpose of porterage in hills. The sick and old men are also carried on backs of porter. Thus man is animal, man is mule, he is pony and he is yak where no other mode of transport is available.

In case of Tarai the position is different. Bullock carts, buffalo carts, trucks, buses and cars can transport men and material where roads are available.

Road construction to contact sparse settlement in mountainous regions is rather a very difficult task. There are very few highways in Himalayan Nepal. In Tarai, however, the position is easier. There is one highway of 1030 km. long, which connects east with west Nepal. It also links the Tarai districts. In the Hill areas only two east-west highways namely Arniko and Prithivi are available which join a few hilly areas. Tribhuvan Highway is the only one which is working as an economic passage to link Nepal with India. In other mountain regions there is no road. It is therefore difficult to cross areas of north due to old, weak and dangerous bridges of various kinds like bamboo log, timber log, ropeways etc.

Hill and Tarai regions have been linked with small feeder roads like :

(i) Dhankuta-Dharan Highway

(ii) Sidharth Highway between Bhairhawa and Pokhara

(iii) Dhangarhi-Dandeldhura Highway.

District to district routes are very crude, rough, difficult and dangerous mostly in remote parts of the country. In this country not only in construction but a huge amount of money is needed in maintenance also. Such huge amount cannot be afforded by a nation like Nepal.

Analysing the circumstances of transport and communication of Nepal it is obvious that up to 1950 human and animal powers were used as means of transportation and communication. Nepal, though a small country, has a gigantic transport problem. To reach the furtherest point it takes several days. Nepal's topography is the main hindrance in thorough passage. In the first half of the 20th century many efforts were made to provide bare transport facilities to people. A ropeway with 8 m. tons per hour capacity was first installed in Nepal in 1922 for 22.5 kms. Stretch of Dhorsing-Mata Tirath ropeway was later in 1947 extended to Teku. Another ropeway with higher capacity was constructed between Hetauda and Kathmandu with 22.5 m. tons per hour capacity.

Similarly, Railway transport was also introduced in 1928 with the installation of Raxaul-Amlekhganj Railway. Janakpur-Jayanagar 53 km. and Janakpur-Brijalpura railway was started in 1935. But this route was not sufficiently utilised.

Further realising the importance of transportation and communication both for people and for development of the country various steps were taken to construct hundreds of kilometres of roads and bridges linking many isolated small villages right from 1950. Ropeway and Railways are now being operated by Nepal Transport Corporation. The first electric-powered trolly bus was introduced linking Kathmandu and Bhaktapur in 1975-76. Up to this day though the network of transportation is not adequate, most of the parts of the country can, however, be reached without entering into foreign land. A promising fact is witnessed in the achievement of road transport for the last three decades.

In 1951 Nepal had only 376 Kms. of road. This figure has now increased to 6306 Kms. in 1987, of which 44 per cent is bitumen-topped. Of the total kilometerage of roade, 31 per cent falls in the category of Highway. The average service of one kilometre road in 1951 was for 22 thousand of population but due to significant increase in Kms. of road in 1987, one kilometre of road is now serving about 22.8 hundred of people. Thus by 1987 one kilometre of road has influenced about 23 sq. Km. of land. The major Highways of Nepal are shown in Table 2.21.

Communications

Nepal is a country of varied altitudes, diversified climates and diversified plain to hillocks habitation; therefore communication is a very important factor. Specially where road transport is difficult, telecommunication and postal services are

Table 2.21

Major Highways of Nepal

S. No.	*Highways*	*Length Km.*	*By aid of*
1.	Mahendra Raj Marg (East-west) Highway	1032	
2.	Prithivi Raj Marg (Kathmandu-Pokhara)	200	China
3.	Tribhuvan Rajpath	190	India
4.	Dhanagadhi-Dadedhura Raj Marg	140	U.S.A.
5.	Sidharth Raj Marg (Sunauli-Pokhara)	181	India
6.	Jogbani-Dharan Dhankuta Raj Marg	100	U.K.
7.	Nepalganj-Surkhet	92	HMG. Nepal
8.	Arniko Raj Marg (Kathmandu-Kodari)	87	China
9.	Gorakha-Narayangadh Rajmarg	61	China
10.	Kathmandu-Janakpur-Bhittamod Rajmarg	100	

only two medias of getting welfare of the society. Keeping in view its importance in the social and economic development of the country special attention has been paid to develop communication sector since the first five year plan.

A. Telecommunication

Telecommunication is simple, easiest and quickest means of communication. This type of service was introduced as far as in 1913 for the first time in Nepal. That time it remained limited to certain pockets of the country only. But after 1951 this service was expanded and in 1955-56, 350 lines of local telephones were distributed and existing trunk telephone services were expanded in other pockets. By year 1988 the country has 29 telephone exchanges, 56 public call offices and 89 wireless stations.

B. Postal Service

Postal service was started only with the transporting of mailing letters in 1956. From that time onwards postal services

Yearwise improvement in road construction in the whole Nepal is as under.

Table 2.22

Total Road Construction (Km.) Progressive Figures

Type	*1977*	*1978*	*1979*	*1980*	*1981*	*1982*	*1983*	*1984*	*1985*	*1986*	*1987*
(a) Black top	1751	1851	1916	2044	2167	2322	2484	2645	2724	NA	2794
(b) Gravel	556	593	685	564	703	719	830	815	918	NA	1180
(c) Earthen	1829	2151	2090	2332	2151	2229	2232	2257	2283	NA	2332
Total Km.	4136	4595	4691	4940	5021	5270	5546	5717	5925	NA	6306

Source : Nepal Road Statistics, Department of Roads, H.M.G., 1987.

have been widened and connected with other economic services such as money order, savings, bankings etc. Extensions and expansions of the services were continuously made from 1956. Up to 1987-88 the total number of post offices opened was 2022.

It is therefore obvious that in spite of many physical hazards and impediments the progress in case of communication has been constantly developing each year. In 1981 telephone exchanges were only 22, they rose to 29 in 1988. Likewise, public call offices position seems more pronounced as in 1981 there was no Public Call Office but in 1988 the number rose to 56. Wireless stations were also increased from 80 in 1981 to 89 in 1988.

Facing the overall adversaries the progress made is appreciable. In the Tarai region, specially in eastern zone and central zone, communications have improved adequately. Industries are put up, business and economic activities are picking up. Therefore, internal and international communications have improved progressively each year.

REFERENCES

Acharya, B., *Sri panch bada maharajadhiraj Prithlvi Narayan Shah*, 4 Vols., Kathmandu, 1968.

Amatya, S.L., *Cash crop farming in Nepal*, Tribhuvan University, 1971.

Bajracharya, B.D., *Licchavikalka avilekh*, Nepal, 2030 B.C.

Banerji, J., 'The glory of the Himalaya', Himalaya, Vol. I, No. I, 1952.

Bhatt, D.D., Natural history and economic botany of Nepal, Orient Longman Limited, 1977.

Bista, D.B., *People of Nepal*, Kathmandu, 1967.

Burathoki, J.B. and U.M, Malla, Ecology of tropical high-lands, 1968.

Dejong, G.F., Demography and research with high altitude population, 1970.

Fleming, Jr. R.L., *The general ecology, flora and fauna of midland Nepal*, CDC, T.U., 1977.

Gurung, H.B., *Nepal dimensions of development*, Kathmandu, 1984.

Hagen, T., *Nepal the Kingdom in the Himalayas*, 1961.

Hagen, T., "Report on the geological survey of Nepal", Vol. I, 1969.

HMG, Central Bureau of Statistics, Population Census—1981. Geographic regions tables, Vol. II, 1984.

HMG, Deptt. of Statics, Statical pocket book, 1986.

HMG, Deptt. of Information, *Mechi dekhi Mahakali*, Vol. 1-4, Kathmandu, 1975.

Kansakar, V.B., "Population projection for Nepal (1970-2000)", CEDA, T.U. Nepal, 1980.

Karan, P.P., *Nepal, a Cultural and Physical Geography*, 1960.

Kihara, H., "Fauna and flora of Nepal Himalaya", Vol. I, 1952.

Kihara, H., *Land and crops of Nepal Himalaya*, Vol. II, Japan, 1952.

Kihara, H., *People of Nepal Himalaya*, Vol. III, Japan, 1952.

Kirkpatrick, C., *An Account of the Kingdom of Nepal*, New Delhi, 1975.

Malla, U.M., *Population growth and environment in the context of Nepal*, Central Panchayat Training Institute, Nepal, 1979.

Sharma, C.K., River systems of Nepal, 1977.

Sharma, C.K., Natural resources of Nepal, 1978.

Shrestha, C.B., *Cultural geography of Nepal*, Bhaktapur, 1981

Shrestha, H., *Water resources of Nepal*, Kathmandu, 1979.

Singh, L.R., *The Tarai region of U.P.*, 1965.

Stainton, J.D.A., *Forest of Nepal*, London, 1977.

Stiller, L., *The rise of the house of Gorakha*, New Delhi, 1973.

Zimmermann, A., *The highest plants in the world*, In Mountain World, New York, 1953.

3

Immigration Pattern and Settlements in Tarai

The problem of national integration vis-a-vis Tarai, has arisen due to the people of one cultural background having migrated into a region of another cultural background. Migration therefore is a very important topic for the study of movements of people in large numbers from one region of Tarai to the other and from one nation to another nation's Tarai region.

Pursuing the reports of the last two censuses it is found that the government of Nepal has become very serious in controlling the population growth of the country. The official population growth in Nepal has increased from 2 per cent in 1961 to 2.07 per cent in 1971. It further rose to 2.62 per cent in 1981 census. Tarai had the highest growth of population: 4.11 per cent annually followed by Hill 1.65 per eent and mountain 1.35 per cent. Population from sub-ecological belts ranged from 5.44 per cent for western mountain to 7.70 per cent for far-western Tarai region.[1]

There are two important factors in this alarming increase. The first is the high natural growth rate of the

1. C.B.S., Population Monograph of Nepal, HMG, CBS, 1989, p. 23.

population combined with reduced mortality rate due to medical advances. The second factor is the high rate of immigration from neighbouring countries. In the later pages I have concentrated much on socio-economic conditions of migrants from India in the Tarai region and shown the impact of such migration on society in general exhibiting two Governments' relations (Nepal-India).

Migration from Gangetic India into Tarai

The early history of Tarai reveals that in spite of the fact that kingdoms arose and disintegrated people have been making their way to Tarai. The first Aryan tribesmen arrived East-ward in Tarai from the area of Prayag, a confluence of Ganga and Yamuna around 900 B.C. During the period 900 to 500 B.C. Aryans penetrated into northern India, called Uttar Pradesh and Bihar now-a-days. The powerful kingdom of Videha (Janak) was established in northern Bihar whose capital was Mithila. It is quite obvious that the same must have been located at the site of Janakpur in Mahottari-Dhanusha district of Eastern Tarai. King Janak of Videha (Jankpur) marrid his daughter Sita to King God Ram of Kaushala (Ayodhya).

Then the king of Sakya dynasty had his capital at Kapilvastu in the mid-western Tarai. Lord Buddha was born in 563 B.C. to a Sakya King at Lumbani near Kapilvastu which is still in Nepal Tarai region. Like Kingdoms of Videha and Kapilvastu another Aryan King had established his kingdom at Simraun Garh in South-east corner of Bara District of Nepal. Archaeologists will discover when excavations are taken in hand that the first king of Simraun Garh may be the chieftain in the Vrijjan confederacy, an Aryan tribe settled in Tarai region around 700 to 600 B.C. In Tarai area there exist many other ruins which when identified will shed more light on long and complex history of Tarai region.

It appears that nearly all the settlers in early History of Tarai were from India's Gangetic plain. They were either Aryan or of pre-Aryan stock. However, settlement pattern in modern times can be traced from three sources, namely from the record of British East India Company, from the record of Nepalese Government officials and the mythical and oral history of Tarai villagers. The British Records and reports of Colonel W. Kirkpatrick and Francis Hamilton provide the information that Col. Kirkpatrick crossed Tarai for taking expedition to Kathmandu in 1773. He has described the settlement pattern of Bara and Parsa districts. He observed that the land was cleared of jungles for about 4 to 5 miles and then partly cleared another 4 to 5 miles. Then people started cultivation by living in small clusters of huts.[1]

Hamilton found that majority of the inhabitants living in Eastern part of Tarai were from plains-tribals like Tharus, Rajbanshis, Mechis and Gangais.[2] The farmers practised slash and burn cultivation and shifted their location after every three or four years when the land lost its fertility. Such land though out of use was also not reclaimed for forest, because of continual grazing of cowherds and buffalos which were brought from Northern India by Ahirs and Caste Hindus.

The Nepali speaking Sen Kings of Palpa and Mukwanpur gained control over mid-western Tarai in 15th or 16th century and extended their control to eastern Tarai as well in mid seventeenth century. They looked upon the dense, malarial forest as a defence wall against invasion from India hence they did not encourage settlement. They rather drew Tarai revenues from trapping and selling elephants and taxing the seasonal pasturing of cattle. Shah Kings rested the Tarai from Sen Kings in 1770 and permitted some settlement.[3]

It was only around 1860, those who controlled Nepal thought that Tarai was of no use for defence purpose.[4] Since

1. Kirkpatrick, Colonel, *An Account of Kingdom of Nepal*, William Miller (London, 1811), pp. 12-16.
2. Hamilton, F., *An Account of Kingdom of Nepal* (Edinburgh, 1819), pp. 156-169.
3. Ibid, pp. 131-132.
4. Nepali Chitranjan, Nepali ma Kariyamochan Ko Itihas, July-Sept. 1964, pp. 10-11.

Nepal gave assistance to Britishers in the mutiny of 1857-58 they got the title for the far-western Tarai which the British had taken away in 1814-16 war and treaty. Jang Bahadur therefore encouraged the settlement of Tarai. He even promised to all Nepali slaves that they would achieve freedom and would be treated as free if they settled in Tarai. Such details of the Rana Government are given in the documents of that period.[1]

The following reasons in general can be accounted for in the settlement of Tarai region.

Causes of Migration

On the basis of the prevailing concepts of scholars about the movement of people and their changing trend of migration it is found that migration itself has undergone into different phases:

(a) Wandering habits of people in the pre-historic period.

(b) Stages of organised settlement and related movement in the ancient periods.

(c) Stages of trade-oriented movement.

(d) Stages of colonization in modern period.

(e) Decolonization and repatriation.

Factors which motivate people for movement and leaving one place for settling at another place can be accounted for as under.

Physical

Physical conditions of the region which vary according to time and place play a vital role in influencing human migration from one region to another physical catastrophe such as volcanic eruptions, earthquakes, landslides, soil

1. Administrative regulation for Tarai District 1816, 3 Vols.

erosion, climatic fluctuation, compel men to move. Deforestation coupled with soil erosion is an important factor in the shifting of human settlement. Epidemics like malaria in Nepal Tarai prevented people to settle there easily. Health resorts also attract people from plains to settle at such places. Modern scientists have changed the whole theory of this natural phenomena. Artificial climatic conditions like air conditioning, invention of disease resisting plants, control over epidemics have enabled men to settle even on unsuitable places if scientific methods are available for help.

Economic Factors

Of all those factors which motivated man to migrate, the economic factor is the most important. In search of better opportunity for occupation people migrate from one place to another. They move from rural areas to urban areas, from unproductive area to a productive one. They move due to population constraints. Little chances of jobs due to dense population also make them move. Industrialisation points, village cottage industry points, excavation of historical sites, digging of canals, preparation of defence line, religious places, attracting usual mela places provide adequate chances for better employment and so better economy.

Development of transport and communication has also influenced people for migration. Transport technology has given enough facilities to people to move to remote places, distant regions and distant countries also.

The wish of men in improving their economic status day by day makes them move for better chances elsewhere. The psycological feeling to live in white collar also attracts people for urban areas. Mining activities like Dhanbad Jharea in Bihar do influence people to migrate. Trade and commerce centres, rail-heads, shipyards, pilgrim centres, power generation centres, places with better facility of cultivation and government's policy for balancing population growth are reasons for human migration.

Social Factors

Although most of the factors for motivating migration are considered economic but social factors are not less significant. Social customs, traditions and prejudices do induce people to migrate. In urban areas people of different cultures and customs are regarded as carriers of diversified culture. But in rural areas people have old and conventional traditions which are not liked by younger generation. The new lights, mod-ways, living in the towns are attractions for young people of rural regions. And sometimes rural area people are so rigid in their customs and culture that anyone who breaks them is an outcaste for non-observance of rules.

After marriage, almost all girls move to their in-laws' houses; so marriage is the highest social factor for migration. Sometimes people have intercaste marriages and are disliked by the locality, they too move elsewhere to live in other places.

Caste, creed and religion, for those people, who have broader ideas with modern social outlook, are the things of the past. So, with independent thinking they wish to adjust themselves in regions where they get the opportunity; consequently they willingly move.

Family restriction, old outdated customs, paternal occupation, rigid religious obeyance, social injustice, non-availability of better education for children and higher education for children, better norms of life open societies; all these factors instigate people to migrate from one place to another.

Political Factors

Political factors are also not insignificant. Several historical reasons and incidents are there to give adequate evidence where people left one country for residing into another. International wars and treaties have, time to time, forced people to move from one region to another in the form of refugees etc. Population transfer from India to Pakistan and from Pakistan to India was the consequence of such political settlement. Military advances and invasions make Kings and their janata to move or run away to safer places.

Demographic Factors

Uneven distribution of population, unbalanced growth of literacy and economic, uneven growth of population etc. do compel people to shift to places of advantage. People migrate to places having low density population. This process not only enables quantitative change but also determines qualitative aspect of population. People with higher education, better technical knowhow and better work experience seek their job elsewhere. Birth rate and death rate do influence people for migration.

All these factors have contributed as reasons of migration and are involved in the settlement of people in Tarai. Brief analysis is presented herewith.

Migration in the Context of People of Indian Origin and People from India

Earlier I have given some of the historical incidents which were instrumental in migrating people from India to Nepal into its Tarai region. The geocultural unity of Nepal and India is radiant in the border area of 800 km. (from Melchi in east to Mahakali in west).

Nepal's social, economic and political ties with India are very old. Relations of people of these two countries rooted deep into the pages of history and into the hearts of the people. Ancient religion and traditions of both countries are common phenomena. Gautama the founder of Buddhism (521 BC) was born in Nepal, learned in India, attained wisdom in India and died in India. Emperor Ashoka (300 BC) came to Kathmandu to spread the sermon of Buddhism and also built many stupas and Chaityas, Kashi, Gaya, Haridwar are considered the most sacred places by Nepalese and they believe that to achieve Moksha they should go to die there. This still continues.

In the Lachhavi period there were some kingdoms on Indian border and northern India, Kapilvastu, Vaishali,

Videha, Shakyas, Kolis, and Malla Kingdoms, all jointly effective in Nepal and India. When greater kingdoms were established in India smaller and petty ones moved to Nepal and settled there in Tarai regions and also in the valley. In the advent of Muslim invasion around 10th century and onwards up to 14th century Northern India was into the grip of Muslim rulers. During this period rulers of Mewar, Chittor, Kannauj, Kumaon, Mithila and Videha fled with their supporters and settled in Nepal for better security. Ruler of Simraungarh who integrated many parts of Tarai fell into the hands of Muslims in 1324 A.D. Sen kings of Palpa and Makwanpur tried their best to consolidate in Tarai region and developed this part economically and made safer politically. These kings brought Maithili language in Tarai and made it official.

During the period of Malla Kings, who too, are of Indian origin, Brahmins and Pujaris were invited from India to perform Puja ceremony at Pashupatinath. Therefore, perior to British rule in India there remained hardly any feeling between the people of Nepal and India for separation.

Indian Immigration after Unification of Nepal

The Shah rulers (during the period from 1768 to 1845) encouraged the Indian people to settle in Tarai. The founder of the present Nepal, King Prithivi Narayan Shah, was also in favour of inviting settlers to Nepal Tarai. He was however cautious not to permit entry to foreign businessmen. In *Divya Updesh* (Pollo) he stated that, "Do not permit Indian traders to go beyond God Pradesh. If they come to our country they will definitely make our subjects pauper".

Between 1860 and 1951 Nepal government encouraged economic development in Tarai and efforts to settle hill people there giving them many concessions but the response from hill people was very poor, because Tarai was unfamiliar and unpleasant to them being hot, and malarious. This played a plus point to Indian settlers. The Government of Nepal had no other option. The economic expansion in Tarai by extension of railhead attracted many business communities like Marwaries, Banias from India.

Muslims of adjoining Indian border provinces like U.P. and Bihar were also attracted to Tarai. As they are good artisans and have better hand skills, and techniques, they also came to Tarai to earn their livelihood. They still maintain their customs like other Muslims in India.

By the seventeenth century, Indian migrants settled in Kathmandu valley as well as in Tarai. There was a high rate of men and women migrated from southern portion of India. The men married Khas and Mangoloid tribes of women.[1] The children were known as Kshatriyas.[2] Brahmans and Rajputs from South mixed with the people of Hill region and formed small kingdoms. Gorakha was one such kingdom out of forty six established in that period. Rajputs, Khas, Magars and Gurung were in command in Nepal up to 17th century rather up to the unification by Prithivi Narayan Shah.

The Measure of Migration

While discussing the scale of migration into the Tarai, the number of people, the caste and communal characteristics of migrants, the location of their previous radiance and their economic factors are very much involved. The study of migration pattern in Nepal is of special nature as necessary early data are not available. Data were collected in 1967-68 field survey.[3]

From the data in Table 3.1, it is apparent that migration into the sample villages of Mahottari, Dhanusha, Bara and Kapilvastu districts is not enough. In Kailali district number of newly arrived settlers is more significant. But in Jhapa District scale of migration is great enough to effect rapid growth of population. But these figures of five

1. Northey, W. and Morris, C.J., The Gurkhas, Cosmo Publications, Delhi, 1974, pp. 124-125.
2. Hodgson, B.H., Essays on the language, literature and religion of Nepal and Tibet, Trubner & Co. London, 1874, Pt. 2.
3. Gaige, F.H., "National Integration in Nepal : A study of Nepal Tarai", University of Pennsylvania, 1970.

Table 3.1

Migrant Families as Percentage of all Families in Sample and Non-sample Villages by District and Sub-region District

District and sub-region of district	*No. of sample villages surveyed*	*No. of families in villages*	*No. of migrant families*	*Migrant families as percentage to families*	*No. of non-sample villages surveyed*	*No. of families in villages 1958*	*No. of migrant families 1958-67*	*Migrant families as a percentage of families*
Jhapa (Total)	10	509	167	32.8	6	133	238	179.0
Mahottari								
Dhanusha								
Sub-Total	16	3487	33	1.00				
P.C.A.								
Sub-Total	8	874	83	9.5				
F.F.F.A.								
Total	24	4361	11[illegible]	2.7	2	124	49	39.5

Bara								
Sub-Total P.C.A.	16	3409	50	1.5				
Sub-Total F.F.F.A.	4	333	46	13.8	No Data Collected			
Total	20	3742	96	2.6				
Kapilvastu								
Sub-Total P.C.A.	15	1348	29	2.1				
Sub-Total F.F.F.A.	4	168	63	37.5				
Total	19	1511	92	6.1	2	118	61	51.5
Kailali Total	18	290	45	15.5	No Data Collected			
Five District Survey Total	81	10413	516		10	375	348	

P.C.A. = Plains cultivated area.
F.F.F.A. = Forests and fringe of forest area.

districts of Tarai should not be applied as normal scale. Table is further broken down for Mahottari—Dhanusha, Bara, and Kapilvastu into two sub-categories. In the plains-cultivated area much of the population is concentrated. In the forest fringe area in the northern part the land clearing is in process and more settlement is being done than in the plains-cultivated area. The settling families are seen more pronounced in the villages under non-sample survey.[1]

Migrations from Hills into Tarai

Demographic and economic problems which are rampant in Gangetic plain also plague Hill regions of Nepal forcing people to leave their ancestral villages and to move for the land which may support them. Although Himalayas have always been a source of attraction to adventurers and mystics but they offer little for living conditions. This phenomenon existed about 3000 years ago. Some of the Aryan tribes moving eastward in the Gangetic plain must have picked up their way towards eastward Himalayan plains and foothills. It seems quite natural that those tribes who were herding cows were attracted to grassy lands of Tarai and further to Himalayan foothills. This tribe must be Gopala that bred cows. History of the Nepal also gives clear evidence that NE Muni installed first King to the throne was a Gopal. His dynasty lasted several years. On a grazing dispute it is also evident that Gopala Kingship fell into the hands of another brother clan named as Ahir in later days.

High altitude Himalayas are inhcspitable, dry and cannot provide enough provision for substance living. When the balance between the living population and available resources receded, people started to come down and moved eastward and gradually this process continued for hundreds of years. So the last limit was the Tarai plain land.

The west to east migration has been documented in Nepalese and Indian censuses. Many Magar and Gurungs families leaving their ancestral villages in the west hills moved

1. Ibid, Table, p. 246.

to East Plains. In 1961 census Nepal enumerates 67,327 Magars and 6938 Gurungs living in the eastern Hills.[1] Indian census 1901 enumerates nearly 200000 speakers of Nepali and Hill-tribal languages settled in India.[2]

In 1954 U.N.O. forestry specialist was one of the first to issue the warning that erosion is slowly but surely robbing the Mahabharat's habitable land; "Because its drainage basins are being deforested."[3]

In 1951 and onward Nepal Government tried to adjust overpopulated Hill areas with meagre living production by shifting Hillmen to Tarai land. They were offered attractive terms also. Migration has three characteristics. First is permanent migration. Studies show that Mr. Mac Dougal found that out of 641 families of 6 villages, 39 had moved away finally, i.e. 6 per cent of population.

Second type migration is semipermanent. This means migration for 6 months, few years or about 5 to 10 years and then returning of people to their own place. The permanent migration involves children and women also but temporary migrations are men-centred.

The third type migration is just seasonal and usually occurs for three to four months.

Tarai is a Population-Hungry Belly

Economic deterioration in the hill areas of Nepal and Gangetic plains has tempted both Indians and Hill people to settle there. Most attracting feature was to acquire land and become land holder either free or on relatively little cash. By the time agriculture developed in Tarai, it provided businessmen new opportunities as well. So Tarai can be called a population vacuum. When we compare the population densities in Tarai and surrounding areas the above fact is identified. In the map enclosed it is indicative of greater population density

1. Census of Nepal, 1961, pp. 18-28.
2. Census of India, 1961, Vol. I, Part II C, pp. 141, 183.
3. Earnest Robbi Report to the Government of Nepal on forestry, Rome, 1954, F.A.O. Report No. 209, pp. 14-15.

in the north and the south of Tarai, then in the region itself. Even if one considers that there is much less cultivable land in Hills than Tarai the density in Hill cultivable land is more pronouncing than in Tarai. The greatest disparity in the far east where, for example, Kanchanpur district of Tarai had a density of population of 31 people per sq. mile in 1961 while neighbouring district Dandeldhura had a density of 146, nearly five times greater.

Repulsion pressure in the hills has persisted for many decades. This has been evidenced by large scale migration of Hill people into northern India, Sikkim and Bhutan over the past 70 years. High death rate caused by malarial fever in Tarai made Nepal Government seek U.N. aid for eradication campaign in 1950. In order to assess the extent of potential for absorbing settlers in Tarai one must find out how much of forest land is still vulnerable to settlers.

Caste and Communal Characteristics of Migrants

Many Nepali officials have formed the idea that migration to Tarai is primarily from Hills and these migrants outnumber others. They will gradually change the Hill-plains' cultural equation and would bring Nepalisation in the region. This conception has been made due to the fact that the Hill settlers are more conspicuous and vocal than settlers of the plain origin. Secondly, plain people try to settle in relatively large established villages where visiting officials have more difficulty for passage and identification. Hill settlers often come in contact with officials with problems like malaria-eradication scheme and to get their huts sprayed with anti-malaria oil. Moreover, Government officials, when they find that a particular settlement was not there in their previous visit they form the idea of a new settlement by Hill stock. In the survey of the five districts of Tarai it was revealed otherwise and was found that 59 per cent settlement belonged to plain people and 35% to Hill origin people.

Migration pattern varies from region to region and part to part. In Kailali 71 per cent migrants are caste Hindus and Tribals from Hills. In other two districts Jhapa and

Kapilvastu, the number of migrants are distributed evenly between the caste Hindus and Hilly Tribal people. In Bara, Mahottari and Dhanusha, majority of migrants are plain origin; 71 percent and 94 per cent respectively. It is also a fact that larger percentage of plain migrants are shifting from one place to another than Hill origin settlers.

Majority of migrants from Hills are high caste Hindus whereas majority of migrants from plains are of low-caste. Bara district has lowest percentage of high caste Hill migrants. 57 per cent of all Hill migrants Kapilvastu had the highest 89 per cent. Low caste migrants from plains represent majority in 4 districts. If we add low caste plain Hindus, plain tribals and Muslims[1], they present 75% in Jhapa, 70% in Mahottari-Dhanusha, 78% in Bara and 77% in Kapilvastu.

Due to the fact that majority of migrants from Hills are upper caste and majority of plain settlers are of low castes, cultural equation can definitely change. Caste ranking of migrants is an important factor as they change the socio-economical, political and cultural material of Tarai. Hill Brahmins and Chhettries are well educated compared to low castes. Therefore, it is quite clear that high caste Brahmins and Chhettries have a dominating leadership part to play. So it is not possible that majority of low-caste people may change the culture. In Jhapa and Kapilvastu where a large minority of Hill settlers dominates society, Nepalization is making rapid inroads in Hill dominant culture.

Another factor for determining the trend of Nepalization is the extent of population. If upper caste hill people settle in an area already occupied by upper caste and business wizards of plains origin, it will be difficult to Nepalize culture. Tharus are also in good number in Tarai who have come from northern Hill region. Due to change in land tenure system from time to time, settlers have been shifting themselves from one region to another to their best advantage.

In few limited areas Hill tribal people such as Magars, Gurungs, Rais, Limbus and Tamangs have settled for number of years. They migrated to Tarai because they lost control

1. Survey of district in 1967.

of their land in the hills mostly to upper caste hill people. Now they seem to lose their control of land again in Tarai due to their indebtedness and vulnerability to eviction. They often mortgage their lands and property to upper caste people and businessmen.

It is therefore to conclude that fringes of forest areas are becoming Nepalized gradually. The tendency to Nepalization has also been witnessed in the far east Tarai forested area of Jhapa and Morang Districts but in other districts like Parsa, Bara, Rautahat, the position is fully under the grip of the people of plain origin.

Economic Standard of Migrants

The cultural dominance of Tarai by Hill or plain people depends solely on the economic status. The low caste migrants usually have low economic status while upper castes are better than others. The economic categories are land owner, tenant farmer, farm labourers, caste occupation worker and shopkeepers, weavers, hand labour and casual workers.

A tenant farmer is one who rents land from a resident or absentee land owner and a farm labour is he, who works on daily or hourly basis for other farmers who are either land owners or tenants who earn their livelihood by tradition. Caste professions are like Sunar, who makes jewellery, Halwai who prepares sweets, charmkar who skins dead animals. Of these groups the tenant farmers, labourers and caste occupation people are generally poor and belong to low-caste stock. Such people cannot exert any influence in social community affairs. As the social and status dominance is concerned, it is still in the hands of the largest landowners and better shopkeepers.

From the study of Jhapa, Kailali and Kapilvastu districts the facts have been revealed in Table 3.2.

The percentage increase of population during 1971-1981 shows a wide variation from 16.83 in the hills and mountains, while in Tarai it was 51.84 per cent. The population pressure

Table 3.2

Population : Geographical Regionwise 1971-1981

Geographical Region	*1971*	*Percentage*	*1981*	*Percentage*	*% increase during 1971-81*
Mountain and Hills	72,10,017	62.39	84,23,849	56.07	16.83
Taral	41,45,966	37.61	65,98,990	43.93	51.84
Total	1,15,56,983	100.00	1,50,22,839	100.00	30.00

Source : C.B.S., Population Census of Nepal 1971 and 1981.

is very high in mountain and hills in terms of cultivated area. Though Nepal is predominantly a rural and a cultural country only 17 per cent of the total land area is under cultivation. Nearly 65 per cent of the total cultivated area lies in Tarai region.

As such people migrate from Hills and mountains to Tarai due to heavy population pressure on cultivated land in Hills and mountains.

Productivity : Productivity of land in Hilly region is very low because production fully depends upon rain. No irrigation facilities and improved input are yet provided here. So the yield rate is critically low. Naturally, Hill and mountain people migrate to seek better opportunities elsewhere like military services, manual services of watch and ward and for agriculture in Tarai.

(a) Study reveals that the larger percentage of migrants who own lands are from Kapilvastu and Kailali districts while there is a different picture in Jhapa district where the percentage of landholders is less. 43% of Hill caste people and 79% of Hill tribal people in Jhapa district are tenant farmers or farm labourers.

(b) A good percentage in Jhapa and Kapilvastu districts is due to shopkeepers. The small businessmen keep small shops and some are moneyed people

Table 3.3

Migrant Families Settling Permanently, 1959-67 as a Percentage of Total Population in 1967 by District and Economic Status

District	*Total migrant families*	*Migrant families who have purchased land*	*Migrant families that are tenant farmers*	*Migrant families that are farm labourers*	*Migrant families pursuing caste occupation*	*Migrant families that are shop-keepers*
Jhapa	167	22.8	31.1	18.0	9.0	16.2
Kapilvastu	92	47.8	10.9	23.9	4.4	12.0
Kailali*	43	64.4	6.7	17.8	11.1	–

Source : Data collected for above districts in field survey of 1967-68.
*For Kailali District migrant families enumerated only for 1963-67

who do large scale business there by earning enough capital.

(c) Some rich shopkeepers may exert some social influence but dominants are big landholders only. In Jhapa district out of 36 migrants who acquired status of landholders 26 are from Brahmins and Chhettries and 6 are from plains who were landholders. No Muslim was found to achieve such status in the surveys done.

(d) Evidently, hill Brahmins and Chhettries made the largest percentage of holding lands in Jhapa district. Break up of the 26 Brahmins and Chhettries who acquired landownership is as under :

4 Obtained from Government's Land Reform Office.
10 From Other Brahmins and Chettries.
7 From Tajpurias and Rajbanshis.
3 From Hill tribals.
2 From plains caste people.

The transfer of land from one Hill family to another does not make any difference in economic standing. High caste Hill people have made their fortune primarily by Hill people.

(e) In Kapilvastu and Kailali districts the position is as under:

44 Migrants acquired land ownership.

37 are from Hill Brahmins and Chhetries.

7 Are from Hill Tribals, plain Hindus and Muslims.

In Kailali district position was:

29 Total migrants who obtained land ownership.

20 Belonged to Hill Brahmins and Chhetries.

1 From Newars.

8 From low-caste Hill families.

Out of 20 migrants of Hill Brahmins and Chhetries 18 got their land from Tharus and Land Reform Office. Newars and 8 low caste Hill families obtained their land ownership from Land Reform Office. It is therefore undoubtedly proved that Hill Brahmins and Chhetries are still in dominant position in Tarai districts.

SUMMARY OF MIGRATION FACTORS

Impact on Sending and Receiving Region

Significance : Nepal has the blended character of migrants. Migrants are of two categories: they are either inter-regional or international. It has become significant due to overpopulation in Hill areas and the opening of Tarai region as a new vista for settlement. Of the total population of 16 million people in Nepal nearly half now live in Kathmandu Valley and in Hills. While 30 years ago the percentage was about 65. So the marked flow of migration indicates towards Tarai.

Dynamics of Migration : The mobility of people from one region to another is due to various factors. Many authors have done good work in the study of Migration problem.

1. Donald J. Bogue[1] is of the view that migrations are of pull and push factors. One who cannot satisfy his needs in atmosphere unhealthy to him, he migrates to the other place. Decline of resources, lack of employment, discriminatory treatment, allevation from caste-community, natural calamities are the push factors.
2. Binay Thomas[2] feels that migration takes place due to unfavourable population pressures. In the nineteenth century migration was stimulated due to rural employment shifting from one region to other.
3. Thomson[3] feels migration takes place due to a desire to improve economical condition of individuals. Also as per desire to freedom from political oppression.
4. Peter R. Cox[4] enumerates personal causes for migration like, service, nearness to relations, congenial neighbours, trade functions.
5. Alfred Souvey[5] feels that people having a certain degree of initiative and enterprise and also possessing higher technical knowhow shift to the place or region to get job satisfaction as well as economic independence.
6. William Patterson[6] is of view that generally young

1. Bogue, Donald J., *Principles of Demography*, John Wiley & Sons, Inc., 1969.
2. Thomas, Binley, *International Migrations*, The study of population, An Inventory & Appraisal, (ed) Philip M. Hansar & Otii Dudley Duncan : The University of Chicago Press, Chicago & London, pp. 510-543.
3. Thomson, Warrant, Population Problems, McGraw Hill Book Co., New York, 1953, pp. 273-314.
4. Cox, Peter R., Demography, 5th Edition, Cambridge University Press, London, 1976, pp. 141-152.
5. Souvey, Alfred, General Theory of Population, Weidenfald & Nicolson, London, 1969.
6. Patterson, William, Population, 2nd Ed., The Macmillan Co,, London, 1969.

youth migrate for seeking better employment opportunities.

7. Ralph Thomlinson[1] is of idea that individual migration may be due to a desire for higher rank and better economic and social living conditions. But for the society it may be for correcting imbalance between the supply of workers and jobs and between the consumer and the producer.
8. Ralph and Beals, Middred S. Levy and Leon N. Meses[2] think that a "Strong will" for migration is best to motivate one to shift from one place to other.
9. Rashi Fein[3] finds that migration is more volatile with young people with their educational standard.
10. Peter A. Morrison[4] feels that general migration is beneficial for individuals because they result into gains in income, better occupational status and reduction to poverty and unemployment.

Analysing the above factors it is found that all the factors given by different authors have their role in migration within Nepal on the whole and the Tarai region in particular. Main reasons for migration from Hills include natural calamities, lack of land ownership, lack of employment opportunities, population pressure, low agriculture productivity, lack of economic facilities etc. Push factors have forced Hill people to migrate to Tarai and other regions of the country and other countries.

1. Thomlinson, Ralph, Population Dynamics, Causes and Consequences of World Demographic Change, Random House,New York, 1965, pp. 210-265.
2. Beals, Ralph E., et al., "Rationality and Migration in Ghana", Review of Economics and Statistics, XLIX, No. 4, Nov. 1967, pp. 480-486.
3. Fein, Rashi, "Educational Patterns in Southern Migration", Southern Economic Journal, 32, No. 1, July, 1965.
4. Morrison, Peter A., "Population Movement : Where the Public Interest and Private Interest conflict". Commission on Population Growth and the American Future Research Reports, Vol. V, Population Distribution and Policy, edited by Sara Mills Maize, Chapter 3, Part II.

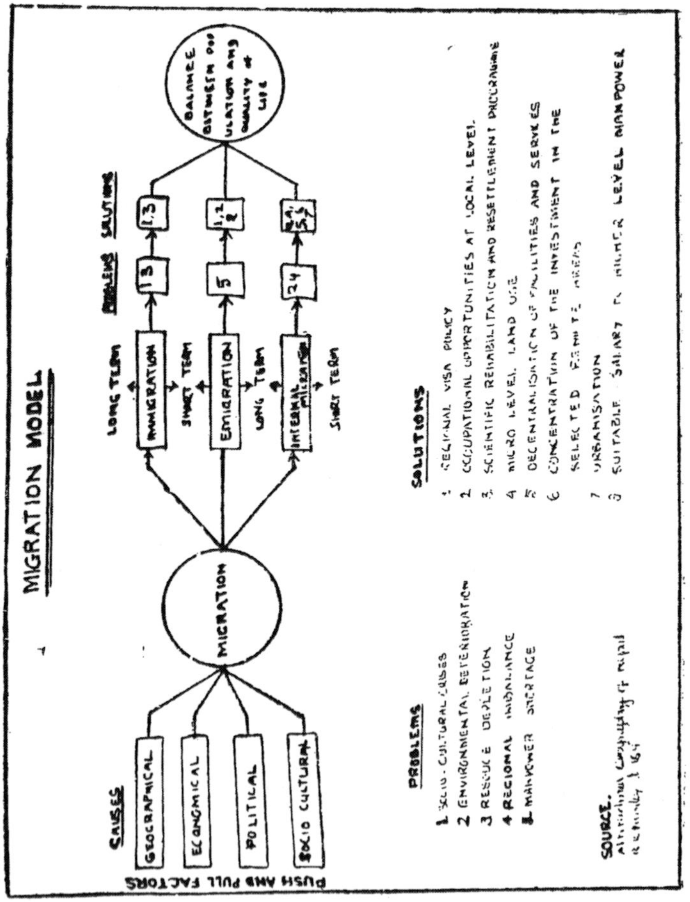
MIGRATION MODEL
CAUSES
GEOGRAPHICAL
ECONOMICAL
POLITICAL
SOCIO CULTURAL
PUSH AND PULL FACTORS
MIGRATION
LONG TERM
IMMIGRATION
SHORT TERM
EMIGRATION
LONG TERM
INTERNAL MIGRATION
SHORT TERM
PROBLEMS
SOLUTIONS
13
5
24
1,3
BALANCE BETWEEN POPULATION AND QUALITY OF LIFE
PROBLEMS
1 SOCIO-CULTURAL CRISES
2 ENVIRONMENTAL DETERIORATION
3 RESOURCE DEPLETION
4 REGIONAL IMBALANCE
5 MANPOWER SHORTAGE
SOLUTIONS
1 REGIONAL VISA POLICY
2 OCCUPATIONAL OPPORTUNITIES AT LOCAL LEVEL
3 SCIENTIFIC REHABILITATION AND RESETTLEMENT PROGRAMME
4 MICRO LEVEL LAND USE
5 DECENTRALISATION OF FACILITIES AND SERVICES
6 CONCENTRATION OF THE INVESTMENT IN THE
7 URBANISATION
8 SUITABLE SALARY TO HIGHER LEVEL MANPOWER
SOURCE.

The Tarai attracted people due to pull factors like availability of land, food surplus, resettlement programmes, industrial and trade activities, high development investment, better education, better transport and markets etc.

Impact on Sending Region

Since the opening of settlement opportunities in Tarai region large number of Hill people migrated to this region. This brings economic development as in the following diagram.

MIGRATION FROM THE HILLS

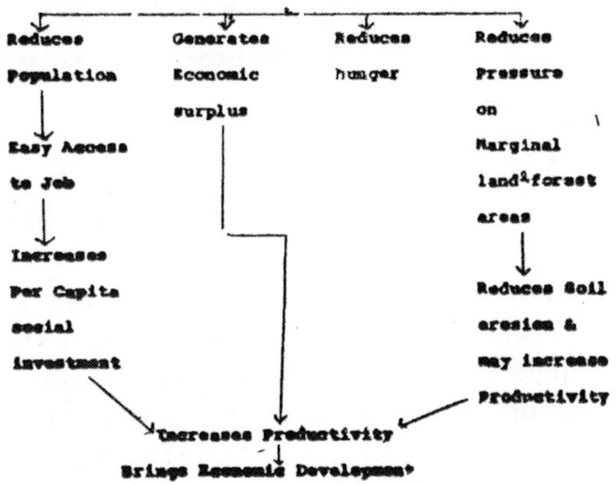

Inter-Regional Migration in Nepal, 1981, New Era, Kathmandu.

Impact on Receiving Region (Tarai)

Population density in Tarai region was very low before opening of this area for settlement. The Ranas in order to increase their revenue from forests, to reduce population pressure in the hills and to stop emigration made attempts to cultivate Tarai land. Tarai is a good resourceful region of Nepal. So migration in Tarai brings economic development as shown in the diagram.

IMPACT ON RECEIVING REGION (TARAI)

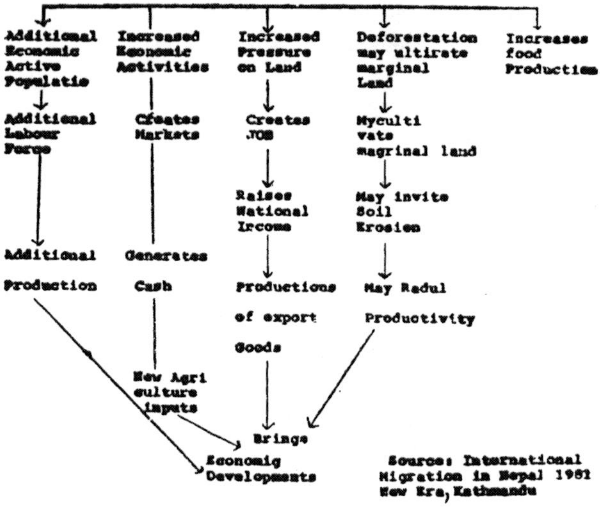

Problem of Identity Citizenship

It is a very important subject with reference to the Tarai of Nepal. Citizenship makes one to take part in the process of governing. It grants access to powers. It is therefore a very important fact for national integra'ion. There has been a complex situation in Nepal for granting citizenship to the people of Tarai belonging to Indian origin on geographical, ethnic and linguistic backgrounds. The people of nationally dominating hill culture and the people of plain culture lived with their own identities for several decades often with a feeling of suspicion of each other.

Citizenship legislation framed by representatives of dominant Hill culture in 1960 is not without suspicion for it makes citizenship more difficult for the people of plain origin living in Tarai.

Status of Tarai Subjects before 1951

Attitude towards people with plain culture was quite

unhealthy by the dominant hill culture group people. In Kathmandu too this attitude prevailed before 1951. In 1769 Prithivi Narayan Shah, a King of western hill principality, Gorakha conquered Kathmandu valley. During the next four years he extended his command over the eastern hills and eastern Tarai creating an entity which made Nepal. After the conquest of Tarai, necessity arose to define responsibilities and rights of people living in Tarai region. The documents around 1850-60 reveal that Zamindaries and minor government posts in Tarai were given to Tarai inhabitants in three preferentially selected categories. The first preference went in "Hill Folks", second to "those who settled in Nepal territory with their family members and who were rich and loyal to government and had respectable origin. An Indian in those days was categorised as a man living in Tarai without his family, living there on temporary basis".[1] It is apparent that this distinction was made after the victory of Tarai by Prithivi Narayan Shah to establish criteria for recruiting people in the local administration. Hill people were given preference over plain people living in Tarai and thus plain people were relegated to the second class status.

Plain people living in Tarai region were not treated on equal terms with hill people up to 1950-51; nothing was done to eradicate their isolation. It was witnessed that only on Shiv Ratri days Indiann were allowed to make pilgrimage to Pashupatinath temple in Kathmandu. While on other days they were not allowed to go upside without obtaining Visa at Birganj. This system continued up to 1950 and was not modified. Before 1951 it seems those who could speak Nepali languages like Nepali, Newari, Magar or Gurung were permitted to go to Kathmandu Valley.

It was actually difficult to trace out plain people living in Tarai and the people of Indian origin or Indians. A hill person whether a merchant or an agriculturist, before the advent of malaria eradication programme, had a very hurried trip to Tarai and across for buying or selling goods. His

1. Administrative regulation for Tarai Districts, 1961, Vol. I, p. 16.

attitude towards Tarai persons was always negative as illustrated by the following saying common among hill people.

"Do not perform the funeral rites for one who goes to Hitaura (a place in central inner Tarai) during spring and to one who goes to Tibet during winter". It means clearly that those who visit such places do not deserve funeral rites at all, a very discriminating and apathetic attitude.

Citizenship Laws in 1950

When the political turmoil was ended in Nepal in 1950-51, the need was voiced for drawing out voters' list for holding elections. Since there was total absence of definition of citizenship in this country the Public Representation Act 1951 was framed. This Act gave the right to vote to those persons only who were living in Nepal for more than 60 years.[1]

This Act at least developed a sense in the mind of Nepali administrative machinery to formulate citizenship laws. Such laws were framed in 1952 under which a little improvement was done. The main relaxation seems as under :

> "Anyone who was born in Nepal and anyone permanently settled in Nepal having at least one parent in Nepal or any woman married to a citizen and any one who had lived in Nepal for 5 years could seek citizenship and a right to vote".[2]

The five years stay condition for achieving bonafideness is also current in India, Pakistan and most other countries. In 1951 the Indian government was instrumental and motivated Nepali administration to modify the laws. Tribhuvan Virvikram Shah was a very powerful king in Kathmandu.

1. Nepal Gazette, Vol. I, No. 27, Feb. 10, 1952.
2. Legal Department, Laws concerning nationality (New York, 1954, pp. 320-321).

Ambassador C.P.N. Singh and Govind Narayan, his personal advisor prepared Nepal to make the Nepali constitution on the pattern of Indian constitution.[1]

Nepali had no experience of framing constitutional laws but at the same time there is no evidence that Indians advised or wrote the Public Representation Act and Citizenship Act. Changes in the Citizenship Act 1950 made it more non-discriminatory. This was due to a change of outlook among educated people. Youngmen from Kathmandu valley and from Tarai obtained their education, together in Northern Indian universities like Varanasi, Patna, Lucknow and Delhi etc. So a sense of brotherhood among both tribes (Hill Folk and plain people) developed gradually. Distinction will slowly move off the minds of both. There was already a Nepali Congress Party, founded in 1946 which was against the political organization of Rana regime and trying to get the style of functioning changed.

The General Election in 1959 resulted into the formation of Nepali Congress government. It showed considerable change of attitude towards India. Among the members elected for parliament on Nepali Congress tickets, twelve were plain people and 11 from the Hill area. Among the names of cabinet ministers names of B.P. Koirala, S.P. Koirala, Rudra Prasad Giri and Shamshad were from the hill people but this had close ties with the plains. Two members Ram Narayan from Janakpur and Parsuram Chaudhry a Tharu from Dang (Western Tarai) were from Tarai region; one deputy minister Shri Suryanath Das Yadav was from Saptari district of Tarai.[2]

Though adequate data is not available to prove the unity of Hill and plain people but the upsurge against Rana government has left many stories in the mouth of citizens together.

1. Bhuwan Lal Joshi and L.E. Rose, "Democratic Innovations in Nepal" (Berkley, 1966), p. 88.
2. Nepal Election Commission, Result of General Election 1959.

1960 Laws of Citizenship

The citizenship enactment of 1960 was done in a different atmosphere when Royal coup was already in the offing. Nepal Congress leaders were in jail and exiled along with many others belonging to other political parties. However, Nepali Congress continued its activities underground in the Tarai region. Thereafter, the Royal government had changed its attitude and it was soft to the interest of Tarai people.

In articles 7 and 8 of the 1962 constitution it was seen that article 7 was just a repetition of article 2 of 1951 Citizenship Act. It gives right of citizenship by birth and by marriage.[1] The major difference in Article and Section 2 of 1962 constitution states:

While making Law in pursuance of clause (i) it shall be inter-alia, stipulated that a foreigner may qualify for the acquisition of citizenship if:

(a) He can speak and write the national language of Nepal.

(b) He is engaged in an occupation, resides in Nepal.

(c) He has taken steps to renounce citizenship of the country of which he is a citizen and

(d) He has resided in Nepal for not less than a period of two years in case of a person of Nepali origin and for not less than 12 years in case of a person other than of Nepalese Origin.[2]

Anti-Indian Sentiments

People migrating from India to Nepal Tarai are of two types, those who establish business and the other who are tenant farmers and labourers. Businessmen learn Nepali very quickly because in course of their business and contracts they come close to Nepali higher officials. More so they are educated people who grasp Nepali language quickly. For

1. Nepal Election (Result of First General Election, 1959).
2. Constitution of Nepal (Kathmandu, 1963), pp. 3-5, Articles 7 & 8.

others it was not possible as they had no good and common bondage with hill origin or Nepali speaking people. In 1968 Citizenship Rules also no provision for language test was made; clause (b) requirements are very unusual. While making application for citizenship one must prove that he is an earning member living in Nepal.

Clause (c) is another requirement for naturalization not given in the earlier Act of 1962.

Clause (d) is more restrictive. On one side it shortens the period of residence in case of hill origin and Nepalese; on the other side it has extended the period abnormally. In this clause discrimination against plain people is quite apparent. There are many such cases where inter-border area and international region area marriages were done due to ancestral reasons and by this law it is evident that Nepali Law makers were imbibed with apprehension for plain origin people who may seek citizenship in good numbers. This suspicion grown in the minds of early rulers is still prevailing in government circles and among Nepal population. The main reason of disbelief is the behaviour of Britishers and their gradual restrictions and demands. Nepal has not yet realised that India is now a democratic country. She is fully aware that her frontier nations should be strong and well guarded.[1] Nepalese still believe that India is following the inherited policy of Britishers.

Attitude of Nepal Towards India

As mentioned earlier India always favoured sympathetic and friendly relations with India. Sentiments have always been guiding India and Nepal to keep loving affinity. Nepal is a Hindu Nation and majority of Hindus come for pilgrimage to India in famous shrines like Vishwanath Temple at Varanasi. Equally a good number of Indian citizens, monks, yogis go to Nepal and Pashupatinath every year, whatever governments' interests on both sides be. Social and cultural background of both countries is a strong string which is binding both countries.

1. Jawahar Lal Nehru, India's foreign policy, New Delhi, 1961.

In 1950 the first feeling of protecting interests of king Mahendra and Nepali Congressmen took this sympathetic attitude by India as based merely for security considerations than to assist Nepal for prosperity and development.

During the premiership of B.P. Koirala, King Tribhuwan scrapped Nepal's democracy but India did not show any sign of protest as they thought Nepal was politically established and more so it was not desired to interfere in the matters of other non-aligned nation.

It is screened by Nepal press that India-Nepal treaty of 1950 was more unhealthy due to multifarious restrictions. In 1956 India modified its treaty, with reciprocal attitude, India gave more bent towards Nepal and she wanted to make Nepal a strong border country.[1] In turn China was also clever enough to open its diplomatic mission in Nepal. This became a source of worry to India.

King Mahendra also never wanted to fully depend on India so he sought unusual help from China. China gave 60 million of the Indian currency in 1956 and a free grant of 100 million of Indian rupees in 1960.[2] China gradually tried her best to isolate India from Nepal. King Mahendra too was adding fuel to fire. He wished to expose himself as the most-patriotic, so he started anti-India tirade and tried to find out those new friends who had no good relations with India.[3]

Since 1963 onward, India has been constantly trying to improve her relations with Nepal. India signed treaties on trade and transit with Nepal to control unauthorised trade. Nepal Press was full of appreciation for this treaty. Thereafter, Karnali Hydro Electric Project was given by India. Panchmeshwar dam, Bridge or Narayani river and many other big and small works were completed by India in Nepal. Premier Kirtinidhi Vista appreciated the help given by India[4]

1. V.B. Karnik, *China invades India*, 1963, p. 164.
2. Peking review No. 13, March, 1960, p. 64.
3. Ibid.
4. Rising Nepal, Kathmandu, Sept. 26, 1978.

in spite of her own pressing needs.

The affinities of religion and culture, socio-economic ties, service rendered by Gorakha in Indian Army and many other factors create a good base for firm friendship. King Birendra on many occasions thanked India for its policy of non-interference in Nepal's internal affairs. The fact is realised that it is India who shaped Nepal's international personality and image. In spite of the gratitude accepted by Nepal she reflected many views against India like Kashmir case. Nepal wants to show herself more independent with separate identity without having much reference to India. Such thinking sometimes irked Indian Government. Many steps taken by Nepal are thorny and damage India-Nepal relations.

1. *Preference to China in the Kingdom*

Nepal permitted many projects by China in the Tarai region just close to India which was detrimental to India's defence. In 1962 when Indian troops were withdrawn from Nepal, China had a chance to cross the whole land of Nepal and stand in Tarai region and establish links across the border. This was very very sorry state of affairs and was against the spirit of understanding between India and Nepal.

2. *Creation of "Stateless Category" of Persons in Tarai*

Nepalese living in Tarai region often complain that they are not regarded in equal terms with Hill area people. They live with the feeling of second class citizens. Their contribution to national service is negligent. They are denied citizenship certificates.[1] Certificates have been denied to lakhs of people in Tarai and a setback is witnessed into national integration. The reason for this behaviour on the part of Nepal has produced unusual influx of population in Tarai. One of the reason of influx is the coming of Muslims who are neither needed in Pakistan nor in Bangladesh. Evidently, Saudi Arabia is spending large amount in Nepal.[2]

1. Kanchan Majumdar, Foreign relations between India and Nepal, Calcutta, 1986, pp. 50-51.
2. In an interview with eastern economic review, July 8, 1983.

3. *River Project*

On sharing the river water by both India and Nepal projects of Karnali and Pancheshwar and Rapti are being delayed abnormally because Nepal has apprehension that large amount of money will flow into the Kingdom thereby giving chance for Indian domination.

4. *Cruel Attitude Against Nepalese Press*

Nepal has been very discriminating against the non-Nepalese. The Government of Nepal does not allow non-Nepali journalists to enter Rastriya Panchayat for covering the proceedings.

5. *Nepal's Proposal for Kingdom being declared a Zone of Peace*

The zone of peace proposal has been irritant between Indo-Nepal relations. China was quick to endorse Nepali demand with the idea that whatever would be termed as loss to India will be gain to China.[1] Consequently, China got her reward in the form of many contracts such as renovating the Chhatra irrigation canal originally built by India. This project was close to Indian border near Naxalbari.

Religion

For understanding the national integration of Nepal, the problem of cultural characteristics must be understood. In Tarai a special feature remains that most of its inhabitants do not share cultural ways with the people of Hills. While Nepal's hill culture is followed in the whole Nepal and this culture alone Nepal's leadership wishes to thrust upon others living in Tarai.

Most Tarai people are just part of the north Indian plain culture. They differ from hill people not only for their language and caste characteristics but also the type of food

1. Vishwa Pradhan, 'Nepal a peace zone', Calcutta, 1980, p. 65.

they eat, style of clothes they wear, implements they use, sports they play, even their ways of shaking hands and head while talking. These actions they share with the people living in the border lands of U.P. and Bihar. Common cultural ties are very much the same for the people of Tarai and northern region people of India.

1. *Religion as Characteristic of the Population of Tarai*

In this chapter three cultural features of Tarai people are analysed in order to assess the extent of Indian culture (northern part) predomination in Tarai and also up to what extent hill culture has penetrated into the region. Actually religion as separate item is not most important than three other characteristics for measuring cultural difference, because religion of both hill people and plain population is predominantly Hindu. Yet there is a fine thread of difference.

According to the census of 1961 about 88 per cent population of Nepal was Hindu. The percentage is, however, the same in hills and in Tarai region. Table 3.4 presents the position religionwise.

Tables 3.4 and 3.5 present data on the numerical and percentage distribution of population of various religious groups from the censuses of 1952-54 and 1981. The overwhelming majority of the population has been and continues to be that of the Hindus. They accounted for at least 88 per cent of the population during 1952-54 to 1981. The Hindu population not only remained the most prominent group in the country but they were also growing numerically as well as in percentage terms. In 1952-54 over 88 per cent of the population were Hindus compared with 90 per cent in census of 1981.

The Hindu population grew at the rate of 2.67 per cent per annum compared to 2.66 per cent growth rate of total population in 1971-81.

Table 3.6 provides the numerical as well as the proportionate distribution of the major religious groups by three Geographical Zones of the country, mountain, hill and Tarai for the censuses of 1971 and 1981. It is obvious that majority of Hindus live in the hill although its share of total Hindu

Table 3.4

Numerical and Percentage Distribution of the Population by Religion Nepal Census 1952-54 to 1981

Religion	*1952-54*		*1961*		*1971*		*1981*	
	No.	%	*No.*	%	*No.*	%	*No.*	%
Hindu	7,318,392	88.9	8,254,403	87.7	10,330,009	89.4	13,445,787	89.5
Buddhist	707,104	8.6	870,991	9.2	866,411	7.5	799,081	5.3
Muslim	208,899	2.5	280,597	3.0	351,156	3.0	399,107	2.7
Others	684	0.0	1,289	0.0	8,377	0.1	378,774	2.5
Unstated	—	—	5,716	0.1	—	—	—	—
All Religions	8,235,079	100	9,412,996	100	11,555,983	100	15,022,837	100

Source—Central Bureau of Statistics 1958, Pop. Census 1952/54, Pt. II.
Central Bureau of Statistics 1968-1961, Vol. II.
Central Bureau of Statistics 1975-1971, Vol. II.
Central Bureau of Statistics 1984-1981, Vol. I, Pt. III.

Table 3.5
Percentage Increase and Growth Rate in Population by Religion 1952-54 to 61, 1961-71, 1971-81 and 1952-54-81

Religion	*Percentage increase in population*				*Growth rate (Geometrio)*			
	1952-54 1961	*1961*	*1971*	*1952-54 1981*	*1952-54 1961*	*1961-1971*	*1971-81*	*1952-54 1981*
Hindu	12 8	25.1	30.2	83.7	1.52 (1.50)	2.57 (2.24)	2.67 (2.64)	2 20 (2.17)
Buddhist	23.2	0.5	7.8	13.0	2.64 (2.61)	0.05 (0.05)	8.81 (8.81)	0 44 (0.44)
Muslim	34.3	25.2	13.7	91.0	3.76 (3.69)	2.27 (2.24)	1.29 (1.28)	2.34 (2.31)
Others	—	214.8	4421.6	—	—	12.15	40.40	—
Others and unstated	929.1	—	—	—	33.75 (29.08)	—	—	—
All Religions	14.3	22.8	30.0	82.4	1.69 (1.67)	2.07 (2.05)	2.66 (2.62)	2.17 (2.15)

N.B.—The figures in brackets refer to exponential growth rate.
Source—Same as Table No. 3.4.

Table 3.6

Religious Composition of Population and Percentage Distribution by Geographical Zone, Nepal—Census 1971-81

Zone	*Census Year*	*All Persons*	*Hindu*		*Buddhist*		*Muslim*		*Others*	
			No.	*%*	*No.*	*%*	*No.*	*%*	*No.*	*%*
Nepal	1971	11,555,583	10,330,009	100	866,411	100	851,186	100	8,377	100
	1981	15,027,839	13,445,787	100	799,081	100	399,197	100	278,174	100
Mountain	1971	1,138,610	938,617	9.1	199,674	23.0	166	0.0	153	1.8
	1981	1,302,896	1,111,967	8.3	159,091	9.9	487	0.1	31,351	8.3
Hill	1971	6,071,407	5,439,279	52.7	617,195	71.2	10,136	2.9	4,797	57.3
	1981	7,163,115	6,447,523	48.0	507,214	63.5	13,447	3.4	194,931	51.5
Tarai	1971	4,345,966	3,952,113	88.3	49,542	5.7	340,884	97.1	3,427	30.9
	1981	6,556,828	5,886,297	43.8	132,776	16.6	385,263	96.5	152,492	0.3

Source—Central Bureau of Statistics 1984, Pop. Census 1981, Vol. II, Pt. II.

population had declined from 53 per cent in 1971 to 48 per cent in 1981. The proportion of Hindus living in mountain has also declined nominally from 9 per cent in 1971 to 8 per cent in 1981. However, the proportion of Hindus living in the Tarai, on the other hand, has gone up from 38.3 per cent in 1971 to 43.8 per cent in 1981, a significant increase of 5.5 per cent. This increase reflects the point of increase and it is due to the movement of Hindu population from the Hill to Tarai.

Buddhists are found in irregular concentration in the Hill area by the Mountain although this concentration decreased appreciably during the last intercensual period 1971-81. The population of Buddhists living in Hill and Mountain declined from 72.1 to 63.5 in Hill area and from 23.0 to 19.9 per cent in the mountains from 1971 to 1981. The proportion of Buddhists living in Tarai increased considerably from 5.7 per cent in 1971 to 16.6 per cent in 1981. This was due to influx of Buddhists from mountain and hill to Tarai region. All this indicates that although majority of Hindus and Buddhists tend to live on Hill, there has been a considerable movement of the people of these two religions following from Hill to Tarai during the intercensual period of 1971-81.

The highest concentration of Muslims has been and continues to be in Tarai. Tarai accounted for 97 per cent of the Muslim population in 1971 and in 1981.

Hinduism in the plain culture and Hinduism in the Hill culture differ somewhat. Village Hinduism in Tarai embraces various deities popularly worshipped in North Indian plains. Hinduism reached to hills at later stages than in plains. Due to Tibetan and Buddhism influences in society, the hill people did not accept Hinduism in its orthodox form. The major differences between the plain and hill culture result from the existence of different religious minorities like Muslims who are quite in good number in Tarai region. Muslims represent 9 to 13 per cent of total population in Tarai and the sub-regions of Tarai while there are very few Buddhists in Tarai.

Table 3.7

Rural and Urban Percentage Distribution and Percentage Change in Population by Religion Nepal—Census Year 1971-81

Religion	1971 % Distribution			1981 % Distribution			% Change in 1971-1981	
	Total Population	Rural	Urban	Total Population	Rural	Urban	Rural	Urban
Hindu	10,330,009	96.3	3.7	13,445,787	93.8 (94 9)	6.2 (5.1)	26.7 (28.3)	120.9 (80.2)
Buddhist	866,411	92.6	7.4	799,081	92.2 (92.7)	7.8 (7 3)	—8.1 (—7.7)	—3.2 (—9.1)
Islam	351,186	95.0	5.0	399,197	90.8 (91.2)	9.2 (8.8)	8.6 (9.1)	109 3 (99.9)
Jain	2,541	78.5	21.5	9,438	83.1 (83.3)	16.9 (16.8)	293.4 (293.9)	191.2 (189.6)

Others	5,836	85.3	14.7	369,326	94.6 (95.0)	5.4 (5.0)	6918.0 (6947.)	221[illegible].0 (2048.5)
Total	11,555,963	96	4.0	15,022,839	93.6 (94.7)	6.4 (5.3)	26.8 (28.2)	107.1 (72.3)

Note—Figures in brackets refer to population of only 16 town Panchayats which were regarded as urban in 1971.

Source—Central Bureau of Statistics 1975—Population Census 1971, Vol. II, Part II and Vol. V and Central Bureau of Statistics 1984—Population Census 1981, Vol. I, Part III and Vol. III.

Not only the above features for whole Nepal and other regions it is found that each district of Tarai has different religious compositions. Table 3.7 presents religious composition living in rural as well as in urban areas with comments on the figures.

Table 3.7 presents the data on rural and urban distribution of population on the basis of religion for the period 1971-1981. It indicates that the majority of religious groups, Jains, Buddhists and Muslims are more urbanised while the dominant religious groups, Hindus were less urbanised in 19Ł1 and 1981. Ranking the religious groups in terms of the proportion living in the urban areas in 1971, Jains were placed first 21.5 per cent followed by Buddhists 7.4 per cent, Muslims 5.0 per cent and Hindus 3.7 per cent. This ranking remained unchanged in 1981.

An example how the growth rate has not been uniform over space is clearly evident from the distribution of districts of Tarai according to their annual compound rates of growth for decade 1971-81 as per Table 3.8. Kanchanpur district in far western Tarai experienced highest growth rate 8.98 per cent followed by Sarlahi 8.26 and Nawal Parsi 7.45 per cent. None of the districts in Tarai region experienced any decline. All the 20 districts have positive growth. 11 districts experienced increase more than 4 per cent, 6 districts increased by more than 2.5 per cent and remaining three below 2 per cent.

The religious composition in Tarai districts has been as per Table 3.9.

From Table 3.9 it is evident that Hindus are a predominant race in almost all the districts of Tarai. In 9 districts they are above 90 per cent while in others around this figure.

Concentration of Mohammadans is very pronouncing in Banke, Shivraj, Khajahani and Rautahat districts while in the Far Western Tarai they seem to be in total absence. Bardia, Kailali and Kanchanpur districts are sparsely inhabited because in the south of these districts dense forests have restricted migration to these districts. Banke with Muslim habitation is the largest due to the fact that Banke is easily

Table 3.8

Population Increase 1971-81 by Districts of Tarai Regions only

District	Increase in Population 1971-81 % Increase	Compound annual growth (%)
1. Jhapa	93 68	6.61
2. Morang	77.31	5.73
3. Sunsari	54.23	4.33
4. Saptari	21.27	1.93
5. Siraha	24.17	2.16
6. Dhanusha	30.84	2.69
7. Mahottari	11.15	1 06
8. Sarlahi	127.16	8.26
9. Rautahat	3.88	0.38
10. Bara	36.66	3.12
11. Parsa	40.66	3.41
12. Chitwam	41.34	3.46
13. Nawal Parsi	110.74	7.45
14. Rupandehi	55.78	4.43
15. Kapilvastu	31.59	2.75
16. Dang-Deokhari	58.74	4.62
17. Banke	63.33	4.91
18. Bardia	94.54	6.71
19. Kailali	100.12	6.94
20. Kanchanpur	145.57	8.98

Source : Central Bureau of Statistics 1984—Population Census 1981, Vol. II.

approachable and there is no forest or hilly range to impede the movement. For the same reason Muslims are relatively large minorities in the three Mid-Western Tarai districts of Shivraj, Khajahani and Majhkhanda. A special feature emerges that Hindu-Muslim ratio in the various Tarai

Table 3.9

Religious Composition of Tarai Population Districtwise

Region and District of Tarai	*Hinduism*	*Islam*	*Buddhism*
Eastern Tarai	89.8	8.9	1.1
Jhapa	95.6	3.4	0.9
Morang	91.0	7.0	1.1
Sunsari	93.0	6.8	0.0
Sirha	93.1	5.6	0.8
Mahottari	89.2	9.0	1.8
Surlahi	87.8	7.8	4.4
Rautahat	83.4	16.9	0.0
Bara	88.2	11.4	0.2
Parsa	87.3	12.6	0.0
Mid-western Tarai	87.1	12.7	0.1
Palhi	91.7	8.3	0.0
Majkhanda	88.9	10.7	0.3
Khajahani	83.1	16.9	0.0
Shivraj	82.3	17.7	0.0
Far western Tarai	91.5	8.5	0.0
Banke	78.0	21.9	0.0
Kailali	99.8	0.2	0.0
Kanchanpur	99.9	0.1	0.0

Source : Central Bureau of Districts Census of Nepal 1961, Vol II, pp. 16-17.

districts has some relation and context to Hindu-Muslim ratio across the border. This is one measure of the cultural ties between the population of the Tarai and northern part of U.P. and Bihar of India.

The cultural bonds in Nepal have the unique character of mutual tolerance and there has never been any occasion when people of one religion might have created a case for Government attention or for the attention of the Nation. Hindus, Muslims, Buddhists and others are following their tenets of religion freely without any objections from others. Hindus, Buddhists, Jains even participate in the rites of each other's religions. Hindus visit Buddha temples and Buddhists likewise visit and pay their respect to Hindu deities. So a kind of blended culture can be witnessed in most of the districts of Tarai.

4

The Political System and the People

Roots of History

Nepal and Indian religions have been common and there is great historical bondage between the two countries which under no circumstances can be separated or isolated. Religions like Hinduism and Buddhism have grown into very big trees in a long span of time of 5000 years. These trees have kept both countries under their soothing and loving sheds. Their roots are extended from Himalayas to Kanya-Kumari. They are so deep that the tree can never be uprooted in a tempest of whatever degree it may be.

(i) Recalling the events of epic times we found that King Janak was a monarch of Videha Kingdom whose capital used to be at Janakpur, which is still a town in Dhanusha district of Central Tarai of Nepal. Sita was born here and Lord Rama's marriage was performed here itself. This is from Ramayana epic time.

(ii) Another episode gives us an idea that our relation and contact with Nepal were there in Mahabharat times also. Reference is available in Mahabharat epic that a Kirata King came from Nepal and took part in the battle of Kurukshetra.

(iii) Gautam Buddha the founder of Buddhism was born in Nepal at Kapilvastu which is presently a district and its Headquarter. Buddha was born in 521 B.C. He attained wisdom at Gaya (Bihar), gave his first sermon to disciples at Sarnath (Varanasi) and died at Kushinagar (India).

(iv) Great King Asoka (300 B.C.) the most powerful emperor of India came to Kathmandu Valley, spread Buddhism and built many chaityas and stupas in the Valley.

(v) Kashi and Gaya are regarded by Nepal people as the most sacred places and Nepalese attach great sanctity to these places. It is their conventional belief that if one dies at Kashi he attains Salvation (Mukti) and then he does not take rebirth for facing the pangs of life. This trend continues in both countries today also.

(vi) During the first century A.D. small petty kings ruled in Northern India. They established their kingdoms in Kapilvastu, Vaishali and in Videha. They made their union as Lichchivi Sangha. Under this Sangha many kings like Shakya, Koli, Lichchivi and Malla were ruling in their small states. But powerful kings like Ajatshatru and Chandra Gupta Maurya overpowered these kings by defeating them and seizing their kingdoms. Many of these kings fled to Nepal and assimilated in their culture. They even felt it a pride to call themselves as Nepali. These kings brought the Guthi system idea along with them as assessed by Mahesh Chandra Regmi. He writes "The Lichhivi rulers during whose period the *Guthi* system appears to have attained a fairly advanced stage of development in Nepal, were originally immigrants from Northern India."[1]

1. Regmi, M.C., "Land Ownership in Nepal", 1976, p. 47.

Thereafter in sporadic cases Indian rulers used to escape under pressure from their own states and settled in Tarai or in Valley.

(vii) In the 10th century A.D. Muslim invasion shook northern Indian principalities and kings. These Muslim invaders continued their wars up to 14th century. By this time they were able to get hold of whole northern-west India. The Hindu kings from Mewar, Chittaur, Kannauj, Kumaon, Mithila and Videha fled to Nepal with their supporters. In this period king Hari Singh Dev who was a ruler of Simraungarh under whom districts of Eastern and Central Tarai regions were included as part of his kingdom also fell into the hands of Muslims (1324 A D.). As such when Tirhutiyas confederation was in trouble, people fled to Nepal.

(viii) The Sen kings of Palpa and Makwanpur applied some intelligence to consolidate Tarai region economically and politically but nothing more they could do to remove the plight of people. They ruled from 15th century A.D. to 18th century. They were defeated by Gorakha kings. The only special thing of attention in this period is that they made Maithili as official language. This was done to consolidate the Tarai and attract the settlers from India.

(ix) One step further to consolidate relations with India was taken by Malla kings. They used to invite Indian scholars for taking their opinion on different subjects. Jagataya Malla in 1715-22 introduced a new tradition of inviting Bhatta Brahmins from south India and putting them as Pujaris (Priests) in Pashupati Nath Temple. This social tradition further cemented the bonds of both countries.

(x) All these historical events prove that religion has been a great transcendental force to keep both countries in friendly and brotherly terms.

(xi) Temples of Kashi and Gaya have been visited by pilgrims of Nepal and thousands of Indians go to Kathmandu to pray Lord Pashupati Nath and Buddha temple, Swambhu Nathji. This trend continues throughout the year.

Prior to British rule in India it was difficult to distinguish between the cultures of both countries.

Nepal's Administrative Structure

Before the advent of democratic Government, particularly before the introduction of Panchayat system, administration during the Rana Regime was highly centralised and feudal in nature. Even after the overthrow of the Romas in 1951, the centralised system persisted for quite some time. It was only after the indroduction of Panchayat system in 1961 that the whole country was organised into a four tier system of Panchayats with the basic idea of decentralisation of administrative structure and decision-making authorities spread to grassroot level.

At the base of the Panchayat system are the village Panchayats or the Town Panchayats. There are at present 4015 village Panchayats in the country, 33 Town Panchayats, 75 District Panchayats and a national Panchayat. The members and chairman of village/town Panchayats are elected through adult franchise. A person, who has attained the age of 21 years is entitled to vote. The district Panchayat consists of elected representatives drawn from Village/Town Panchayat. The village and town Panchayats are given the authority to levy taxes and undertake their own development projects.

With the enactment of the Decentralisation Act 2039 (1982) the Village/Town Panchayat and the District Panchayat are given clear-cut responsibilities and adequate authorities to formulate, implement and supervise Village/Town and District development plans to synchronise with the Five-year Development Plans of the country. The National Panchayat, i.e., the Rastriya Panchayat is a unicameral legislature consisting of 140 members of whom 112 are elected by the people through adult franchise, while the other 28 members are nominated by His Majesty, the King from among the leading public citizens.

The country at present is divided administratively into 5 development regions, 14 zones and 75 districts. The District Administration is headed by a Chief District Officer (CDO). He is mainly responsible for maintaining law and order in his district and coordinates the works of field agencies of different ministries. Similarly, in each of the 75 districts of the country a local development officer (LDO) is posted by the ministry of Panchayat and local development to help supervise and coordinate development plans and projects of the various Panchayat and class organisations.

Under the recent Decentralisation Act, the District Panchayat is the main body responsible for District Development Planning. LDO is the member secretary of the District Panchayat. Each zone is headed by a zonal commissioner who coordinates the activities of CDOs and LDOs of the districts under his jurisdiction and also ensures co-ordination between districts and supervises the development activities of the zone.

A diagram to indicate the Panchayat system in practice is given on next page. How far this system has been successful is a subject of debate. On many occasions there have been agitations against the system and people wanted a constitution based on democratic principles. But the King in Nepal has the unique position. He does not wish any system which may make him isolated or in which the country may be made to lose his grip. Recently from April 1990 there has been great upsurge and commotion in the country for change of system. Nepali Congress headed by Ganesh Man Singh and other political parties agitated against the system and feudal authority of the King of Nepal. Agitation was so powerful that the king had to yield to the wishes of the public. A multi-party election system based on democratic principles was accepted and Shri K.P. Bhattarai of Nepali Congress was installed as the first Prime Minister under the new system.

NEPAL'S PANCHAYAT STSTEM

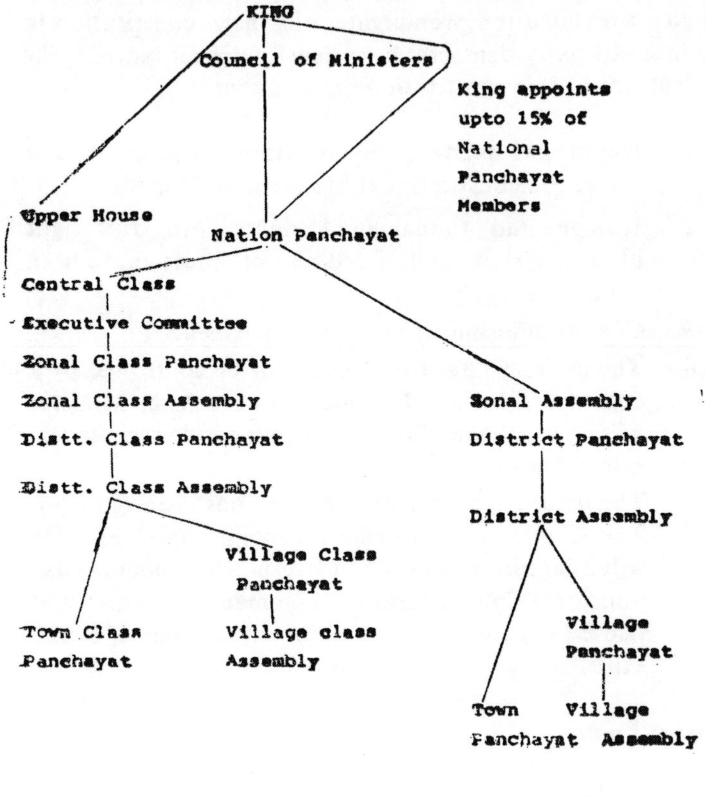

New constitution was drafted by the government headed by Shri K.P. Bhattarai and put before the King for his approval. This constitution was cleared and signed by King Virendra Vikram Shah on 9th November, the Friday of 1990. Thus new constitution got its birth on this auspicious day.

Vide this constitution, nearly 250 years of old Shah dynasty's autocratic and feudal rule ended when King Virendra through a proclamation promulgated the new constitution to bring in multi-party democratic system of Governance. The main features of this constitution are as under :

1. Nepal has made a democratic Sovereign Hindu under the constitutional Monarchial Kingdom.
2. Human and fundamental rights with full right of expression and freedom of press have been confirmed.
3. Capital punishment has been abolished.
4. The military affairs of Nepal will be controlled by a constituted National defence council. Prime Minister will be chairman. Defence minister and commander-in-chief will be its members.
5. The name "Royal Nepal Army" has been retained. The King will be supreme commander-in-chief. He will administer and deploy it on the recommendations of Prime Minister. Commander-in-chief will also be appointed on the recommendation of Prime Minister.

Panchayat Politics at Village and District Levels

It is evident that in the regional politics there is a large chunk of big land owners who dominate. The land owners controlling over thousand of acres of land are influential villagers. There are examples also, when smaller landholders have also good command in village politics. Such people are active only at the local level. They cannot present their case to the government administrative machinery in a forceful way.

In what way village land owners and others manage their representation in village panchayat is a question of intensive study. The social order, caste system, traditional ways, strata of social ladder, all count for much in shaping of village administration. Some data as extracted from the researches will reveal the correct position. Following tables deal with land ownership and village panchayat membership by regional and communal groupings. Further details will follow as to how people of Indian origin living in Tarai fared castewise in panchayats and where they stand in the caste ladder.

Table Observations

From Tables 4.1 to 4.5 it is observed that five different districts namely (i) Jhapa, (ii) Mahottari Dhanusha, (iii) Bara, (iv) Kapilvastu and (v) Kailali were surveyed. These five districts' samples cover the whole Tarai region from east to west. These districts have settlement of both Hill and plain communities. By giving these data an observation to conclude the varied form of attitudes of Hill and plain people in the contribution of panchayat system is to be drawn.

From these data the following results can be derived :

(i) Percentage of large land owners among the Hill people is considerably higher than the percentage of Hill people in total Tarai population. This indicates that Shahs and Ranas have made Hill people to settle in Tarai and also gave them many gratuities to encourage like *Birta* lands.

(ii) These data reveal that among the 4 largest land owners and single largest land owner in the villages, in each of the five districts the percentage of single largest land owner is higher and are better economically despite their small numbers.

(iii) Despite the larger share of upper caste Hill Brahmins, Chhatriyas, Newars in land ownership, these people have no interest in affairs of Tarai

Table 4.1

Land Ownership and Village Panchayat Membership in 10 Sample Villages of Jhapa District by Regional and Communal Groupings, 1967

Regional & Communal Groupings	*Total Population*	*4 largest land owners*	*Single largest land owners*	*Village Panchayat members*
Hill Castes	14.1	25.0	30.3	13.3
Hill Tribes	2.0	—	—	—
Hill Sub-Total	16.1	25.0	30.3	13.3
Plain Hindus	18.1	12.5	10.0	—
Muslims	4.3	—	—	—
Plain Tribes	56.2	62.5	60.0	86.7
Plain Sub-Total	78.6	75.0	70.0	86.7
Caste not identified	5.3			
Total	100	100	100	100

Note : Data collected during field survey in 10 sample villages
Source : A study of Nepal Tarai, University of Pennsylvania, 1970, Part II, p. 480.

because most of them are living in Kathmandu Valley and in Valley towns still. Therefore, Hill people who like to stay at site of their land ownership in Tarai villages due to lesser grade economy share better percentage as single largest land owners.

(iv) Some of the plain castes, particularly Baniyas, Marwari, have more capital backing than hill people.

(v) There is definite correlation in participation between all castes and tribes to the total population in maintaining Panchayats.

(vi) The caste Hindus of plain origin and the Muslims are not participating in Jhapa district, their

Table 4.2

Land Ownership and Village Panchayat Membership in 24 Sample Villages of Mahottari-Dhanusha District by Regional and Communal Groupings

Regional & Communal Groupings	*Total Population*	*4 largest land owner*	*Single large land owners*	*Village Panchayat members*
Hill Castes	6.4	13.4	30 0	8.80
Hill Tribals	7.4	15.5	10.0	11.00
Sub-Total	13.8	28.9	40.0	19.80
Plain Hindus	77.9	69.1	60.0	76.9
Muslims	7.1	—	—	—
Plain Tribals	1.2	2.1	—	1.1
Plain Sub-Total	86.2	71.1	60.0	80.2
Caste not identified	—	—	—	—
Total	100	100	100	100

Source : A study of Nepal Tarai, University of Pannsylvania, Part II, 1970, p. 481.

representatives in Bara District Panchayat are, however, 17 per cent below their total population. In both cases it is tribals of plain origin who came forward to send representatives in village Panchayats. This is mainly because plain tribals tend to live in concentration and in groups in villages where they are in majority. There are many such villages in Bara and Jhapa districts which are very close to dense forests and where people from hills and plains have not yet liked to settle.

(vii) On the whole it can be inferred that the people who have better economic control of land have not taken much interest in village Panchayats. The percentage of land owners participating in the Panchayat is low as per Table 4.6.

Table 4.3

Land Ownership and Village Panchayat Membership in 20 Sample Villages of Bara District by Regional and Communal Groupings, 1967

Regional Communal Groupings	*Total Population*	*4 largest land owners*	*Single largest land owners*	*Village Panchayat members*
Hill Castes	1.2	10.5	25.00	1.3
Hill Tribals	0 4	—	—	—
Total	1.6	10.5	25.00	1.3
Plain Hindus	79.4	63.2	45.00	62.7
Muslims	13.7	15.00	20.00	18.7
Plain Tribals	5.4	10 5	40.0	17.3
Total	98.4	89.5	75.00	98.7

Data collected during field survey 1967-68

Source : A study of Nepal Tarai, University of Pennsylvania, 1970, p. 482.

Table 4.4

Land Ownership and Village Panchayat Membership in 20 Sample Villages of Kapilvastu District by Regional and Communal Groupings, 1967

Regional & Communal Groupings	*Total Population*	*4 largest land owners*	*Single largest land owners*	*Village Panchayat members*
Hill Castes	8.5	13.2	20.0	10.7
Hill Tribals	0.5	1.3	—	—
Sub-Total	9.0	14.5	20.0	10.7
Plain Hindus	66.4	48.7	70.00	60.7
Muslims	18.6	25.0	10.00	16.1
Plain Tribals	6.6	11.6	—	12.5
Sub-Total Plains	91.0	85.5	80.00	89.3
Total	100	100	100	100

Table 4.5

Land Ownership and Village Panchayat Membership in 8 Sample Villages of Kailali District by Regional and Communal Groupings, 1967

Regional & Communal Groupings	*Total Population*	*4 largest land owners*	*Single largest land owners*	*Village Panchayat members*
Hill Castes & Hill Tribals	9.6	21.9	37.5	10.0
Hill Sub-Total	9 6	21.9	37.5	10.0
Plain Hindus	8.9			
Muslims	1.2			
Plain Tribals	88.3	78.1	62.5	90.0
Plain Sub-Total	90.4	78.1	62.5	90.0
Total	100	100	100	100

Note : Data were taken from the unpublished thesis of Gaige, F.H. entitled "National Integration in Nepal Tarai", University of Pennsylvania, 1970.

Table 4.6

Percentage of Land Owners Participating in Village Panchayats, 1967

District	*Single Largest Land Owners*			*Four Largest Land Owners*		
	Number	*Panchayat Participant*	*Per-cent*	*Number*	*Panchayat Participant*	*Per cent*
Jhapa	10	4	40	40	8	20
Mahottari-Dhanusha	24	10	41.7	97	38	39.2
Bara	20	4	20.7	76	9	11.8
Kapilvastu	20	8	40.0	76	25	32.9
Kailali	8	3	37.5	32	9	28.1
Total	82	28	34.2	321	89	27.7

Data collected in Field Survey 1967-68.

Source : A study of Nepal Tarai, University of Pennsylvania, 1970, p. 486.

From Table 4.6 indications are clear that out of 82 villages surveyed in single largest land ownership category there was 34.1 per cent representation in village Panchayats while this representation in the category of four largest land owner group was only 27.7 per cent below the earlier one. This justifies the observation as per item III that there are absentees i.e. many wealthy people living in Kathmandu and Valley, though their land is in Tarai, do not associate in Panchayat elections.

For example two castes are referred herewith. In the first caste which relates to a village of southern Bara district the biggest land owner is a Brahmin who resides in Kathmandu during most of the year. He is a descendent of the priest family of palace and owns Birta land (free gift). He pays no attention to local politics.

In another case a Yadav, a biggest land owner living in village does not like to be a member of Panchayat, though he is a most influential man in the village. His disinterest is due to his suspicion in the hill people. He thinks that these Hill people may harm or embarrass him at the district level politics. Therefore, he backed one Kalwar but in the local village Panchayat he is still non-officio chairman. Cases are decided only by his judgement.

Reasons for such attitude towards village Panchayat have been derived after experiences. It has been realised that influential village leaders who are immune to village Panchayats, when they become actual members, the Panchayat becomes a facade. Moreover, Government has not been interested to persuade respected people like Yadav land owners to take effective part in Panchayats. The Government failed rather to inculcate confidence among such people. Due to mutual suspicion antagonism is present between the Plain people and the Government officials of the Hill regions. This is the main barrier to mutual communication.

The second reason is that the Government has failed to delegate real power to village Panchayats to ensure that they are adequately funded and can spend in need for overall development of a village. It has also come to light through the record and information maintained by district level officilsa

Table 4.7
Participation in Village & District Level Panchayat Bodies by Caste, Tribal and Regional Application of Jhapa District Participation, 1967

Regional & Communal Groupings	*Village sample of Population*	*Village Panchayat Members Chairman*	*District Assembly Members*	*District Panchayat Members*
Hill Castes	14.2	41.9	55.6	54.6
Hill Tribals	2.0	4.6	4.4	—
Total	16 1	34.5	60.0	54.6
Plain Hindus	18.1	2.3	—	—
Muslims	4 3	—	3.2	—
Plain Tribals	56.2	51.2	37.8	45.4
Sub-Total	78 6	53 5	40.0	45 4
Total	100	100	100	100

Table 4.8
Participation in Village and District Level Panchayat Bodies by Caste, Tribal and Regional Application of Mahottari-Dhanusha District Participation, 1967

Regional & Communal Groupings	*Village sample of Population*	*Village Panchayat Members Chairman*	*District Assembly Members*	*District Panchayat Members*
Hill Castes	6.4	19.1	18.8	34.8
Hill Tribals	7.4	01.6	3.1	—
Sub-Total	13.8	20.7	21.9	34.8
Plain Hindus	77.9	72.7	74.0	65.2
Muslims	7.1	4.9	2.6	—
Plain Tribals	1.2	1.6	1.6	—
Plain people Sub-Total	86.2	79.2	78.1	65.2
Total	100	100	100	100

Table 4.9

Participation in Village and District Level Panchayat Bodies by Caste, Tribal and Regionai Application of Bara District 1967

Regional & Communal Grouping	*Village sample of Population*	*Village Panchyat Mhmbets Chairman*	*District Assembly Members*	*District Panchayat Members*
Hill Castes	1.2	7.4	12.2	18.2
Hill Tribals	0.4	—	—	—
Total	1.6	7 4	12.2	18.2
Plain Hindus	79.4	56.5	64.5	81.8
Muslims	13.7	6.5	1.9	—
Plain Tribals	5.4	21.3	14.9	—
Plain People Sub-Total	98.4	84.3	81.3	81.8
Position Vacant	—	8.3	6.5	—
Total	100	100	100	100

Table 4.10

Participation in Village and District Level Pauchayat Bodies by Caste, Tribal and Regional Application of Kapilvastu District, 1967

Regional & Communal Groupings	*Village sample of Population*	*Village Panchayat Members Chairman*	*District Assembly Members*	*District Panchayat Members*
Hill Castes	8.4	14.8	13.6	25.0
Hill Tribals	0.5	—	—	—
Total	8.9	14.8	13.6	25.0
Plain Hindus	66.4	55.6	67.9	25.0
Muslims	18.1	18.5	12.03	—
Plain Tribals	6.6	11.1	6.2	8.3
Total	91.1	85.2	86.4	78.0
Total	100	100	100	100

Table 4.11

Kailali District Participation in Village and District Level Panchayat Bodies by Castes, Tribals and Regional Application

Regional and Communal Groupings	Village sample Population	*Village Panchayat*			*District Assembly*			*District Panchayat*	
		Members 1962	*Members 1967*	*Chairman 1962*	*Chairman 1967*	*Members 1962*	*Members 1967*	*Members 1962*	*Members 1967*
1	2	3	4	5	6	7	8	9	10
Hill Castes	9.6	15.3	14.9	61.9	52.4	59.5	59.5	54.5	54 5
Hill Tribals		0.3	0.2						
Hill People Sub-Total	9 6	15.6	15.1	61.9	52.4	59.5	59.5	54.5	54.5

1	2	3	4	5	6	7	8	9	10
Plain Hindus	0.9	0.8	0.2						
Muslims	1.2	0.3							
Plain Tribals	88.3	80.4	73.6	38.1	47.6	40.5	40.5	45.5	45.5
Plain People Sub-Total	90.4	81.5	73.8	38.1	47.6	40.5	40.5	45 5	45.5
Position Vacant		0.5	9.5						
No Caste		2.4	1.5						
Total	100	100	100	100	1C0	100	100	100	100

Note : All data collected in the survey of villages of different districts was done in 1967 by research scholars.

Source : A study of Nepal Tarai, Pennsylvania University, 1970.

and chief development officer that a significant progress has been done by Hill people living in Tarai. Hill people and Hill caste people obtain a larger percentage of positions in the Panchayat bodies as they move up in the Panchayat ladder. Chairman, Village Panchayat, district assembly members and district Panchayat seats are mostly filled by Hill caste people.

The following observation came to the surface by analysing the data of five districts :

(i) The Hill caste people obtain a larger percentage of positions in the Panchayat bodies. In all the five districts they are in larger number as chairman than as village Panchayat members. In Kailali District the difference is evident. Here 15.6 per cent Hill people are members while Hill caste fellows were incharge of 61.9 per cent of chairmanship.

(ii) In Jhapa, Bara, Mahottari-Dhanusha the percentage of Hill people serving as village representatives to the district assembly was higher than the percentage of village panchayat chairman, although chairman's position is more lucrative.

This indicates that Hill people preferred seats which could earn them better status in society.

(iii) In Panchayat ladder, there seems a better percentage of Hill people in the district Panchayats than in District assemblies. This fact is quite obvious in the districts of Mahottari, Bara and Kapilvastu. While 21.9 per cent is seen in district assembly, 39.1 per cent is visible in district Panchayat membership.

Political Status of Castes and Tribes among the Hill and Plain People in Tarai Region

Among the hill people Brahmins, Chhetriyas and Mewars nominate the lower castes and Hill tribes in Tarai as they do elsewhere in Nepal. Other than these three castes, not a single member was elected from other castes in 1967 to any of the five district Panchayats. The exception was in 1962 when one wealthy man of Thakali tribals was elected from Kapilvastu district.

The low caste plain people do face the same fate against high class plain castes. For example in Kapilvastu about 8 per cent of the population is Chamar—a caste known as untouchable among Hindus. The representation of Chamars in the district Panchayat was however only 1.3 per cent. In 1962 there is one example when one Chamar was elected as Chairman in the village Panchayat. But no Chamar could reach district level body in Kapilvastu.

In Mahottari-Dhanusha, the distribution in plain caste groups has a little differenee. Although Brahmins, Rajputs and Ahirs are well represented yet at the district level Panchayat Sudis, Telis and Dhanuks, all untouchable groups also figure as members. Some Telis and Sudis after discarding their caste occupation have switched on to business and have become wealthy persons.

Sudis in Mahottari-Dhanusha district though have 2 per cent population only, they secured 3 out of 23 seats at the district Panchayat level in 1967 i.e., about 13 per cent, an amazing fact.

The plain tribals are perhaps the most exploited people under the traditional system of Hindus. They have been pushed to interior jungles and their lands have been acquired by hill and plain people. The distinction in various tribes has to be studied :

(a) The Tharus who were predominant in the Far-Western Tarai are politically and economically not better to others; they are now being dominated by Hill people who are settling there. This fact is available in Kailali District.

(b In the Far-Eastern Tarai the position is different. Here Rajbanshi, Tajpuria and Gongai still predominate. Although there is larger percentage of Hill and plain people in Jhapa and Morang districts, these tribal groups are united and are maintaining control of their lands and are competing effectively in political system.

(c) Muslims, however, also fared poorly with regard to Panchayat representation. In the three districts, Bara, Kapilvastu and Mahottari-Dhanusha, they could not succeed in securing a single seat at the district level politics. The position seems worst in Kapilvastu where population of Muslims is 18 per cent. This indicates that the concentration of Muslims in different pockets is not effective or Muslims, due to other considerations, do not like to involve themselves into higher politics in a Hindu Nation. There may be another reason that general caste people have no good liking of Muslims in Nepal.

There are examples which show that Hindus and Muslims reared traditional differences and in 1960 the worst and serious disturbance broke out in Mahottari district spreading further to Rautahat district. A few people were also killed. In April 1967, riots occurred in Kapilvastu and Rupandehi districts also. Yet Hindu-Muslim problem in Nepal has not been worrying to Nepal as it is in India.

(d) As the final observation regarding district politics it has come to light that representation of the Hill people in district Panchayats is declining progressively from 1962 to 1983. Plain people and tribals are now more conscious for their rights and they now have courage to stand on equal footings with other caste people. Yet there is a long way ahead.

After collecting the oral evidence from general walk of people it has come to the surface that plain people still refuse to become involved in the Panchayat system. This indicates their calm, non-interfering attitude towards general society. Plain people's suspicion towards Hill people has not yet been wiped out. But the process has begun when plain people stand boldly and on many occasions they have forced out wealthy people of Hill tribes. The trend is very much pronounced in Eastern and Central Tarai where Yadavas having courageous traditions collected or united themselves and started getting present action in village level politics. Such action may not be palatable to Kathmandu Hill people as they advocate for only Hill culture orientation.

In 1967 eight national Panchayat members were elected from 5 districts. Out of 8 representatives 5 were Hill people, 3 Hill Brahmins, 1 Chhatri and 1 Sanyasi (Giri). Three plain people included 1 Brahmin, 1 Rajput and 1 Marwari. Why 5 Hill people were elected when their population was not more than 10 per cent? Allegations are levelled against the Government machinery Nepalese press has been very critical about the part played by Anchaladhish in such elections. Though Anchaladhishs have nothing to do with elections yet they were seen instrumental in getting the results in favour of the Hill people.

Politics at the Zonal Level

The strucure of Panchayat system itself is responsible for disproportionate representation. Zones are the tiers of the Panchayat system just below the top. They were created to pull Tarai and Hill people together into super-district economic and political units with the main goal of integrating the two regions and different castes and communities. But the zones have failed in effective pursuit of economic growth; instead they have retained political function. However, awareness in Kathmandu is witnessed for integration of Hill and Tarai people into one unit.

In 1961 the king appointed a committee to suggest more suitable system other than parliamentary which could bring the masses economically upward. The report of this committee explains:

"It has been felt that administration uniformity in the various geographical regions is essential for all round progress of the kingdom . . . and it has been considered desirable to create zones extending from the Northern border to Southern border of the kingdom. The Hill districts have regional problems as do the Tarai districts. It may be suggested that districts with common problems should be grouped together; however, this may perpetuate existing economic disparities. For example, foodgrain deficits in Hill districts and surpluses in Tarai districts have persisted.

The Hill region will only be able to achieve rapid development if the zonal units are drawn up not only to include the resources of the Hill but the Tarai also . . . . In addition, it will encourage and perpetuate unity among the people living in the mountains, in the hills and in Tarai."

Source: "Nepal Ministry of National Guidance Report of Development Districts and Zones Demarcation Committee" (Kathmandu), 1961, pp. 4-5, by Regmi Research Project).

The report gave much emphasis to National integration. It stressed that the Hill Region can be developed without the resources of Tarai. The committee's recommendations for roads, markets, light industry and coordination were the main items. These economic factors though figured very much but the stress was given for political integration also. The necessity was realised for total unity among Hill and Tarai people.

According to the demarcation committee, 14 zones were recommended. 2 western zones Mahakali and above it Seti, 4 Easternmost zones Mecchi, Kosi, Sagarmatha and Janakpur were organised to run affairs right from Tibetan Border to Indian Border. 4 other zones Bagmati, Gandaki, Dhaulagiri and Karnali did not include any district of Tarai. Remaining 4 zones Rapti includes inner Tarai district of Dang-Deokhuri. In Lumbini and Bheri zones, however, Hill and Tarai districts have been grouped together. Thus demarcation committee was partially successful for geographical integration.

Development in Road Transport

After carving the zones in 1962 the road communications were very limited. There was only one motorable road between Tarai and Hills called Tribhuvan Rajpath from Birganj to Kathmandu which was built by India Government.

Another road built by India is from Bhairawa to Pokhara via Tansen. Other fair weather roads exist between Bhadrapur in Jhapa district and Ilam. Plans for roads from Dharan to Dhankuta, from Janakpur to Kathmandu and Dhangari to Doti were also there but due to various reasons they are still to be completed in full.

A lot of controversy developed after implementing zonal system. Zonal system was seen not effective for economic developments in Panchayats. Reasons for non-functioning of system to a desired scale are as under :

(i) As units of economic activity the zones are artificial and the zonal boundries seldom bear resemblance to commercial spheres either in Hills or in Tarai.

(ii) When both the zonal and district level Panchayats initiate some development programme there is a chance for its duplication and sorting out the cases generally creates friction at the two levels.

(iii) The only function assigned to the zonal Panchayats is propagating Panchayat philosophy among masses. But this job or philosophy could not get a way ahead due to (i) political philosophy being mainly beneficial to educated people, intellectuals in Kathmandu and about a dozen of towns. (ii) Secondly, only palace-related people and higher caste hill intellectuals who are generally elected to zonal Panchayats are to gain and none else. This means the articulation of Panchayats has been rewarded only within national secretariat or within colleges and universities whose young educated folk try to secure official favour.

Through the zonal assemblies, the Tarai people of plain origin are reduced to a minority. In the election of Tarai district representative it is surprising that 9 of the 18 development districts of Tarai are grouped together in zones dominated numerically by Hill districts. It is clear that two or three districts of Tarai are linked with three or four districts of Hill area giving clear advantage to Hill origin people. Narayani is the only zone where 2 inner Tarai districts are grouped with three Central Tarai districts. Although plain people form majority in Kapilvastu district Panchayat but they are less represented in Lumbani zone assembly.

Politics at National Level

After considering the working of Panchayat system at village, district and zonal levels I am giving brief details of the systems working at National level. A table is presented herewith to understand the working with more clear ideas.

Table 4.12

Regional and Communal Groups in 1959 and 1967 National Panchayat

Regional and Communal Groupings of representatives	*1959 Parliament*		*1967 National Panchayat*	
	No. of Representatives	*% of Total*	*No. of Representatives*	*% of Total*
Hill Brahmins	31	28.4	30	24.0
Chhetris	30	27.5	47	37.6
Newars	5	4.6	15	12.0
Low caste Hill people	1	0.9	1	0.8
Hill tribals	22	20.2	19	15.2
Sub-Total Hill people	89	81.7	112	89.6
Caste Hindus & Muslims in plains	13	11.9	11	8.8
Plain Tribals	7	6.4	2	1.6
Sub-Total Plain people	20	18 4	13	10.4
Total of all Representatives	109	100	125	100

Note : Caste identification made from the list of members of 1959 Parliament and 1967 National Panchayat.

The above table presents the actual position as up to what extent plain people participate in the top level politics. One point is that the background should be kept in mind while appreciating the trend of representation to Parliament and to National Panchayat. The trend is that a member of Parliament is more influential than a member of National Panchayat. This makes National Panchayat less attractive. The trend indicates that the Hill people have been more benefited by this system than plain people. Chhetris, Newars and Brahmins have gained advantage of this change. In 1959 and 1967 the Chhetris increased their representation in the National Panchayat by 10 per cent and Newars too increased by 7 per cent. Hill Brahmins, though, have some decline in representation in 1967 but that is due to dissensions in the ruling groups and Brahmins helping one or the other group.

So, overall assessment is evident that at all levels whether district, zonal or national, only educated, intellectuals, Brahmins, Chhetris and Newars are dominating the political scenario. Caste Hindus and Muslims of plain belt decline by 2 per cent. The traditional ruling groups particularly Chhetris and Newars along with Brahmins are the main architects of National politics and the Tarai plain people have no significant representation to influence top level politics. Their say has no ground.

5

The Organisation of Land and Reform Patterns

Land Tenure System and Consequent Reforms

Nepal's Tarai land is situated on the southern part of the Hilly region from west to east. It is a flat land area, level and plain like Gangetic plain with temperate climate. It is imperative to understand the history of Tarai. How by means of local level trials the whole patch of Tarai has been developed is a case of important attention.

Up to the beginning of 20th century the whole Tarai land was covered with dense forests where even sun-rays could not penetrate. It was called a "Death Valley" or "Kala Banzar" due to malarial infestation. Whosoever tried to enter these forests was attacked by malaria fever and thus made to die. The whole belt of about 32 to 40 Km. width was very dense with forests. Yet the history has a lot to tell us of the circumstances under which this *Kala Banzar* was converted into granary or most fertile and productive land of Nepal.

In 1857 mutiny in India the Nepal Government helped British India Government by offering Gorakha soldiers to subside the feelings of independence in India and to control the Indian mutineers by means of force. Britishers were successful with this help and they totally subsided the tempest raised. So, in gratitude of this friendly hand extended by Nepali Government towards British India the latter restored Tarai land comprising twenty districts to Nepal. This portion of land was taken as of no use to British India. But Nepal this time was more wise. She pressed its administrative machinery to make use of this land. Nepalese Government also encouraged Indians to migrate to this land. For quite some years even Government servants were seen very reluctant to live in Tarai but gradually when Indian people started coming in, Hill people too were not lagging behind.

After 1950 the settlement of Tarai region was patronised by both Indian immigrants and hill people. The process of deforestation and clearance of shrubs and grass commenced stage by stage. Two to three Kms. of forest was cleaned first, ploughed and made the land cultivable at first stage. Thereafter, another batch of immigrants cleared another three Kms. and started cultivation. Thus, the whole land of Tarai was cleared and made the most fertile patch of Nepal. It has become not only the granary of Nepal but also the source of almost all her exportable surplus.[1] Many extra privileges were offered to Hill people to settle down in Tarai. So, the land once unpopular and called *Kala Banzar* is now become densely populated. The place of trees and shrubs was taken by human jungles. The density of population has become 140.47 persons per square kilometre as per 1971 census. It is therefore safely inferred that the policy of Nepal Government adopted in 1964 to attract Indian settlers had become so successful that the Nepalese Government at later stages started thinking in reverse direction. She started discouraging Indian settlers as she had the apprehension that more Indians, if absorbed, would create more problems to Nepali Government. Official figures of Indians in Nepal are given in the last pages of this chapter. The settlement of Tarai can be attributed to those factors which attracted settlers on the one side and those which made Indians to leave their homeland and to select better livelihood and dwelling in Tarai on the other.

1. Gaige, F.H., Report 1968-69, Rana and Thapa, 1975.

Opening of Gateway to Outer World

Tarai land being situated in the foothills of Himalayas and landlocked by India in the south, west and east, it was not possible for Nepal to door away to the outer world without the gracious attitude of India. In 1950, foreign aid programme was launched and a treaty of trade and transit was signed with Indian Government. Nepal was able to obtain facility of gateway through India. At about 14 points transit and passage were permitted by India. Up to 1950 almost 90 per cent foreign trade of Nepal was limited to India barring a small quantity from Tibet side. At present Indian ports are the only means of export and import for Nepal, without which Nepal's products like jute and other raw materials cannot get passage to any of the world's country. The 800 Km. border with India is almost open without any physical barricading. Therefore, Geo-cultural units of Nepal and India are reflected through the people of these countries. Citizens have no passport or visa restriction between both countries. The passage is free without any time restriction. Religion is another great factor which links the hearts of two nations.

Indian Migration in Nepal Tarai after the Unification

After the unification of Nepal in 1768 Shah rulers boosted Indians to settle in Tarai in their regime 1768-1846. The founder of present Nepal, Prithivi Narayan Shah was favouring one side settlement in the Tarai region but he had another mind on not permitting entry of foreign businessmen. In 'Divya Updesha' he has clearly stated that the Indian traders should not be permitted to go beyond Divya Pradesh[1] (God's land). If they come to our country they would certainly make our subjects pauper. Shah was thus very shrewd and his main object being encouraging settlement in Tarai region was to increase production as well as earn more revenue. Screening the above statement it is clearly inferred

1. Kirkpatrick, Colonel, *An Account of the Kingdom of Nepal*, 1826.

that the Indian traders were already in Tarai. Their attitude of business was well recognised by the ruler. Later on, Pratap Singh Shah even issued royal declaration, "Cultivate the land and set up Farmsteads."[1] It was widely circulated during 1775-1777 and in the period of Rajendra Vikram Shah in 1826.

Progressive Incidence

In Tarai abundant virgin lands were available. Eastern and central Tarai was forested densely. So, the clearing of forests and developing virgin land was not possible due to acute shortage of manpower. Hill people were firmly reluctant and local people living in some pockets were not in ample numbers. The different incidences forced people in stages to settle in Tarai.

The first incidence of calamity broke out in Bihar and Bengal in 1769-70. There was a severe blow of famine in these provinces of India. The blow was so serious that on estimation it was found that one-third population of Bihar had died.[2] Famine stricken Bihari people were in search of better and richer fields with wider facility. Such land was available in Tarai so Bihari people were ultimately attracted and they shifted their original home and moved in batches to settle in Nepal Tarai. The next step taken by Rana Bahadur Shah was that he issued decree to send people to Tarai lands in Saptari, Mahottari, Bara, Parasa, Rautahat and Morang districts.[3]

The second, third eighth and ninth articles clearly say that Nepal wished to attract settlers from India or wherever possible to cultivate farms in Tarai. Nepal also attracted farmers by giving subsidies for small periods like a year or

1. Lal Mohar issued by Pratap Singh Shah 1774-1777 and Rajendra Vikram Shah 1826.
2. Regmi, M.C., *Land Tenure and Taxation in Nepal*, Vol. I, 1963, p. 25.
3. Stiller, Ludwig F., *The Silent Cry of the People of Nepal* (1816-1839), 1976, p. 56.

two. It did not charge revenue or collect production in this period of term settled. It also supplied seeds and grains to start with.

Likewise, contractors whether they were Nepalese or Indian, were also given many privileges to develop the land and to tempt settlers from India or from Birta lands in Nepal.[1] This fact has been proved by a contract issued by Ambar Singh for developing virgin land.[2] On the other hand East India Company was mainly interested in trade with Nepal; therefore the treaty of Commerce and Trade was signed between Nepal and the East India Company in 1792. But gradually it was realised that the situation did not improve. Col. Kirkpatrick therefore made another mission to Nepal in 1793 just to improve further trade with India.[3] However right from 1768 (King Prithivi Narayan Shah and Bhemsen Thapa) to 1836, Prithivi Narayan Shah was very careful and he never wanted that English influence should increase in Nepal. The tensions in the minds of both Nepal and East India Company persisted for long. Consequently, another war broke out in 1814-16 between Gorkhas and East India Company.

At the end of war a treaty was signed in which Gorakhas had to yield western territory. But the bravery of Gorakha soldiers was, however, recognised and many Gorakha soldiers were recruited in the British Army.

Second Stage for Encouragement for Immigration to Nepal Tarai

The Indian immigration to Nepal Tarai was boosted between 1846-1950 due to the following reasons :

(i) Abundant *Birta* and *Guthi* lands were available in Tarai. Therefore, to cultivate the land, manpower was needed.

1. Regmi, M C., op. cit., 1963, p. 25, State granted land to individuals.
2. Stiller, Ludwig F., op. cit., p. 93.
3. Kirkpatrick, Colonel, op. cit.

(ii) The Government of Nepal also tried to get maximum agricultural production and revenue from the land.

(iii) The Tarai was sparsely populated and there was a need to encourage more people to settle in the region.

(iv) Natural calamities (like famine in India in the bordering districts) compelled people to shift to Tarai to seek fresh livelihood.

(v) There was a need to develop Tarai in the form of market towns.

(vi) Socio-political reasons cropped up either in India or in Nepal. This further encouraged Indian people to migrate to Nepal Tarai.

Policy of Nepal Government to Maximise Agricultural Produce

During the Rana period, plots of lands were given to Rana family members as *Birta* and to religious institutions as *Guthi* and other personal belongings, such as *Kipat, Jagir* and *Rakam.*

Guthi : The lands assigned for use of charitable, religious or philanthropic institutions.

Kipat : It is essentially a form of communal tenure as only members of certain ethnic groups are permitted to own land. The individuals have definite right in this land by virtue of their membership in the relevant social unit. The title to land has a communal character and it is perfunctory rather than absolute.

Birta : *Birta* is a term of Sanskrit word *Vrithi* meaning livelihood. It is an assignment of income from the land by the state in favour of individuals in order to provide them with a livelihood. In Nepal society we find that by virtue of religious tradition or due to social and political system many people are not directly participating in any economic activity. But they have to be supported by state. Their maintenance depends generally at the cost of agrarian class. To divert the ownership rights in the land through *Birta* grants in favour of priests, religious teachers, soldiers and members of nobility and members of Royal family. This was the pivot on which rested the social and political framework of the state. *Birta* ownership ensured stable and secured income to the beneficiary and also left the idea of social high and rich economic status. *Birta* was thus regarded as a form of private property with defined rights.

Jagir: Before 1951 it was a common practice in Nepal to assign the income of *Raikar* land, as emoluments of office to Government employees and associated functionaries. Such assignments were called *Jagirs* while Raikar land, not so assigned, was called *Jagira*. The *Jagir* system as it evolved in Nepal is little different than that practised in India. While in India *Jagirdar* has not to perform certain special duties but enjoys the benefit which he got as a result of services rendered in the past in the shape of a form of compensation for current services. While in Nepal *Jagir* land is the outcome of reward for the current services. The land granted for past services comes into the category of *Birta* system.

Birta, Guthi and *Jagirdars* acquire their right through Royal grants or assigument that made them Lords and members of the land and the peasant in every sense. In the course of time, with the development of a central state authority, the type of ownership was changed. The rights of *Birta* owners and *Jagirdars* were not absolute but the land was said to be secured only in cases where law permitted to be so. Therefore only a few categories of *Birta* owners enjoyed fullfledged proprietary rights in the land.

Rakam : *Rakam* is not like *Birta, Guthi* or *Jagir*. It refers to *Raikar* lands including those assigned in *Jagir* and *Guthi*. By this system cultivators are required to provide unpaid labour on a compulsory basis to meet the governmental requirement. It is unique in Nepal that the right of unpaid labour rests with the state. *Rakam* tenure imposed obligation on the peasants in the form of both kind and cash payments and labour services. It remained limited to Kathmandu Valley only.

Inter-relationship of Different Forms of Land Tenure System

In Nepal the basic forms of land tenure are *Raikar* and *Kipat*. While *Raikar* land belongs to the state the *Kipat* land belongs to the community under a customary form of Land Tenure that was gradually merged into state tenure system. *Raikar* land was known as *Birta* when it was alienated by the state in favour of individuals and called *Jagir* when it was assigned as emolument to Government employees and functionaries.

Guthi tenure originated from the attention of *Jagira*, *Birta* or *Kipat* lands by the state or by private individuals for religious and charitable purposes. Fiscal and tenurial concessions granted to cultivators of Jagira, Guthi, Jagir and Kipat lands led to the emergence of Rakam Tenure. Although raikar was a reflection of the unlimited prerogative of an absolute government which identified land-ownership with sovereignty.

The Birta system, thus, helped to create a feudalistic class that rendered social and political support to the rulers. The Guthi system contributed to the satisfaction of religious propensities of both the rulers and common people. Jagir and Rakam systems enabled the Government to support an administration and functionaries without the use of much cash in a situation where an exchange economy was yet to develop.

CHART SHOWING LAND TENURE SYSTEM IN NEPAL

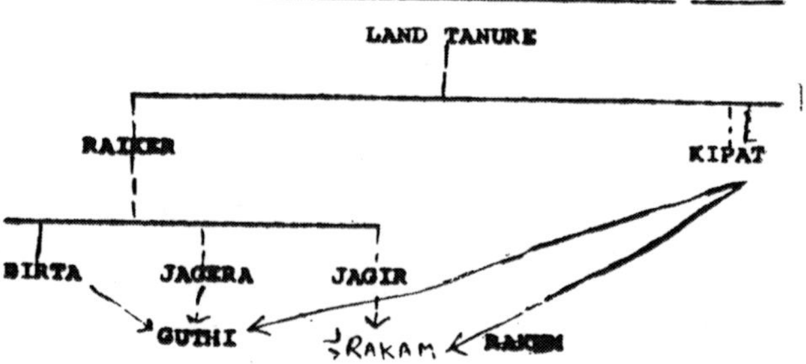

BIRTA TENURE

A Privileged Land Ownership

As explained earlier the Birta land ownership is only a privileged ownership granted under social, religious or political consideration. It remains in evidence that in 1356 king of Dullu in western Nepal bequeathed land to Brahmans on the plea that those who donate land to Brahmans would dwell in Heaven for 60,000 years. And those who confiscate such grant would become worm and live in human excreta for 60,000 years.[1] So in several cases the grants also invoked the blessings of the recipient for spiritual well-being of the donor and his relatives and successors as well. The land being the valuable natural resource in the Nepal Government policy, the following are the objectives:

(a) To maximise agricultural production and augment land revenue.

(b) It was used as instrument for implementing above policies.

(c) To extend the area of agriculture thereby increasing more cultivable land.

(d) On religious considerations that is assuage one's sins by donating such land to Brahmans.

(e) For encouraging settlement (new) the *Birta* land was distributed for residential purpose also.[2]

(f) To satisfy the settlements of spiritual obligation. The Idea of Heaven and Hell dwelling in the minds was motivated as such by Brahmans and Brahmanical writings.

(g) In society land-ownership is assessed as a grade of status—bigger the lands better the status and consequently bettet respect from poorer and less privileged people.

1. Kautilya Arthashastra (R. Sharma, 8th Ed., Mysore, p. 45).
2. Govt. of Nepal, "Construction of houses", Ministry of Law and Justice, 1965, Kathmandu, p. 540.

(h) To give benefit to members of the ruling party and obtain sustained loyalty.

(i) To encourage valour and bravity the *Birta* lands were also given to such soldiers who displayed extra-ordinary prowess in military campaign. Many victorious generals got such lands as reward.

(j) Likewise Shah Rulers granted *Birta* lands to chieftains and members of the nobility in Jumla, Dailekh, Doti and Baglung districts which were later annexed in the process of unification.[1]

(k) During the period of Rana Regime in 1846 rulers were able to exploit the Birta system for personal gains. Rana rulers were hungry of land and they continued to grant Birta lands to their kith and kin for more than 100 years.

Status of Birta Owned Class

Birta ownership became the symbol of higher status and the feeling created in the mind of such land owners is that of an ego which indicates that it is not the land alone but the resultant respect which *Birta* owner gets from society which is the main consideration. Such ownership was concentrated only among Brahmans, Chhatris, Gurangs, Magars, Limbus and Tamakas. Some cases do appear when Newar community was also benefited by *Birta* land.

Birta lands were, however, transferable, hence the system did not create a stable and excluded landed aristocracy. Though the sale of such land was harmful for *Birta* owners but due to many social and other obligations or compulsions lands were sold also in many cases like pressures of debt. Thus *Birta* lands shifted into the hands of moneyed people.

When such a trend of transferring the lands was witnessed the Government and *Birta* land owners themselves made rules

1. Order regarding *Halbandi Birta* of Vishnu Shahi, Aug. 30, 1948 in Regmi, Vol. II, pp. 31-32,

to restrict such practice; however, transfer was permitted under certain unavoidable circumstances with the sanction of Government. *Birta* owners were able to retain their lands if they stated under oath that these had been acquired through valid means.

For several reasons such restrictions remained ineffective. Grant of waste and forest lands in the old territories remained in force for Prime Minister and his family members. It was really an indirect way of legitimizing Jang Bahadur Rana acquisition of far western Tarai region comprising the present districts of Banke, Bardiya, Kailali and Kanchanpur. Therefore there is enough evidence that Jung Bahadur Rana acquired cultivated area as *Birta* on various pretexts.

Area of Land Sanctioned by Nepal Government as Birta and Guthi

Dr. M.C. Regmi has given the following figures for areas of land under various forms of Land Tenure up to 1952:*

Form of Tenure	*Area (Hectares)*	*% of Total Area*
Raikar	963,500	50.0
Birta	700,000	36.3
Guthi	40,500	2.0
Kipat	77,000	4.0
Jagir Rakam etc.	146,500	7.7

The bighas of land were allotted in the name of Guthi in the western, central and eastern Tarai regions in Nepal. Most of the holders were religious teachers, soldiers and members of the royal family. During Rana period many Acts were enacted to encourage cultivation of land in Tarai e.g. The Madhesh Malko Sawal (Revenue Regulations for Tarai District). Jamindar Patwari Sawal enacted in 1936 and 18

*Regmi, M.C., *Land Ownership in Nepal*, 1976, p. 79.

other orders followed for obligatory following by Jamindars and Patwaris. Article 18 of this regulation states "If there is barren land under your disposal and if someone comes to cultivate it you cannot sue the cultivator because the land is already cultivated."

Article 28 of Madhesh Malko Sawal states that "If Raitis are not available, they are to be purchased and should be kept in one's own Mauja (particular area of land under supervision of Jimidar). Seed should also be provided to raise if he does not hold it." An interesting law was promulgated at the time of King Surendra Vikram Shah (1847-1881) which states:[1]

Raitis are to be invited from all sectors irrespective of whether they be Nepali or Indian to cultivate the land in Morang district. Necessary items needed (*bhotopotadi*) for agriculture are to be facilitated and land should be given to them for cultivation. Any *Raiti* if he has arrears of payment to Government or loans repayable he should settle in the area and cultivate the land up to the period when he is able to pay the government or the creditors the arrears or the loans. The office of the region or Amal should prepare a document of his land and revenue and loans. The slave who has already settled one year in Muglan (India) but returns to Morang district and cultivates the land, the creditors should not hold him for loans, but if a slave of Gorakha raj has settled in Morang district in a similar situation he could be held by the creditors and they could sell him, this is no penalty. These documents clearly show that the Government tried to attract settlers to the Tarai from different areas, particularly from India. The main object of Government was to maximise the agriculture production and thereby to increase revenue from the land.

Another interesting document was also recorded by Elder et al. study (1974-8). They have noted:[2]

1. Sh Panch Surendra Vikram Shah Devka Shahan Baneko Mulki Ain (Kathmandu, 1965), 2022.
2. Elder, J.W., et al., *Planned settlement in Nepal's Tarai : A Socio-Analysis of the Khajura/Bardia Punrvas Project*, INAS and CEDA, Tribhuvan University, Kathmandu, 1976.

> "The Government... established settlement offices at Birat Nagar in the Eastern Tarai and at Hetauda in mid central Tarai and announced that any one could acquire as many bighas of land as he wished simply by settling on them and clearing them of forests".

Tarai is fertile with abundant rainfall yet it was sparsely populated due to endemic malaria. Even poor people of hills did not migrate to Tarai until the malaria eradication scheme was implemented with the help of World Health Organization. The Indian people could settle and adopt the area from the very beginning due to similar geographical settings of Nepal Tarai, and plains of northern India particularly up to portions of Uttar Pradesh, Bihar and Bengal.

Natural Calamities in (Bihar) and Adjoining Regions of Nepal Tarai which Contributed Shifting of Indian Population

Most of the rivers originating from Nepal flow down to Gangetic plains and meet Ganges at different points. The problem of flooding of all these rivers remains a cause of worry for north Bihar people. River Sapt Kosi comes from East Nepal and flows down to the plain at Chatra in Nepal, then enters Bihar at Birpur and further flows through the area touching districts of Sharsa, Madhubani, Darbhanga, Munghyr and eventually reaches Kurusela in Katihar district of Bihar. It thus covers a distance of 260 kms. This river has been continuously a source of flood. In 1763 the Kosi river flooded up to a mile of west of Purnea, changed her course and swept miles of land in 1807-8, 1873-92 floods. The entire sector of northern Bihar covering 33 to 36 thousand square Kms. is inundated with ravaging floods every year. So like Hwang-ho of China this river is called the "river of sorrow". India, to save futher damage, built a strong barrage in 1958 at Hanuman Nagar with the cooperation of Nepal.

In 1770 there was a devastating famine and in 1783 another drought followed. So, sometimes by floods and at other times by droughts and famine, northern Bihar has always been a victim of calamities. Not only this, there was a very severe earthquake in 1934 in which Purnea and Darbhanga districts suffered badly.[1] So all these natural calamities, added to other sufferings, resulted into migration of the poor, the landless, hungry and suffering Bihari people into Nepal Tarai.

Socio-Political Reasons

Mutiny of 1857 : Sepoy mutiny in 1857 was also one of the important factors that encouraged Indian migration into Nepal Tarai. During the mutiny many Hindus and Muslims fled to Nepal and made their residence in the Western Tarai region. As Nepal also helped the British Government during mutiny, the present districts of Banke, Bardia, Kailali and Kanchanpur were restored to Nepal in 1861.

Revolution of 1950 : In 1950 Indian Government helped Nepal to overthrow the Rana Government. Hundreds of Indians entered Nepal to help Nepali Congress in this movement. So those Indians who entered Nepal for political reasons were later encouraged to settle down as Nepali citizens.

Developing of Market Towns in Tarai : There arose need for development of commercial centres in Nepal Tarai. Indian railheads were extended close by the border towns of Nepal between late 19th century and early 20th century. Township of Birganj, Janakpur, Birat Nagar. Bhadrapur, Bhairahwa, Nepalganj and Dhamgarhi flourished when railheads were extended to border towns of Raxaul, Jayanagar, Farbisganj, Jogbani, Nautanwa, Rupdeo and Gautiphants. Birat Nagar became the largest trading centre of Nepal. Indian railhead was extended 20 kms. to connect Farbisganj in 1914 and further 4 kilometres to Jogbani in 1916. Col. Tej Bahadur consequently shifted his headquarters from Rangeli to Birat Nagar.

Construction of Roads : About the year 1950 the British constructed a road between Jogbani and Dharan. Due to this

1. R.C. Roychaudhury, Bihar District Gazetteers, Darbhanga and Purnea, Patna, 1964, p. 119.

road Dharan bazar became the largest trading centre. So by the construction of roads many bazars and towns in Tarai picked up humming business. Marwaris of Rajasthan, Baniya, Halwais, Rouniyar, Kalwar and Telis of Bihar gave all round boost to these towns. Local people like Newars, Thakalis and Sherpas also started migrating to Tarai and took part in business. A special document was issued that those Indian businessmen who could migrate to Nepal would be given two bighas of land, about 142,576 sq. feet free. This further encouraged Indian settlement in Tarai.

Establishment of Industries in Tarai Towns : After the development of railhead and the construction of roads, many industries and factories were established in Tarai towns. Some of them can be enumerated as under :

The Birat Nagar Jute Mills	1936
Raghupati Jute Mills Ltd.	1947
Judha Match Factory, Birganj	1938
Judha Match Factory, Birat Nagar	1943
Nepal Plywood and Balimco. Ltd., Birat Nagar	1943
Nepal Church Co. Ltd.	1947

Many rice mills and Biri factories were also established in Bhadrapur, Birat Nagar, Janakpur and Birajganj by Indian businessmen.

Post-Independence Migration of Indian People to Nepal : After the signing of treaty between the Government of Nepal and India in 1958 relations with both countries became very cordial. Citizens of both countries were allowed free movement to and from Nepal without any check. The article 7 of this treaty clearly states :

"The Government of Nepal and India agree to grant on a reciprocal basis to the nationals of one country in the territories of others the same privileges in the matter of residence, ownership of property, participation in trade and commerce, movement and other privileges of similar nature" (Bhasin, 1972, p. 122).

Such treaties were also signed on July 31, 1950, September 11, 1960 and in August 1971. So these trade and commerce treaties not only strengthened the bonds of two countries but further encouraged Indian nationals to do their business in Nepal. A treaty concerning irrigation and water development was signed on 14th July 1954 and for Kosi barrage it was signed on 25th April 1954.

Up to 1964 Indians were encouraged to settle down in Nepal, Citizenship Acts of Nepal 1963, 1964 and 1968 made it simpler to obtain Nepalese citizenship. In the general election in 1958 most of the Indian settlers were included in the voters' list. The liberal attitudes of early interim Government towards migrants from India were responsible for increase of Indian population in Nepal.

Even during the period of King Mahendra 1956-71 Indian capitalists were encouraged with many subsidies to set up industries in Tarai. Birla opened cotton industry in Nepal.[1] In the Industrial Policy Act of 1962 it was evidently found that no distinction in nationality would be made where bigger industries are being set up. Foreign nationals were further allowed to take back their sum plus 10 per cent profit in foreign currency to their home country.[2]

Business Sector : In this sector establishment of National Trading Ltd. 1962 in Nepal also encouraged Indian businessmen to invest their money in Nepal. According to Marwari businessmen of Birat Nagar it was foreign goods which fetched good amount of money for them.

Land Reform Policy

Land reform policy was decided in 1964 under which Indian tenants were often forced from one place to another in search of land. The policy of 1964, however, gave secure right to many Indian tenants and thus they became permanent occupants. This also prevented and restricted many hill people from holding land in Tarai. Those hill people who could not secure land were forced to deforest jungle and make cultivable

1. Nepal Ain Sangraha (Collection of Legal Code), Part I, 1964, HMG, pp. 840-945.
2. Ibid, pp. 856-861.

lands. Substantially, it can be inferred that because of land reform policy, temporary Indian cultivators established cultivation for their livelihood. A sample progression of Indian migration into Panchayat of Morang district of Tarai at different periods is given below. Figures also present wards 4, 6, 7, and 9 of Katahari Panchayat.

Figures indicate that maximum number of Indian immigrants into Tarai were up to 1963. After 1963 the number of permanent settlers were curtailed. This was due to successive malaria eradication programmes in Tarai after 1960. The Development Programmes, New Legal Code 1963 and Land Reform Act 1964 helped hill people to settle in Tarai. It checked the permanent infiltration of the Indian population only in the agriculture sector of the Tarai.

Conclusion

The pattern of Indian immigrants into Nepal Tarai is a definite case of historical development. Migrants to Tarai came due to many reasons stated earlier not only of their own but also they were encouraged by Nepal Government to settle down in Tarai. Indians were invited to clear jungles, cultivate lands, increase agricultural products, set up industries, start business and instal markets, and construct townships. For quite sometime, say up to 1965, it was not in the mind of the Government that due to unchecked migration to Tarai it would become a land of overpopulation thereby compelling administration to revise its policy. So, in 1964 Nepal Government realised that continued inflow of foreign nationals must be restricted.[1]

Restrictions to foreign nationals came rather late in the development context of Nepal. Today it is very difficult to differentiate the immigrant Indians and local Tarai people. The ethnic groups living in Nepal Tarai are physically and culturally

1. Land Reform Act 1964.

Table 5.1

Immigrants to Katahari Panchayat of Morang District by Indian Ethnic Groups during 1933-1966

Indian Ethnic Group	*Total families or households in 1976*	*Total family members*	*Up to 1933*	*1934 to 1943*	*1944 to 1953*	*1954 to 1962*	*1963 to 1966*
Koeri	12	66	—	—	12	—	—
Dhanuk	4	21	—	—	1	3	—
Saha	13	33	—	2	4	2	4
Kewat	58	296	—	17	15	22	4
Sahani	16	69	1	3	4	6	2
Das	2	7	—	—	—	2	—
Singh	2	15	—	—	—	2	—
Sahu	1	2	—	—	—	1	—
Mahato	4	20	—	—	4	—	—
Tamta	1	6	-	—	—	—	1
Mistri	1	5	—	—	—	1	—
Minga	12	62	—	1	4	6	1

Mansuri	1	3	—	1	—	1	—
Raya	1	1	—	1	—	—	—
Paswan	30	135	1	9	11	6	3
Yadav	1	2	—	—	—	—	1
Kaona	1	4	—	—	1	—	—
Thakur	1	2	—	—	—	1	—
Dhobi	2	7	—	—	1	—	1
Mochi	1	3	—	—	—	—	1
Harijan	11	47	1	9	1	—	—
Total	175	806	3	43	58	55	18

Source : Dahal, B.R., "Indian Ethnic Groups in Nepal Tarai", Ph.D. report, CNAS, 1978,

the same people living in the border districts of U.P., Bihar and Bengal. Languages, food habits, style of wearing clothes and other socio-cultural patterns and religious behaviour is the same. International marriage is also permitted. Any settler (Madhesia) of Nepal can marry his daughters in India and can get bride for his son from India. This makes people cross the borders as and when required to meet their social obligations with their affinal relations.

These days lot of controversies and tensions have developed in Tarai and a distinction between who is a local Nepali and who is an outsider (Indian citizen) is making its inroads. Rana and Thapa (1975-58) have outlined the following categories of Indians in Nepal:

1. Those who are still Indian citizens.
2. Those who were born in India but have not taken Nepalese citizenship.
3. Those who were born in Nepal but are descended from Indians.

Whatever the social, political or economic consequences, Nepal is passing through Indian immigrants, it is quite obvious that Tarai has become Nepal's vital economic zone. It has become the granary of Nepal. Much of the revenue comes from products of Tarai like jute, cigarettes, matches, cloth, sugar, rice and oil, industries located in Tarai. The most outstanding indigenous economic development ever to occur in the history of Nepal is present in the Nepal Tarai.

Agriculture in Tarai

Tarai's topography is dominated by level plains resting on low lying Churia Hills of Siwalik range system to the north and continues to south to merge with Gangetic plains of India. From the air, Tarai seems flat green with agricultural fields contrasting sharply with chaotic escarpments of Churia Hills and steep slopes of Mahabharat mountain in the north. Hundreds of parallel rivers and streams rush away from Hills and very eagerly run south to meet the holy river Ganga about a hundred fifty kilometres south. On ground level, most district plains are called Dehaut.

Villages can be detected by concentration of trees and brown earthen huts. Eventually from air the view down resembles the flanks of some huge forest as the trees, villages and fields together blend into a vast, verdant wall described as "Monotonous" by a traveller.[1]

The expanse of plain was formed by the flow of numerous rivers like Mechi, Kamala, Gandiki, Sone, Mahakali etc. along with hundreds of their tributaries. These rivers eroded the uplands of Mahabharat and Churia ranges and deposited alluvium into Indo-Gangetic area which is supposed to be the older structural plain of North India.[2]

These rivers transport tremendous amounts of materials during the monsoon rainy season. They are full of rich brown earth which is deposited in plain Tarai. This feature is very prominent in the case of Kosi river as noted by Karan "From June to September the Kosi is a rolling mass of water carrying the heaviest charge of detritus known in a tropical river."[3] The depth of these sediments as estimated throughout plains in general is between 6000 to 20,000 feet.

Gradient of Plain

Gradient from the base of the first range of Hills to the south is slight only. The distance from Muskar (500 ft. above sea level) to the Indian railhead at Jaya Nagar (230 ft. above sea level) is 27 kms. which indicates the downward slope of 10 ft. per kilometre.

Bhabar Tarai

The slope in feet is more sluggish than indicated earlier. The total gradient is aggregated slightly due to BHABAR

1. Wilhelm Filchnor, Der Fieberholls, Nepal (Wlesbadeneherhard Brockhans, 1953, p. 191).
2. Memoirs of Geological Survey of India (Calcutta,1939) pp. 128-130.
3. P.P. Karan, *Nepal: A Physical Culture and Geog.*, Kentucky Press, 1960, p. 24.

TRACT. A somewhat more pronounced slope is running along the outer edges of the hills resembling a coalescent alluvial Fan.[1] In this tract the coarser gravels are depsited first, allowing rapid percolation of edaphic drought. This region might be better delimited by a survey of water depths in open wells. In April 1970, such depth was measured and approximately found to be 35 feet at Jiba and 40 feet at Phulbaria which are north of Mircheya. The Bhabar Tract appears around East-west Highway or Rajmarg. In general it is safer to say that the tract merges into Tarai just South of national highway and slope; from there it is not prominent as it is only 10 feet per kilometre.

Hillocks in Tarai

Hills present an even front along the northern border of the plain area except between towns of Mirchaya and Golbazar where a low ridge extends south. This feature rises 100 ft. above the plain of Mirchaya and is about one and half km. long. The area where Rajmarg runs east-west Tarai has been cut through this ridge. There are other low mounds between the upper reaches of Mainswati and Gobarjal rivers but they also contain alluvial genesis.

Inner Tarai

Throughout the entire Tarai region the land north of Churia Hills descends into a series of elongated valleys before rising abruptly into the Mahabharat Ranges. These are called as dunes. They are not continuous but actually are formed where rivers are merging. Bhitari dune north of Sirha or dune of Udaipur is situated on the confluence of Kamala and Udaipur rivers. This large open plain about 1000 ft. above sea level is surrounded by densely wooded forests.

1. Sharan Shrestha, *Modern Geography of Nepal* (Kathmandu, 1960), p. 9.

Administrative Divisions of Tarai

For administrative convenience the whole Tarai region has been divided into the following districts. These twenty districts have been further grouped locationwise into five regions. Table 5.2 represents districts and their Headquarters. For better understanding the level of Tarai, each district Headquarter is shown with its altitude. 11 districts are 100 metres MSL, while some are between 100 to 200 mts. Only one Headquarter Ghorahi of Chitwan district is more than 600 mts. i.e. 2210 ft. This height is also not much to influence climate and monsoon or temperatures.

Table 5.2

Tarai Districts

Region	*District name*	*Area in sq. km.*	*Headquarter*	*Altitude (m)*
Eastern	1. Jhapa	1606	Bhadrapur	75
	2. Morang	1855	Birat Nagar	72
	3. Sunsari	1257	Inaruwa	83
	4. Saptari	1363	Rajbiraj	78
	5. Siraha	1188	Siraha	76
Central	1. Dhanusha	1180	Janakpur	73
	2. Mahottari	1002	Jaleswar	61
	3. Sarlahi	1259	Malangwa	83
	4 Rautahat	1126	Gaur	76
	5. Bara	1190	Kalaiya	99
	6. Parsa	1353	Birganj	88
	7. Chitwan	2218	Bharatpur	191
Western	1. Nawalparsi	2162	Parsi	111
	2. Rupandehi	1360	Bhairahawa	106
	3. Kapilvastu	1738	Taulihawa	103
Mid Western	1. Dang Deokhuri	2955	Ghorahi	663
	2. Banke	2337	Nepalganj	152
	3. Bardiya	2025	Gulariya	149
Far Western	1. Kailali	3235	Dhangadhi	171
	2. Kanchanpur	1610	Mahendra Nagar	116
Total	20	34019		

Geographical elements like topography, climate, temperatures, rainfall, rivers etc. have already been given in separate chapter.

Tarai being plain and lying in temperature and monsoon, the climate is very suitable for cultivation. The proportion of cultivated area is just double i.e. 65% than hill area 29% and a nominal agriculture about 5% is done in Himalayas. Eastern Tarai produces surplus foodgrains. Rice as food crop and oilseed and sugarcane as cash crops are very common in Tarai.

Nepal is pre-dominantly an agricultural country. About ninety per cent of economically active population of the country as per 1981 figures was engaged in Agriculture and allied Industry. This sector contributed about 52% of GDP in 1986-87.

Foodgrains production in the country depends greatly upon nature. However, there are many reasons why agriculture dominates the economic life of people in Tarai.

(a) Tarai region is well suited for farming as moderate and good soil go hand in hand to create prosperous conditions.

(b) Water for irrigation and for human and livestock consumption is in abundance. Large number of rivers and streams further make position conducive to farming.

(c) There are no other developed natural resources which could stand in competition with agriculture.

(d) It is the culture and technique of the people living in Tarai which is more important as to how they plough? how they sow seeds? how they select and examine the suitability of field for growing a particular crop?

(e) The peasant doing farming develops a sense of satisfaction, rather ego, to own a piece of land. Thereby he gains wealth. There is no other honourable way to make a good living. Even a low paid employee or a primary school teacher feels great honour in possessing farming land of any size.

So, cultivation in Tarai is done with the natural aptitude of people. According to the 1981-82 national sample census of agriculture, land-use in Nepal is dominated by holdings with temporary crops. Of 3,984,298 holdings reported with multiple land uses in 1981-82, 2,157,431 i.e. 54.15% holdings have temporary crops. As such more than ninety one per cent of total area of holdings (2,463,717 hectares) is under temporary crops.[1]

The estimated 2,193,956 holdings in Nepal in 1981-82 were small with an area of 1.13 eectares. The average number of parcels per holding was 4.3 and they were dominantly owned by operators.

In 1978-79, the average yield per hectare of Paddy, Wheat, Maize and Millet was in the order of 1853 Kg., 1166 Kg., 1635 Kg. and 1079 Kg. respectively. The average yield per hectare of the cash crops, sugarcane, oilseed, tobacco and potato was respectively 16823 Kg., 642 Kg., 123 Kg. and 5499 Kg.

In 1987-88, the average yield rate of paddy, wheat, maize and millet reached 2095 Kg., 1248 Kg., 1338 Kg. and 911 Kg. respectively. Similarly, there has been insignificant change over a period of one decade in the per hectare yield rate of cash crops except sugarcane and tobacco. In 1987-88, the yield rate of sugarcane was 27588 Kg., oilseeds 625 Kg., tobacco Kg. and potato 7071 Kg.

Jute is grown in fewer of Tarai districts. The yield rate for this cash crop was 1399 Kg. per hectare in 1978-79 which reached 1093 Kg. per hectare in 1987-88. One of the main reasons for low productivity in agricultute has been inadequate use of approved seeds, particularly in paddy and maize. Of the total improved seed it is only wheat which shares about 85% of the total improved seeds used.

In order to obtain maximum yield it is imperative to use improved seeds and chemical fertilizer. Fertilizers are imported and used in agriculture production.

1. CBS, A Comparative Study of Ecological Belts based on National Sample Census of Agriculture for Nepal, 1981-82, HMG, 1988.

The total import of chemical fertilizer (N.P.I.C.) rose from 21073 metric tons in 1978-79 to 42376 metric tons in 1987-88 while actual consumption rose from 18544 M.T. to 54422 M.T. during the above period.

Food Crops and Cash Crops Grown in Tarai Districts

Food crops and cash crops grown in Tarai districts are discussed exclusively here.

Food Crops

Paddy : Paddy is the foremost crop which covers an area of about 55% of the total area under cereal crops in Nepal Tarai. Jhapa, Morang, Saptari, Rautahat, Rupandehi, Kapilvastu etc. produce the largest amount of paddy. Otherwise in other places it is grown in the valleys of rivers. Wet paddy is grown where plentiful of water is available and dry paddy is sown with the low amount of water or where water is not filled in fields throughout the crop standing. In Tarai even three croppings of paddy are popular. Rice is the chief foodgrain in Tarai. Its production is 1.9 M.T. per hectare. Like India (Bihar and Eastern U.P.) Masuli the improved variety of rice is becoming very popular and is a real gift to Tarai people.

Minikit programmes for villages are being emphasised and modern technology is also being imported to increase agriculture production. Japanese variety of rice is also planted in some areas to save the plants from hail-storm and heavy wind blows.

The rice grown in Tarai not only fulfils the national requirement but is also exported to other countries.

Wheat : Wheat covers about 15% of the total cultivated land under food crops of Nepal. It is a winter crop, so generally, it is grown in Tarai region. In the western hilly region wheat is also adequately produced due to suitable weather and water availability.

Analysing the area of wheat engaged in Tarai districts it is found that in 10 years from 1978-79 to 1987-88, out of

20 districts 19 have increased their acrage. Consequently, production of wheat has also gone up in 19 districts. It shows a very satisfactory position, visualised for improving both area of cultivation and production per hectare. Eastern and central zone districts have switched on to wheat production with good impetus. Kailali and Kanchanpur districts are also not lagging behind. The Bara district is the largest producer of wheat. Though in earlier stages i.e. about a decade back the wheat was not a countable crop and it was not very popular among Tarai farmers.

Maize : Maize is also one of the major food crop produced in Nepal. About 19% of the cultivable area of Nepal is covered by maize. However, people have started disowning this crop and prefer wheat and rice. It is indicated that out of 20 districts producing maize in Tarai two have already decreased the area and production. Chitwan and Dang-Deokhuri are the two districts which produce maize in good quantity. The main feature is that maize sown and grown in each district of Tarai leaving none to exception.

Millets : This is also a coarse foodgrain and grown mostly in hilly region. It is confined to the central region. It indicates that millets though produced by each district of Tarai year after year, the area under production has gone down; out of 20 districts 17 have already stopped growing this grain. However, without much effort Kodobuck wheat is available in valleys and waterlogged places which poor people collect after rains when it is ripe.

Barley : Barley is also produced in the land where wheat is sown. But due to its 2nd gradation after wheat it is not very much patronized by people. A very small quantity is produced in Tarai districts. Rautahat is the only district which produced 749 M. Tons of barley in 1987-88.

Cash Crops

Apart from food crops the economy of a country depends much on cash crops. Such crops are the only source of income to farmers, by which they can imporove their living; they can purchase better seeds and implements for agriculture. They can manage their obligation and duties towards their children for their food, education, marriage etc. and can build house for better living. By cash only he can purchase better cattle like cow, buffaloes, sheep, goats etc. to augment his income. Therefore, cash crops play a vital role in the life of a farmer. Like all other countries Nepal is also doing cash crop farming in large scale over the land where it is possible. Where soil, climate and temperature are suitable for a particular crop, sugarcane, oilseeds, tobacco, potato, jute and ganja or marijuana fetch good income. Nepal is one of the few countries in the world which has not declared marijuana as an illegal crop.

1. *Sugarcane* : Sugarcane is one crop which does not require much labour and attention. It occupies the field for the whole year. Its cultivation is mainly confined to the Tarai Region of Kosi, Narayani and Lumbani zones. Large areas are given to sugarcane in Morang, Sunsari, Sarlahi, Bara, Parsa, Nawal Parsi, Rupendehi, Kapilvastu and Rautahat districts of Tarai. Apart from above districts sugarcane is grown in almost all remaining districts of Tarai. It depicts the correct position as to how sugarcane cropping progressed within 10 years.

2. *Oilseeds* : Next important cash crop is oilseed which covers about 45% of the land devoted to winter crops. It grows higher in Tarai, Udaipur, Sindhuli. Makwanpur, Chitwan, Rautahat, Rupandehi, Dang-Deokhuri, Banke, Bardia, Kailali and even in Kanchanpur districts. It clears the position as to which place and district has produced maximum quality of oilseed in 1987-88. Chitwan, Dang-Deokhuri and Bardia districts are very prominent.

3. *Tobacco* : Tobacco as a cash crop is also grown mostly in the Tarai region. It is more suited for cultivation in low land areas like Saptari, Mahottari, Dhanusha, Sirha and Sarlahi districts. It shows what little or more tobacco is produced in each district of Tarai. Since it requires lot of pre-requisite conditions like excise license, it could not grow to the extent people needed. Tobacco cigarette factory installed in Tarai has boosted up its cultivation. Tobacco is

also used in Biri-filling which is done locally in the Tarai region.

4. *Potato* : Among the cash crops potato is gaining sudden favour from farmers of lower hilly parts and Tarai districts. It is evident that during the last 10 years potato has been on increasing trend every year. Out of 20 districts of Tarai, barring none, each district produces potato. Every year, the yield is growing. Even Nawalparsi and Kanchanpur districts which used to produce less than 500 M. Tons of potato have improved considerably. In 1987-88 Nawalparsi produced 3520 M.T., Kapilvastu 1900 M.T. and Kanchanpur 4500 M.T. which is an appreciable increase.

Since India is also a good producer of potato its foreign trade is bleak and mostly the crop is consumed locally with a small quantity to the uphill land of Tibet.

5. *Jute* : The most precious among the kinds of cash crops is the jute. Eastern and central Tarai lands have more potential areas of jute growing. It is produced mostly in Jhapa, Morang, Sunsari districts and other areas also grow jute but they are not very prominent. The production in the later years has gone down due to people having started the use of synthetic packing.

Other Small Crops

Coffee : Coffee is grown mostly in Gulmi.

Cardamom is prosperous in Illana, Panchthar, Terathum, Taplejung, Sankhuwasawa, Dhankuta, Bhojpur and Khotong.

Ginger : In the western part of Nepal mostly in hill area, like Palpa, Tanahu, Syanja and Salyan, ginger is produced as the most prospective commercial crop. It is sent to India in large quantity.

Cotton : Cotton is not a very yielding crop in Nepal However, it is grown in Banke, Bardia and Dang-Deokhuri districts of Tarai. To some extent, it is also tried in lower parts of the Arun valley. This crop should be given due attention, as the cotton is the most relevant commodity for a cold country like Nepal. It can save foreign exchange too.

Table 5.3

Area and Productiou of Jute from 1978-79 to 1987-88

Financial year	*Total area hect.*	*Mtrs production*
1978-79	46853	65551
1979-80	56714	67514
1980-81	51959	59284
1981-82	35320	42663
1982-83	30400	39039
1983-84	23666	25043
1984-85	27200	33142
1985-86	47191	61102
1986-87	19840	23452
1987-88	14450	15800

Source : Statistical data on Jute and Jute products published by Jute Development and Trading Corporation.

Cumin : Seeds are grown in Sedgan only.

Vegetables and Fruits : There is no dearth of any kind of vegetables in Nepal. Land and climate is suitable for all types of vegetables in some or the other part of Nepal. Tarai terrace farming of Kathmandu valley and other low lying areas produce vegetables in large quantity. Markets can be seen full of vegetable shops even in the remote villages.

Methods and Equipments

The methods and equipments used by typical Tarai farmers have undergone no change for the last two thousand years. The same primitive ways are being followed up to this day. Man is the chief tool and the main source of power. There are very few machines, such as tractors and mechanical ploughs. Every activity like ploughing, sowing, planting, harvesting and thrashing is done by arduous hand labour. Transplanting, not really necessary for most crops, remains in use due to cultural inertia of past centuries.

The wooden plough is the main tool for tilling the field. It consists of a carved wooden pole with a metal bit attached on a yoke. The bullock is the main draft animal. In Nepal Tarai a special feature of ploughing is that one bullock should be higher than the other because the plough is to turn constantly in one direction. Fields are very small. This plough system is very vague and inefficient as it just scratches earth and does not do deep plouging which is very essential for better yields.

Improved variety of seeds are not procured. Generally neither local farmers take interest nor central machinery has been active so far, yet it cannot be said that nothing has been done by the Government.

It will not be improper to say that Nepal is a very rich country inhabited by poor people. Tarai and mid-lands are pertinent for peasants. Possibilities of various crops, and fruit trees along with vegetables can be explored in the hill region but not yet exploited. So many areas having potential for one or the other crops are not in use yet. Monsoon does not directly effect floods and droughts and in turn scarcity and famine. Therefore during the bad season when main crops fail farmers should adjust by a variety of different cereals and beans, edible roots and fruits. But all this requires proper awareness and a central agency to render proper guidance and assistance to farmers in times of need.

Conservation of natural resources is needed to protect all the vulnerable and endangered flora and fauna species. Man, even by adopting to modern technology should adjust himself with nature without disturbing ecology. In the name of development though immediate results are sweet but their distant repercussion is very sour and bleak. Policy makers and activists of elite circles totally failed to impress upon the grassroot level groups in making themselves aware of basic problems regarding the country's degrading environment and ecology.

Nepal seems to be one of the countries of the world where people of different parts cooperate and help in the development of the nation. So the war between population and production should be fought with intelligence. The growth rate of population is 2.6 while production is 2.5. So the challenge is always there. On many occasions the foreign aid is deemed as a rightful weapon to overcome this disparity but the cost of such efforts itself makes a government bankrupt.

Development is not an easy job. Most of the higher level planners and executives are not fully conversant with lower level local problems; so a concerted effort should be made in the form of meeting the lowest tier of people, holding seminars, keeping good contact with all levels of society.

Corruption and contradictions should be nipped and the staff should be suitably trained to get the schemes percolated to the grassroot level. Without translating the knowledge into realistic and practical surface, the quality of life cannot be improved. Research reports, resolutions, decisions and suggestions of various brain are shelved in the almirahs of red tapism. They should be taken out and plausible ones should be given practical life.

Rural Technology

The conventional technology is still being used in Nepal and by community in rural areas. Yet many of them can be improved. Agricultural Development Bank (ADB) has initiated many programmes for socio-economic upliftment. In the villages people are being made aware for better cleanliness. Construction Pit for latrine is being encouraged to make villages more healthier. Community irrigation, afforestation, mobile Banking Service through saving camps and similar other programmes should be implemented. For villagers, occupations like goat-raising, cow and buffalo raising, piggery, fisheries, poultry, cottage industry, agriculture, ceramic pots etc. are some of the simple works which could be done without any special apprenticeship.

Identification and development of rural technologies should be introduced in villages. Nepal has now a number of agencies, organisation and projects to deal with rural development. Simple and cheap technology should be introduced in villages like smokeless oven. Some of the cheaper and feasible projects can be started immediately without incurring much expenses.

1. *Hydro Pump*

The lift pumps without consuming any energy are needed for villages. The stream water has been lifted up to the extent of 50 m in three stages. So electricity can be produced by the stream current itself.

2. *Solar Cooker*

This device is not costly and saves about 50% of the fuel. It can be very useful in Tarai region where sunshine is adequate.

3. *Water Turbines*

This small water mill can fulfil the basic needs of villages like grinding, powerloom, and pumping of water.

4. *Solar Water Heater*

It can also save the limited resources of the country.

5. *Bio-Gas*

Small size plant is useful to agro-based villages. In Tarai region farmers along with cultivation keep a number of milch animals and bullocks also. From their dung it is very cheaper to instal Bio-Gas plants in each village and to those houses who can afford it individually. The problem of cooking meal and the lighting of house can be served by this simple application. It is assessed that Nepal produces 27 million metric tons of cowdung per year from household animals, out of which only 62,000 M. Tons is consumed as firefuel. There is thus a total loss of 46,000 M. Tons of nitrogen and 32,000 M.T. of phosphorus. It should be tapped for best use.

6. *Windmill*

Nepal's altitude creates high potential to instal windmill. They are very common in Tarai and also in Jumla and Pulpa. This energy should be fully harnessed.

7. *Rope Line*

To carry goods from upper hill region to low altitudinal settlement, short ropeways should be installed. Steep slopes are very conducive for rope lines and cable cars.

8. *Training of Local Technicians*

The traditional techniques of Nepal require immediate improvement for which local craftsmen like carpenters, blacksmiths, leather workers should be trained in use of improved implements and tools. This will not only enhance the dexterity in the job but also increase the income of the workmen, because with better and improved tools he can do the job in lesser time and can add his income by undertaking more jobs in hand in the time thus saved.

Use of Fertilizers

There being no local fertilizer unit in Nepal all chemicals and fertilizers have to be imported. As per Table 5.4 it is revealed that the interest of Nepali farmers in use of fertilizer was not dim. Ten years figures show that in 1978 a total of 18544 M.T. of fertilizers were consumed by them. Every year the trend of consumption continued to rise and in 1987-88 consumption rose to 54422 M.T. just five times more than in 1978-79. Though the increase indicates the farmers' inclination towards chemical manures but as all these chemicals are being imported from outside either on purchase account or as aid their input cost is so high that the average peasant cannot muster courage to purchase the same.

Table 5.5 indicates that except for potash all other chemical fertilizers were consuming higher and higher value. Therefore, it is not always possible to make available the

Table 5.4

Import and Consumption of Chemical Fertilizers in Nepal

(in M.T.)

Year	Nitrogen (N)		Phosphorus (P)		(K-20) (K)		Total	
	Import	Consumption	Import	Consumption	Import	Consumption	Import	Consumption
1978-79	15240	13746	3763	3341	2070	1457	21073	18544
1979-80	21455	15501	3825	4285	75	1178	25355	20964
1980-81	15582	16767	3682	5105	1665	686	20929	22458
1981-82	20052	17976	7239	5073	—	775	27281	22824
1982-83	36665	22882	7110	7459	—	938	43775	31279
1983-84	22509	28058	9786	8463	—	779	32295	37300
1984-85	34386	31656	13640	10623	1200	550	49256	42829
1985-86	42223	31698	12601	11053	—	657	54824	43408
1986-87	26025	32900	14257	12064	3250	210	43532	45174
1987-88	27854	38233	11579	15309	2943	880	42376	54422

Source : Agriculture Input Corporation. Figures from Statistical Year Book of Nepal, 1989, p. 171.

Table 5.5

Price of Agriculture Inputs 1978-1987

(*in Rs/MT*)

Chemical fertiliser	*1978*	*1979*	*1980*	*1981*	*1982*	*1983*	*1984*	*1985*	*1986*	*1987*
a. Sulphate	1870	1870	2400	2400	2400	2400	2400	3000	2850	2850
b. Urea	2440	2440	3100	3100	3500	3500	3500	4200	3990	3990
c. Complex	2770	2269.5	2800	2800	3250	3250	3200	4200	3990	3990
d Compound	—	2210	2740	2740	3200	3200	3200	3200	3990	3990
e. DAP	—	—	—	—	4500	4500	4500	5620	5339	5339
f. Potash	3375	2250	1572.5	1572.5	1572.5	1572.5	1572.5	2100	1995	1995

Source ; Agriculture Input Corporation. Figures from Statistical Year Book of Nepal, 1989.

adequate quantity of chemical manures as per demand of the farmers. From foreign import duties, transportation charges, porterage charges to carry them to the field together fetch a large amount which is a total extraordinary expense not always bearable by a country like Nepal.

Problematic Agro Sector

Our analysis shows that the agriculture sector has been the most important sector in the economy and also the most important contributor to the nationwide growth. One fact emerges that the share of agriculture's contribution has not changed during the last one and a half decade. The contribution to GDP, the employment structure and foreign trade patterns have remained unchanged. Labour shifting out of agriculture sector has not changed. Rather it is likely to be more significant once the agrarian reforms are implemented to their full intente, which may sometime stir up the landlord class sufficiently to make employment policy outside the ambit of agriculture an important variable in overall planning.

An examination of growth in real per capita income and increase in agriculture production indicate that the slow rate of growth in the agriculture sector has been the main reason for the slow rate of growth in economy. The growth in average annual real per capita income fell short of targeted growth rate of 1.8% to 0.9% in the first four years of the third five year plan. Thus the actual growth rate was realised in 50% of the expected growth rate.

Since the share of agriculture sector in the economy of Nepal is exceedingly high the poor performance in this sector has retarded the speed of overall economy. The average annual growth rate in the non-agro sector during the above period was 4.7% whereas growth in the overall economy came to 3% because the growth rate in agriculture sector remained only 2.22%.

The share of the agriculture sector in the GDP was 65% but its contribution to the growth was lower to the tune of 46% only. Compared to the targets, the realised consequences ave shown a wide gap in performance. Yet the economy has shown positive results which reveal that with some success new elements have been introduced in the economy. The failure element still persists in the system. Consequently, these elements have contributed to or impeded the growth of agriculture and thereby growth in overall economy.

HORTICULTURE IN NEPAL

Horticultural Belt

Due to topographical variations a wide variety of fruits of tropical to temperate trees are grown in Nepal. Lacking the pertinent market facility this sector is not developed as desired. Lack of packing technique of protection like cold storage etc. and lack of proper transportation and handling, has left this sector undeveloped.

About 43000 hectares of land is under fruit growing area in Nepal. Mango, apple, junnar and bananas occupy 32% of land in fruit category. Junnar is concentrated in Dhankuta, Kaski, Dailekh while mango is abundantly produced in Sarlahi, Dhanusha, Saptari districts in Tarai Region. The apple is grown in Mustang, Jumla, Sidhupalchok, and banana in Jhapa, Tanehu and Dhading.

Temperate fruits like lemon, orange, peaches, appricot and apples are potential fruits for the hill area. Plantain, orange, pomegranate and jack fruits are grown in Tarai as well as in low hills. Consumers of fruits are generally service holders who really purchase some fruits. Trees such as guava, plantain, orange, mango, shaddok, peach, pear, pomegranate, plum, paw-paw, jack fruits, lemon, lime and citrons are found in most parts of the country. However, local markets do not lift all and on many occasions fruits are allowed to decay. Arun valley alone produces more than a dozen variety of plantain such as :

(i) Malbhog,
(ii) Kurche,
(iii) Madmanie,

(iv) Jhapre,

(v) Charmanent,

(vi) Baraker

(vii) Bayamgo,

(viii) Chiniya,

(ix) Jahaji,

(x) Hazára,

(xi) Lalchini,

(xii) Nangra,

(xiii) Lalkera,

(xiv) Sakharchini,

(xv) Dhusra

The varieties are famous as per their intrinsic value.

The quality of some fruits is low. Localisation of fruits can be done, like orange orchards in Mangtewa, Dhankuta, Bhojpur, Polhara, Manakamana, Panaute localities. Citron fruits are also very widely distributed. Kathmandu valley is able to produce pears and persimmon also. Otherwise economically beneficial fruits are plantain, orange, jack fruit and lemon. Plantain does not require any higher technical know-how and can be put to market without much botherations.

Now-a-days coconut and banana are being patronised in Mechi and Kosi regions. In the southern part of Arun Valley, every household has one or more plots of plantain garden. If fruit canning and preservation factories are installed in Tarai and Nepal it would definitely make Nepal a great fruit producing nation. Because its diversified climate and different altitudes are suited to all kinds of fruits and according to their choice of land and locality.

Tarai could well be considered the belt of fruit trees in terms of number of holdings reported, Tarai having the largest total number of holdings grown with permanent crops, Guava 18,141, Jackfruit 14,914, Banana 24,609 and Pineapple

Table 5.6

Distribution of Holdings by Species of Permanent Crops and by Ecological Belt in Nepal, 1981-82

Permanent Crops	*Nepal*		*Mountain*		*Hill*		*Tarai*	
	No.	%	*No.*	%	*No.*	%	*No.*	%
Orange	10,372	100	990	9.54	9,142	88.14	240	2.31
Lemon	7,815	100	1,385	17.72	5,713	73.08	719	9.20
Lime	11,924	100	2,215	18.58	8,998	75.46	711	5.96
Sweet Orange and Anar	1,800	100	501	27.85	1,171	65.06	128	7.11
Other citrons	4,512	100	1,894	41.07	2,604	56.46	114	2.47
Jackfruit	19,840	100	105	0.53	4,821	24.30	14914	75.17
Guava	24,983	100	393	1.57	6,449	25.82	18110	72.61
Lichi	3,383	100	—	—	66	1.95	3317	98.05
Pear	4,652	100	1,062	22.83	3,234	69.52	356	7.65

Peach	8,932	100	3,915	48.83	4,792	53.65	225	2.52
Papaya	14,634	100	130	0.89	4,282	29.26	10222	69.85
Mango	51,331	100	407	0.71	6,318	11 02	50606	88.27
Banana	39,441	100	2,590	6.58	12,242	31.03	24609	62.39
Pineapple	3,326	100	128	3.85	1,388	41.73	1810	54.47
Other fruits	116,167	100	9,069	7.81	13,149	11.32	93949	80.87
Total	329,214	100	24,784	7.53	84,369	25 63	220061	66.84

Source : HMG, Central Bureau of Statistics, Kathmandu, 1988, p. 402.

Table 5.7

Distribution of Area of Holdings under Orchards by Species of Permanent Crops and by Sub-ecological Belt of Tarai—Nepal, 1981-82

Permanent Crops	Tarai		Eastern		Central		Western		Mid-Western		Far Western	
	HAS	%	HAS	%	HAS	%	HAS	%	HAS	%	HAS	%
Orange	1	100	—	—	1	100	—	—	—	—	—	—
Lemon	7	100	—	—	5	71.43	—	—	2	28 57	—	—
Lime	8	100	—	—	7	87.50	—	—	1	12.88	—	—
Sweet Orange and Anar	1	100	—	—	—	—	—	—	1	100	—	—
Other citrons	—	—	—	—	—		—	—	—	—	—	—
Guava	746	100	61	8.18	527	10.64	99	13.27	6	0.80	53	7.11
Jackfruit	934	100	185	19.81	419	51.28	258	27.62	1	0.11	11	0.38
Lichi	128	100	48	37.50	32	25.00	47	36.72	—	—	1	0.78

Pear	—	—	—	—	—	—	—	—	—	—	—	—
Peach	—	—	—	—	—	—	—	—	—	—	—	—
Papaya	327	100	102	31.18	106	32.42	56	17.13	8	2.45	55	16.82
Mango	4944	100	1208	24.43	2553	51.64	1061	21.46	45	0.91	77	2.56
Banana	2056	100	721	35.07	836	40.66	156	7.19	92	2.53	251	14.15
Pineapple	171	100	44	25.73	121	70.76	6	3.51	—	—	—	—
Other fruits	10468	100	4044	38.68	5187	49.85	986	9.42	45	0.43	206	1.97
Total	19791	100	6413	32.40	9854	49.70	2669	13.49	161	0.81	694	3.51

1,810 were found to be abundantly grown in larger number of holdings than other two belts.

Source : Comparative study of ecological belt based on the national sample census of agriculture for Nepal, HMG, National Planning Commission, Central Bureau of Statistics, Kathmandu, 1988.

The above table indicates that mango, banana, jackfruit, guava and papaya are most important in the sub-ecological belt of Tarai. Hectares of fruits grown in each sub-section of Tarai is given in the above table. Mid-western Tarai seems not very conducive for growing variety of fruits.

Livestock Position

Nepal is not only the sanctuary of floral variations but fauna is also rich to some extent. Being a Hindu Kingdom Nepalese regard cow a sacred national animal. Cow and oxen have contributed a lot in agriculture. The cow has a definite culture in India and Nepal. She is regarded as a mother. Every Nepali, after getting up in the morning, bows before the cow if she is physically available in front. Some even walk few steps to have darshan of the mother cow before starting their daily core. So it can be safely said that the cow culture in Nepal has a definite mention. It has penetrated into Nepalese life. A cow has made her abode in the heart of a Hindu. Animals like elephants, buffalo, bull, lion, tiger, ram, dog, antelope, rats, and birds like peacock, goose, vulture all are regarded as sacred according to occasions. Hindu Mythology has so intensively advocated for compassion to animal that such example cannot be found in any other religion. Ethno-botanical and ethno-zoological knowledge of Nepalese was supreme and vast to control local milieu.

In the high humidity and rich vegetation of the land area, villages are using local herbs for animal like titepati, to save animals from juga leaches. People also identify a wide variety of fodder crops and trees fodder for their domestic animals.

Among the domestic animals there are cows, chouri yak, buffaloes, cattle, sheep, goats etc. Sheep and goats serve the double purpose. They provide wool and their own meat where needed.

The transporters are mainly mules, asses and horses. Ghee is one of the most important product of milch animals. Butwal Ghee is exported to India and other countries. All sweetmeat shops and Halwai sweets are prepared by pure ghee of animals. Even Puries and Paranthas are cooked in pure ghee which is called by the name of Deshi ghee. The other oils used are vegetable oil which is not very much liked in Nepal.

Due to altitudinal differences, cattle herding also differs. In the plains and Tarai area animals bearing milk, wool and meat are reared. Cow and buffaloes are the chief milk producing animals so they are popular in Tarai Region and suitable fodder is available for them. Above 3500 metres Chouri Yak is very prominent. Yak has two varieties Jhapa or Zopkiogai a cross-breed of Yak and cow. Yaks are reared in Himalayan grasslands which give milk, meat and chouri. They are also used for the purpose of carrying loads. This animal seldom survives below 3500 metres. In trans-Himalayan trade only yak can traverse the difficult terrains and passes. Donkeys, mules, yak and even sheep carry loads through the high passes of the north. But donkeys and mules are limited to southern regions only.

Pastures in the winter lie around 4000-4500 metres but in summer they are on lower altitudes. Himalaya as well as Mahabharat regions consist of many useful pastures; therefore sheep and goat rearing is done by large number of rural people. Some people are fully devoted to sheep grazing job and they ascend and descend according to the temperture and climate along with their flock of animals.

Holdings Reporting Cattle

The estimated total number of holdings in Nepal with cattle was 1,261,916. Out of this number 595,515 were in the hills and 527,479 in Tarai and the remaining 138,929 were in

Table 5.8

Distribution of Holdings Reporting Cattle by Sub-ecological Belt, Nepal, 1981-82

Ecological Development	Mountain		Hill		Tarai	
	No.	%	No.	%	No.	%
Eastern	36,829	26.51	132.960	22.32	150,610	28.55
Central	42,292	30.44	131.292	22 05	206,230	39.10
Western	1,509	1.08	159,682	26.91	91,563	17.36
Mid-Western	28,155	20.27	114,019	19.15	44,132	8.37
Far Western	30,144	21.70	57,616	9.67	34,937	6.62
	138,939	100.00	595,515	100.00	527,472	100.00

the mountain. Distribution of holdings reporting cattle by sub-ecological belt of Nepal in 1981-82 is given in Table 5.8. The details as given in this table are further sub-divided regionwise to give true picture as to which region has what number of holdings.

The following table indicates that hills are suitable places for animal grazing, yet in Tarai the number of holdings is so large that it reveals the fact that in this region ample land is still available for animal grazing in spite of intensive farming.

Table 5.9

Distribution of Cattle Population by Ecological Belt, 1981-82

Cattle	*Mountain*	*Hill*	*Tarai*
Numbers	810,966	3,171,227	2,519,384
Percentage	12.47%	48.78%	38.75%

Total cattle population in Nepal is 6,501,577.

Source : His Majesty's Government of Nepal, Planning Commission Secretariat, Central Bureau of Statistics, Kathmandu, Nepal, 1988.

The ratio between male and female cattle by ecological belt were 0.63 in Mountain, 0.70 in Hills and 1.06 in Tarai region.

As my study is centred to Tarai region only, therefore, by overall picture of the whole Nepal country when we look to Tarai region it is safely inferred that this region is not only rich in agriculture but also shares a good percentage in cattle rearing and bird breeding. Poultry percentage is highest in Tarai, while for pigs it stands second to hill area. Pigeons are quite in good number which indicates the culture of people. As Mohammadan population in Tarai is larger than other regions so is the poultry and pigeons' population because Mohammadans carry this occupation in good number than any other community.

Table 5.10

Population of Cows and other Animals including Pigatory and Birds by Ecological Belt in 1981-82

	Animals	*Mountain*	*Hill*	*Tarai*
1.	Cows in milk	199,513	894,406	608,823
2.	Buffaloes	255,416	1,411,227	713,060
3.	Buffaloes in milk	97,432	583,853	263,634
4.	Goats	466,602	2,024,223	1,152,834
5.	Sheep	233,147	350,050	93,906
6.	Pigs	44,260	299,329	90,018
7.	Duck, pigeons and birds			
	(a) Ducks	4,711	27,113	110,501
	(b) Pigeons	41,423	212,275	577,044
	(c) Other birds	2,466	13,511	4,393

Comparing the figures given as per Table 5.10 for 1981-82 a significant increase in all type of animals is revealed as per Table 5.11. This increase is reflected in all the ecological belts.

Tarai region where no spare land can be allotted for cattle grazing surprisingly does a good job in cattle breeding also. The main reasons can be :

(i) Its overwhelming population.

(ii) People living in Tarai belong to different ethnic groups who have interest for rearing some or the other type of animals like the Gwala keeping cows, Shepherd's goats and sheep, Dhanuk's pigs, Mohammadan's poultry and pigeons etc.

Table 5.11

Livestock Population and its Distribution 1984-85

Belt	*Cattle*	*Buffaloes*	*Sheep*	*Goats*	*Pigs*
Mountain	800,654	280,621	351,863	755,425	51,949
Hill	3,230,028	1,706,821	355,904	2,799,177	268,376
Tarai	2,317,312	851,927	97,385	1,327,733	121,622
Total	6,356,994	2,839,369	805,152	4,882,335	441,946

6

The Ethnic and Linguistic Characteristics of Settled Groups

Tarai is the creation of not only "Organic activity"[1] but of alluvial action in the Siwalik and higher Himalayan ranges. Dozens of snowfed rivers and streams which flow only during the monsoon season originate from the Siwalik range itself. These rivers and streams deposit rocks, gravel, and sand, the fertile top soil on the edge of the plains, thereby further raising the level of the plains. During the dry months of the year, from mid-September to mid-June, most of these river-beds are no more than broad expanses of bone—white and gray rocks and gravel, with an occasional spring fed trickle of water threading the way amid the alluvial debris.

However during monsoon these rivers convert themselves into raging torrents and emptying out of the hills flow south across the Tarai. They widen rapidly and slow down depositing materials they have dislodged from hillsides. As they slow down they deposit first heavier materials, huge boulders, then gravel and thereafter silt and sand. The area closest to the foothills where coarsest materials are deposited

1. Ibid. p. 16.

is called 'Bhaber' in geological terms and area further away where finer materials like alluvium, silt and sand are deposited is called the Tarai.[1]

Ecology of Tarai

The ecology of Tarai has been changing over the past several hundred years and specially past many decades. The pattern of change is just identical to the pattern that took place in the Gangetic plain. In the sixteenth and seventeenth centuries Mughal emperors were in the habit of hunting wild elephants, buffaloes, bisons, rhinoceros, lions and tigers in the Doaba of Ganga and Jamuna.[2] Along with the process of hunting deforestation of doaba also continued simultaneously. The same process was implemented in Tarai region of Nepal also.

There are about 6,258 nucleated villages, usually clustered around under the shades of big trees like Pipal, Pakar and Banyan. The village structure is just a hut constructed of Bamboo, mud and thatch. There are some two storey brick houses also. Drinking water is drawn from open dug wells with the help of a rope and earthen pitchers or iron bucket, Dol (iron container).

The villages situated in Nepal Tarai and in the Gangetic plain have numerous similarities like the style of houses, way of living, way of clothing. Daily life, customs and rituals are identical in both portions. But a visible difference is also there by which villages of Tarai (Nepal) can be distinguished by villages of Gangetic Tarai.

Some of these are—Indian villages have cracking sounds of gears of motor vehicles and buses along metallic roads, while in Nepal Tarai either there are no roads or where they are, they are kachcha, rough and dusty. Vehicular traffic is seldom seen. Only bullock carts, buffalo carts carry the bulk of loads. Some load is shared by mules

1. Earnest Noble report of Government of Nepal on Forestry (Rome, 1954), F.A.O. Report No. 209, pp. 7-8, 10-11.
2. Spate, op. cit., pp. 78-79.

and donkeys. Indian villages are lit with electricity while in Tarai the electric has not yet touched villages and after the sunset it is difficult to locate a village in the shady and grassy land of Nepal. Administration has just commenced in Nepal villages of Tarai yet significant improvement is not visible. Modern facilities of roads and electricity are limited to a dozen of commercial towns only. Without hard surface roads and bridges, life seems inactive during the monsoon season specially.

Another feature which is accountable is the culture of some of hill people of mangoloid features. These hill people have been motivated to settle down in Tarai due to population constraints in hill areas and valleys. Though they are lesser in number yet more influential than Indian origin people but they keep their identity alone by strictly following their own ways of life as they were doing in Hills.

It is evident that Indian nationals into Nepal remained totally scheduled in their way of life. So in the process of social integration efforts should be made so that Indian origin people should feel that they are full-fledged members of Nepali Society.

Therefore a detailed socio-cultural study of Indian ethnic groups living in Nepal Tarai has been done to find out the changes and diffusion of cultural traits. It is also the aim of study to find out as to which customs and habits could be integrated into the Nepali culture and which factors are susceptible to change.

Linguistic Composition

Nepal is a multi-linguistic, multi-religious and multi-ethnic country. According to the census definition used, the mother tongue is the language spoken in childhood. In the case of babies or persons who cannot speak the mother tongue of the mother, the mother's tongue is considered as their mother tongue. However, the classification of mother tongues was not uniform in the census. In 1952/54, information on 35 languages was collected but was provided duly for 24 languages. In 1951, 52 languages' information was collected but tabulated for 36 only. In 1971 tabulation was done for 17 languages and in 1981, 18 languages were tabulated.

The changes in the number and classification of mother tongues over years was firstly due to ambiguity in classifying distinction between language and dialect. Sometimes a dialect was taken as language. This could lead to an over-numeration of languages spoken in the country. Secondly, the different ways of classification of languages included only those languages to which data was collected but tabulations were not made separately. Thirdly, there is the problem of overlapping among those sharing common ancestral descent. For example, Hindi has been the rallying point of Maithili, Bhojpuri and Awadhi—the languages predominantly spoken in Tarai. The transfer of people across the languages was considered a plausible explanation for finding the decrease of Hindi speaking population.

Linguistic Distribution of Population

The census from 1952-54 to 1961 recorded 11 languages and this number was reduced to 10 in 1981. These languages were spoken by at least 94% of the population in the census year.

The proportion of Nepali speaking people has been increasing numerically as well as in percentage terms over years. Nepali was spoken by 49% of the population in 1952-54 which rose to 58% in 1981. Table 6.1 represents the position of all languages in different censuses.

Numerically Maithili speakers occupied the second position although their proportion declined slowly and continuously over the years. Maithili was spoken by 12.44% in 1952-54 and in 1981 it was 11.11%. The position of Tamang was taken over by Bhojpuri in 1961 and continued in the third position up to 1981. The population of Tamang speaking people declined from 6% to 3.48% in 1981. Likewise Newari also had declining trend. It was 4.65% in 1952-54 census and came down to 2.99% in 1981 census.

Table 6.1

Numerical and Percentage Distribution of Population by Mother Tongue, Nepal Census 1952-54-1981

Mother Tongue	*1952-54*		*1961*		*1971*		*1981*	
	No.	%	*No.*	%	*No.*	%	*No.*	%
Nepali	4,013,567	48.74	4,796,528	50.96	6,[illegible]50,758	52.45	8,767,361	58.36
Maithili	1,024,780*	12.44	1,130,401	12.01	1,327,242	11.49	1,668,309	11.11
Bhojpuri	477,281*	5.80	577,357	6.13	806,480	6.98	1,142,805	7.61
Tamang	494,745	6.01	518,812	5.51	555,056	4.80	522,416	3.48
Awadhi	328,408*	3.99	477,090	4.75	316,950	2.74	234,343	1.56
Tharu	359,594	4.37	406,907	4.32	495,881	4.29	545,685	3.63
Newari	383,184	4.65	377,927	4.01	454,979	3.14	448,746	2.99
Magar	273,780	3.32	254,675	2.71	288,383	2.50	212,681	1.42
Rai-Kirati	236,049	2.87	239,749	2.55	232,264	2.01	221,353	1.47
Gurung	162,192	1.97	157,748	1.68	171,609	1.40	174,6[illegible]4	1.16
Limbu	145,511	1.77	138,705	1.47	170,787	1.48	129,234	0.36

Others	335,236	4.07	360,835	3.89	675,594	5.85	955,442	6.36
Unstated	752	0.01	6,452	0.07				

Source : 1. Central Bureau of Statistics 1958, Population Census 1952-54, Part II.
2. Central Bureau of Statistics 1968, Population Census 1961, Vol. II.
3. Central Bureau of Statistics 1975, Population Census 1971, Vol. II, Pt. II.
4. Central Bureau of Statistics 1984, Population Census 1981, Vol. I, Pt. III.

*In 1952-54 census there were 300,768 Maithili, 16,385 Bhojpuri and only 27 Awadhi (Pt. II, census 1952-54). This was based on wrong classification of Tarai language (Maithili, Bhojpuri and Awadhi). If classification of Tarai languages were made on the basis of textual comments (Appd. in Part II, Section 2, pp. 60-71 of Population Census 1952/54) we would find that those classified as dialects of Central East and Far-East Tarai were actually Maithili. Dialects of Eastern Tarai were Bhojpuri and those of Far-west Tarai were Awadhi. According to this classification, the number of people speaking Maithili, Bhojpuri and Awadhi turned to be 10,247,80, 477,281 and 328,408 respectively in 1952-54. In 1981 there was no unstated category. This was merged with the category 'Others'.

Language Equation in Tarai Region

The main characteristics of linguistics in Tarai region reveal that—

(i) Majority of the people speak their mother tongues which are not spoken by Hill people.

(ii) These languages are also spoken across the border in Northern Indian parts of U.P. and Bihar.

(iii) In the four eastern districts Sunsari, Sirha, Mahottari and Sarlahi, Maithili is spoken by more than 85% population. Another similar language Awadhi is spoken by more than 87% of people in four districts of Mid-west Tarai namely Palhi, Mujhkhand, Khajahani and Sivraj. It is also spoken by 27% of the population in Banke district.

(iv) In the three districts of Far-western Tarai i.e. Baradia, Kailali and Kanchanpur, Tharu is spoken by more than 80% of population. Maithili is a predominant language spoken in northern Bihar districts of Saharsa and Darbhanga contiguous with Tarai districts of Sunsari, Sirha, Mahottari and Sarlahi.

(v) Bhojpuri is spoken mainly by the people living in Champaran, Arrah districts of north Bihar just contiguous with districts of Tarai—Rautahat, Bara and Parsa. Awadhi is spoken in Gonda, Basti, Gorakhpur and Devaria districts of Uttar Pradesh but in the contiguous mid-west districts of Tarai—Palhi, Majkhanda, Khajahani and Sivraj—Awadhi is not the actual body of the language. In Tarai, terms used are basically Hindi.

(vi) Tharu, though has been taken as language in the Census for simplicity's sake, it is a blended form of Nepali, Hindi, Maithili and Bhojpuri.

(vii) Up to what per cent Nepali and other hill languages are spoken in Tarai ? From the figures of Census taken in 1961 it has come to light that 21% in Jhapa district and 26% in Morang district people speak Nepali. Out of these 20% people of Jhapa and 14% in Morang districts are actually Nepali, the remaining speak hill languages. In Sarlahi district also above 12% population speak Nepali. In Mahottari and Sarlahi there are concentrations of Tamang speakers.

(viii) About 50% of all the Newari speakers living in Tarai are enumerated in Birat Nagar. Newars are business oriented people and always try to locate urban pockets. The town of Birat Nagar is the largest commercial centre in all of Nepal which possesses largest chunk of Newari population.

(ix) Pattern of migration of hill people has been from west to east. The Magars and Gurung though belong to western hills, have migrated in good number to Eastern Tarai.

(x) Only Newars are businessmen and for better consideration come out of their original Kathmandu valley and hill area in search for trade and business. They have no temptation for lands and cultivation. Consequently in each Tarai district they selected towns and big villages to settle themselves. Markets were their main life. So Newari language speakers can be traced in each town of Tarai where they may be in large numbers. They have infested each town.

(xi) In addition to the hill languages included in the table ahead, a few other hill languages are spoken in Tarai. In Eastern Tarai Jhapa, Morang, Sunsari 1836 Limbus, 98 Sherpas, 240 Sunwars, 136 Pahari, 2 Thakalies and 10 Tharus were also enumerated. 57 Thakalies in Mid-western Tarai and 38 Sunwars in Far-western Tarai were located.

In all the districts of Tarai as per census of 1961, only 6% of population speak Nepali as mother tongue and 3% population speak other hill languages. These figures reveal

Table 6.2

Hill Languages spoken in Tarai

Region & District	*Nepali*		*Hill Language*		*Tamang*	*Newari*	*Magar*	*Rai Kirati*	*Gurung*
	No.	*%*	*No.*	*%*					
Nepal	4,796,528	51.0	—	—	518,812	377,727	254,675	236,749	157,778
Eastern Tarai	115,611	6.6	204,066	9.2	9,615	13,624	15,850	6,520	524
Thapa	24,464	20.4	30,464	25.5	1,232	663	1,734	1,205	68
Birat Nagar	45,491	14.0	68,460	21.0	3,662	7,526	5,296	4,927	371
Hanuman Nagar	10,360	3.5	10,812	3.6	51	372	24	—	4
Sirha	10,556	5.0	15,106	7.2	2,560	608	1,211	170	—
Mahottari	30,526	6.3	43,260	6.9	5,325	789	6,203	110	20
Sarlahi	12,243	7.5	20,361	12.4	6,449	537	1,106	23	1
Rautahat	3,875	1.3	4,538	2.1	25	366	190	77	4
Bara	7,221	2.9	10,262	4.1	313	1,517	85	8	35
Parsa	775	0.6	822	0.6	—	46	1	—	—
Mid-west Tarai	11,665	2.8	14,456	3.6	14	2,266	548	34	469
Palhi	3,064	2.2	3,463	3.[illegible]		187	189		23

Majkhanda	6,229	4.4	8,962	6.3	9	1,834	353	34	446
Khajahani	1,393	1.1	1,601	1.3	5	195	5	—	—
Shivraj	529	1.0	430	1.2	—	50	1	—	—
Far-west Tarai	12,625	4.7	12,856	4.3	1	164	27	—	1
Banke	5,341	5.6	5,495	5.8	—	136	17	—	—
Bartia	2,509	3.7	2,539	3.8	—	7	6	—	—
Kailali	4,182	4.7	4,203	4.7	1	19	1	—	—
Kanchanpur	593	3.1	599	3.2	—	2	3	—	1

Source : Census of Nepal 1961, Vol. II, pp. 18-25.

Note : Hill languages are defined as those which are spoken mainly within the Hill region being loosely defined as all parts of Nepal North of Tarai districts.

the fact that hill culture and hill languages are significantly seen in Tarai.

The fact remains that most of the population in Tarai speak plain languages or those languages which people have brought with them while they migrated from Northern plains. Table 6.2 presents the overall picture for making out measurement. The decisive factor is that all those who speak Maithili, Bhojpuri and Awadhi speak regional Hindi.

The proportionate distribution of major languages by rural and urban sector is given in Table 6.3. Newari people seem highly urbanised followed by those who speak Gurung. Although Newari people account for only 3% of the total population nearly half of them live in urban areas namely in Kathmandu Valley. This indication gives clear idea that Newari speaking people have no participation in rural activities like agriculture. On the other hand their

Table 6.3

Percentage Distribution of Major Languages by Rural/Urban Sector 1981

Mother Tongue	*Proportion in the Total Population*		
	Total	*Rural*	*Urban*
Nepali	100	94.35	6.65
Maithili	100	95.70	4.30
Bhojpuri	100	96.71	3.29
Tamang	100	97.26	2.74
Awadhi	100	97.09	2.91
Tharu	100	96.25	3.75
Newari	100	56.61	43.39
Magar	100	98.40	1.60
Rai-Kirati	100	94.93	5.03
Gurung	100	93.09	6.61
Limbu	100	97.32	2.68
Others	100	91.04	8.96
			Total %

Source : Central Bureau of the Statistics 1984, Pop. Census 1981, Vol. I, Part III, Table 12 and Vol. III, Table 9.

participation has encouraged trade, commerce, handicraft business and industry in Kathmandu Valley as well as in other towns.

The Gurung community is the traditional supplier of soldiers working in the Armies of India and United Kingdom. So, after retirement and returning back from services as they are in a better position economically, they select to settle in towns. Those Gurung who serve Nepal Defence forces also like to settle in urban regions.

The proportionate share of major languages in the total population of rural and urban areas is given in Table 6.4. By this table it is observed that the majority of the people both within urban and rural areas speak Nepali. Therefore, Nepali has been introduced in Nepal as the medium of instruction in

Table 6.4

Numerical and Percentage Distribution of the Population of Major Mother Tongues for Rural and Urban Areas—Nepal Census Year 1981

Percentages		*Total*
Rural	*Urban*	
58.80	51.78	58.36
11.35	7.49	11.11
7.85	3.92	7.60
3.64	1.49	3.47
1.64	0.76	1.55
3.73	2.14	3.63
1.80	20.35	2.98
1.48	0.35	1.46
1.49	1.16	1.47
1.15	1.26	1.15
0.89	0.36	0.86
6.18	8.94	6.35
Total 14,066,118	956,721	15,022,839
% 100	100	100

Source : Central Bureau of Statistics 1984, Pop. Census 1981, Vol. I, Part III, Table 12 and Vol. III, Table 9.

education and it has been recognised as a duly official language. However, one fact emerges that though Nepali speakers are in majority in urban and rural regions, yet 41% of the whole population still speak languages other than Nepali.

Newari is the second most important language spoken in urban areas. Twenty per cent of urban population speak Newari as per Table 6.3. Newari people are mainly concentrated in Kathmandu Valley which is the urban scenario of Nepal. In rural areas Maithili, Bhojpuri and Tharu are the important languages spoken by different groups vide Tables 6.3 and 6.4.

7

Castes and Tribes of Tarai : Socio-economic Description

Caste

Like religion and languages the caste factor is also a very important one. While analysing the cultural scenario of Nepal this element is very pertinent and cannot be sidetracked. There are clearly different sets of castes among hill and Tarai people. The caste system among the people living in Tarai of Indian origin is the same system prevalent in Northern part of India, U.P. and Bihar provinces. Caste names and traditional occupation which they follow in India is the same in Tarai also. However, the caste system of hills is not likely to be familiar to those who live outside Nepal.

For deriving particular ideas regarding ethnic groups, labour has been done to demarcate different castes. To localise them in respective regions and to study their present occupation, a detailed study in some pockets has been done to show the present status of each caste and its contribution in national integration.

The difference between the caste system of hills of Nepal and the north Indian plains go beyond the different names for those who carry on the same occupation. For example Sunars

Table 7.1
Population Trend in Tarai Districts 1971-81 and Density 1971-1981

Districts	*Increase between 1971-81*		*Density*		*Density per Km. available land*		*Population of Tarai Zone-wise*	
	%Increase	*Comp. Increase*	*1971*	*1981*	*1971*	*1981*		
1. Jhapa	93.68	6.61	154.2	298.7	221.7	429.4	Tarai—6556828	43.6%
2. Morang	77.31	5.73	162.6	288.2	295.6	524.2	Eastern development	
3. Sunsari	54.23	4.33	177.8	274.1	341.6	526.9	Region—2113442	14.1%
4. Saptari	21 27	1.93	229.3	278.1	341.8	414.4	Central Development	
5. Sirha	24.17	2.16	254.5	316.0	396.7	492.6	Region—2387721	15 9%
6. Dhanusha	30.84	2.69	280.2	366.6	508.0	664.7	Western Development	
7. Mahottari	11.15	1.06	324.2	360 3	515.6	573.1	Region—952969	6.4%
8. Sarlahi	127.16	8.20	139.4	316.7	306.7	697.8	Mid-Western Development	
9. Rautahat	3.88	0.38	294.3	285.3	398.8	414.3	Region—670,760	4.4%
10. Bara	36.66	3.12	106.1	268.0	304.7	416.4	Far-western Development	
11. Parsa	40.66	3.14	149.4	211.2	437.5	615.5	Region—426,876	2.8%
12. Chitwan	41.34	3.46	82.8	117.0	301.5	501.0		
13. Nawal-Parasi	110.74	7.45	67.8	112.8	332.2	700.0		
14. Rupandehi	55.78	4.43	178.9	228.7	301.4	461.5		

15. Kapilvastu	31.59	2.75	118.1	155.1	263.6	346.9
16. Dang	58.74	4.62	56.8	90.1	336.1	533.5
17. Banke	63.33	4.91	53.8	87.9	326.2	500.1
18. Bardia	95.54	6.91	50.8	98.3	180.7	353.4
19. Kailali	180.12	6.94	39.5	74.7	263.1	526.6
20. Kanchanpur	145.27	8.98	42.8	105.0	234.4	575.1

Source : Central Bureau of Statistics 1975, Pop. Census 1971, Vol. I.

of hills and Sunars of the plains are gold and silver workers—makers of jewellery. In plains Sunars have highest status among the various Sudra castes of craftsmen. However, the Sunars of hills have a much lower status surprisingly below the status of blacksmiths.

Tarai has twenty districts and there is none where Indian plain origin people have not settled after migrating from India. Their population varies from east to west. Eastern regions have better concentration of Indian origin people.

The figures in Table 7.1 are just to bring my point to light that the Tarai region population is 43.6 per cent of the population of whole Nepal. More than 65 lakh people live in Tarai. Though data for Indian origin people living in each district of Tarai are not available yet we have one measuring rod and that is language. More than 20 per cent people in Tarai speak Maithili, Bhojpuri and Awadhi. This 20 per cent is in the context of the whole population of Nepal and not only for Tarai districts. In the rural areas of Tarai districts 95.70 per cent speak Maithili, 96.71 per cent speak Bhojpuri and 97.09 per cent Awadhi. So it can be safely inferred that population of speakers of those languages is quite large and this chunk of 65 lakh 56 thousand and 8 hundred twenty eight belong to Indian origin people and none else.

Among the Indian origin people settled in Tarai there are Hindus, Muslims, Jains and Christians also. The Indian based population is a compound of many castes, creeds and tastes. These castes are still being maintained in Tarai regions. Many of them share normal stream of activities like agriculture, trade, business, crafts, industry etc. while some of them are marginal contributors. But all have established their shelter under the open sky and contribute economically and socially to the cause of national integration.

Table 7.2 is added to highlight the population density along Indian and Nepal Tarai Border (1971).

These ratios indicate that population in eastern districts of Tarai has lesser ratio difference from 1.97 between Saharsa district of India and Saptari, Sunsari districts of Tarai (Nepal).

This ratio goes on increasing gradually as we go to western district of Tarai and their counterpart districts of India.

Table 7.2

Population Density along Indian and Nepal Tarai Border (1971)

Nepal Tarai Distts.		*Ratio*		*Indian Distts.*	
Region District	*Popn Density*	*Nepal*	*India*	*Popn. Density*	*State District*
A. West					*A. Uttar Pradesh*
Kanchanpur	43	1	5.00	215	Pilibhit
Kailali	42	1	4.60	193	Kheri
Banke	54	1	4.65	251	Baharaich
Dang-Deukhuri	63	1	4.98	314	Gonda
B. Central					
Kapilvastu Rupandehi	118	1	3.46	408	Basti
Nawal Parasi	121	1	3.98	481	Gorakhpur
C. East					
Chitwan Parsa Bara Rautahat	149	1	2.58	385	Champaran
Sarlahi Mahottari	249	1	2.48	618	Muzaffarpur
Dhanusa Sirha	267	1	2.26	603	Darbhanga
Saptari Sunsari	203	1	1.97	399	Saharsa
Morang Jhapa	151	1	2.37	358	Purnea

Between Gorakhpur and Nawal Parsi (Nepal), the ratio is 3.98. This has increased while going westward. Kanchanpur district of Tarai and Pilibhit district of India have ratio 1 and 5.

The ratio table indicates that the population density in Nepal Tarai is greater in eastern and central belts of Tarai. As we go to the west the density decreases.

Number of Indians in Nepal

I said earlier it is difficult to arrive at certain calculations as to how many Indians are there in Nepal. According to the census of 1961 Nepal enumerated 75311 Indians which accounted for 70 per cent of total foreign citizens. In 1971 this figure rose to 128,289 Indians which constituted 94 per cent of total foreign population.

These Indians, as reported earlier, settled mostly in the eastern, central and western Tarai. Mid-western and far-western districts also represent such population but it is not very large. Banke district has the largest concentration of Mohammadan people.

Why Indians Liked to Settle in Tarai Districts Only

From the figures given it is apparent that Indian people still tend to settle in Tarai districts in spite of the facts that they are already densely populated. The main reasons for such a trend are :

(i) The climate of Tarai is similar to that of Indian frontiers so the working conditions are least effected.

(ii) Tarai Region has great agriculture and industrial potential, so it has become the oasis of Indian industrialists as well as hungry and job seekers.

(iii) Tarai is situated close to the border towns of India so it is very convenient to have easy access to Indian goods, friends and family members.

(iv) Any technical expertise, if needed, can be sought from Indian towns nearby.

(v) Produce can be sent out of Nepal through many transit points legally and illegally also. Smuggling has been encouraged in both countries whenever it could be possible.

(vi) For discharging religious, social and family obligations like marriages etc. it is very convenient from Tarai which is close to the original land of Indian population.

Patterns of Indian Immigrants

Indian immigrants can be divided into 6 sectors under which all types of people could be put to denote as to what was the purpose behind migration of an individual or community. These sectors are :

1. Agriculture
2. Menial labour
3. Industry
4. Construction projects
5. Business and self-employment
6. Service in private business, firms, hotels and teaching jobs.

1. *Agriculture Sector*

In the agriculture sector there are three categories (a) Landlords, (b) Tenants, (c) Agriculture labourers.

(a) Landlords are those who, out of their sweat labour, earned so much that they purchased or acquired some lands and have become their masters. They own just small holding of one Katha to three Bighas. They constantly keep and maintain touch with their original homes and return when possible to discharge their family obligations. Their holding in Tarai is so small that they cannot keep their family there without hardships.

(b) Tenants are just temporary field tillers who work either on contract (kut) or *Adhiya Batai* (half share) or any *Batai* terms with the landlords. Some of them hold tenancy rights also. Temporary tenants give 50 per cent production to landlords though they plough the lands and put all care and labour required. As food was always in shortage in Bihar and U.P. such farmers sought the opportunity to earn their livelihood in Tarai.

(c) Agriculture labour force is also migratory and temporary. They do not hold any land or property. They visit Tarai in seasons of crops, earn money or grains and come back to India in slack season or change their profession and stay in Tarai itself.

2. *Menial Labour*

Such class is very large. Some of them are skilled, some are semi-skilled and others are non-skilled labour. They can be put in the following classes :

(i) Those who castrate animals like bullocks, buffaloes, goats and horse. Only Muslims perform this job.

(ii) Cobblers and Chamars who prepare shoes and manufacture tannery goods and leather articles.

(iii) Sweepers or Doms for cleanliness.

(iv) Washerman—Dhobi for washing clothes.

(v) Tailors—Darji mostly Muslims and low caste Hindu groups are doing this job.

(vi) Repairers of umbrellas, torches, lights and other petty things.

(vii) Rikshaw pullers.

(viii) Bullock cart drivers.

(ix) *Thelagadi* puller, i.e. two wheeled wooden cart pullers.

(x) Lumbers.

(xi) Porters for carrying small loads.

(xii) Mason labourers, earth workers.

(xiii) Vegetable carrying jhalliwallas—those who carry vegetables and small loads in a basket and carry it on their heads.

(xiv) Miscellaneous all purposes. Labourers who have no definite skill for doing a particular job but handle whatever is given them like stone crushing, brick laying etc.

3. *Industry*

In this sector two categories of Indians are working :

(i) Those who are capital investors and are either factory and industry owners or shareholders. Sometimes they hold managerial posts like Directors and General Managers.

(ii) Those who work in factories and industry as skilled, semi-skilled and non-skilled workers. These are labourers, carpenters, blacksmiths, lathemen (turners), masons, fitters, toolmen, engine operators, drivers etc.

4. *Construction Projects*

In this sector many Indians are involved. They are working as contractors of some project, road, building construction or suppliers of labourers for construction work, at different sites of work. Many more labour force is augmented with varying skills of men pertinent for particular job.

5. *Business and Self-employment*

In this category Indians are found mainly in permanent, semi-permanent or seasonal business. Permanent businessmen are those people who have established their business on good footings and so have settled in Tarai towns permanently with their families and have built houses also for their living. Many businessmen of Indian tribes have put cloth-shops, grocery, stationery, hardwares and medical store shops. Some doctors are also working there.

Semi-businessmen are doing the same job as is done by permanent businessmen, the only difference is that these people, apart from keeping their shops in Nepal, are maintaining their shops and kinsmen in India also. Whenever they find position not favourable to them they return to India without facing abnormal trouble in shifting.

The seasonal businessmen are (i) Fruit sellers. (ii) Rice, mustard and oil dealers, Jute produce dealers when the product is ready for sale. (iii) Hosiery and ready-made goods' sellers either keep their temporary shops or sell their goods by roaming in the villages. (iv) There are Churiwallas who sell glass bangles of Firozabad or bracelets of lac on chemical extracted from lac trees. (v) There are cosmetics sellers, ribbon, combs, looking glass sellers and those who move on ferry i.e. carrying cosmetic goods specially for ladies of villages who cannot reach towns to purchase them. They sell like *Bindi*, creams, nail polishes, face powders and talcum powders etc. (vi) There are some shopkeepers who put up their shops in village markets. These shops are of varying commodities. (vii) Sellers of seasonal agricultural produce which is used by people immediately like groundnuts, grams, peas, maize, bhuttas and other edible items.

Servicemen

Nepal started higher education very late by 1956; till then students of Nepal used to obtain higher education from Indian Universities like B.H.U., and Patna. Then, on initial stage when Tribhuwan University was started, Indian teachers were engaged in good numbers.

Apart from it teachers in other stages like primary and secondary, were also recruited and they are working in good numbers.

Other avenue of employment exploited is the hotel business. There are many hotels in Kathmandu and other Valley towns. Indians are working either as Managers or attendants. In the Tarai towns most of the hotels belong to people of Indian origin.

Some truck, bus drivers and cleaners are also seen on the job. Accountant, Munshis, salesmen, etc. in private shops are also engaged in good number.

Caste-ethics in Tarai

Tarai Region of Nepal has 20 districts. It has an area of 30937.55 square kilometres which is 21.77 per cent of the total area of Nepal but as per census of 1981 the population of Tarai contributes 43.6 per cent of the whole population of Nepal. Average density is 140 persons per sq. km. A study of this region was undertaken due to special reasons namely:

(i) Tarai has immense economic importance for the survival of whole Nepal.

(ii) Tarai is a 'melting pot' for various ethnic groups.

On one side where we have indigenous groups like Tharus, Rajbansis, Dhimale and Gangains, on the other side there are Indian ethnic groups like Jha, Thakur, Teli, Ahir, Yadavas, Halwai, Rauniyar, Muslims, Kewat, Kewarat, Godi, Marwari, Bengali, Dhobi, Dhanuk, Paswan, Chamar and Sweeper, Dome etc.

(iii) In addition lot of malaria eradication staff was employed by the government of Nepal that eventually settled down in Tarai.

(iv) Tarai was regarded by Nepal Government as the best place for settling down retired military personnel and also establishing rehabilitation offices for settling the needy people.

In Tarai there was a lot of tension among different ethnic groups while they were engaged in deforesting and making land arable. Those tensioners were both social as well as economic. The problem of national integration cropped up due to lack of understanding between Hill tribe groups and Indian ethnic groups. Controversy remained quite hot for some time.

(v) The flow of all types of Indian workers as well as competitive businessmen has been high in Tarai due to improvement in transport and communication, opening of new roads, and, putting of many factories. The industrial units in Tarai were other alluring elements for the migration of Indian people.

Though Tarai is a very long and vast area consisting of 20 districts but settlement to Eastern Tarai districts is older than any other district. The geo-cultural unity of the people of both countries is reflected all along the 800 km. long border from Mechi (in East) to Mahakali (in West) river zones. Both countries allow free crossing of people without any permit, visa or other restrictions and documentary or oral formalities.

Ranking of Castes

Those people who migrated from India carried their traditional culture. That culture which was inherited by Hindu religion and status of different castes is still maintained without a significant change whether of caste Hindu, or a tribal or Muslim; whosoever migrated from India could not evolve any new system in the other country. The main reason was that Nepal itself is a Hindu Nation and all the tenets of Hindu religion and caste system were already present in the local society. So there was no opposition to the Indian ways of social customs and all castes carried out their tradition and occupations freely.

For the student of Sociology, the Hindu caste system is an important study to know about the social and economic status of a particular caste. How castes play their role in weaving the thread of religion? How from top to bottom castes interact among them? Is there any reaction to old traditions? Has any caste been upgraded due to the change of occupation? All these queries are discussed herewith.

I am giving a list of all the castes inhabiting different districts and villages of the Tarai region. One will find that in one village only a small number of groups as given in the list are found which depend on the size and location of the village. Naturally smaller villages have fewer groups of castes or tribals. Moving from far west to east in Tarai one will find general increase in the number of groups living in any one village. For example, in Kailali and Kanchanpur the typical village is inhabited by Tharus only and that too by one group of Tharus.

In the far eastern Tarai district of Jhapa in any one village there are various number of castes and tribes. Moving from north to south except in those of the far west areas nearer to hill, tribals are settled. As one moves south and south, one finds caste Hindus and Hill Hindu populating the area in large numbers. The hill people and tribals have less complex social systems than plain Hindus at least in terms of number of castes and sub-castes. A greater variety of groups is found in southern parts of the districts than in the northern.

To appreciate the status of different castes a standard definition has been given to the terms used in compiling the list.

1. *Hill People*

These are people who speak hill languages as their mother tongues. Hill people are generally born in the hills or Pahar, Pahari is rather perjorative term for hill people.

2. *Varna*

In Hindu social order there are four tiers or classes of people. These are Brahmins, Kshatriyas, Vaisyas and Shudras. Yet below these classes there is one category called the untouchables. Only two varnas Brahmins and Kshatriya form important social units and other two categories forming untouchables are further divided into numerous castes. For them caste is more important and not Varna.

3. *Castes*

A social unit in an hierarchically organised social system of Hindu people. Castes are generally endogamous and are occupation or craft-exclusive.

4. *Tribes*

A group's members live in a fairly limited geographical area such as western hills and eastern Tarai and which is only tangentially tied to the caste system. Usually at the bottom of the caste hierarchy, the religion of tribes may be either Hindu, or Buddhist or they could be animistic.

5. *Hill Castes and Tribes*

There are castes and tribes, whose many members live in the hills.

6. *Plain Castes and Tribes*

These are the castes and tribes, most of whose members live in the Gangetic Plain.

The ranking of caste in the list is on general assumption and belief prevalent in religion and society. The higher castes are not willing to accept food and water from lower castes. The ranking, however, varies from one part of Tarai to the other but no significant difference of opinion is shown by villages in deciding the rank and status of a particular caste.

The castes and tribes are made to clarify by a column in which their location has been given. These locations are where they are more prominent. The sub-regions in which they are reported in the list to be located, is based on sub-regions in which they were found living during survey in 1967-68. It should be kept in mind that members of some castes and tribes may live in parts of Tarai where they were not found during the course of field survey. Except for hill tribals locations outside the Tarai where the castes and tribes may be found are not mentioned. For example since Ahirs live in the Eastern Tarai, they are found in Northern Bihar. The various hill castes live throughout the hill region of Nepal.

The assumption has been made that the castes or tribal groups found in one of the five districts surveyed would be found in the neighbouring districts of the same sub-region of the Tarai. The use of the far west Tarai, central Tarai, is just giving locations on Tarai for various groups. List of the districts included in different Tarai sub-regions is as follows :

1. Far east	—Jhapa and Morang
2. Mid east	—Sarlahi, Mahottari, Dhanusha Sirha, Saptari, Sunsari
3. Central	—Parsa, Bara, Rautahat
4. Mid west	—Kapilvastu, Rupandehi, Parsi
5. Far west	—Banke, Bardia, Kailali, Kanchanpur
Eastern Tarai	—includes districts of mid and far east Tarai
Western Tarai	—includes districts of far and mid west Tarai.

In the column "status and occupation" a few descriptive notes have been given for each group. The description includes traditional occupation. Theoretically all castes have traditional occupation but in case of tribes it is not so. After the introduction of industry in the area some castes have to change their occupation like Bherihars who were producing woollen goods by hands now find no patronage as these goods are prepared in woollen mills, so Bherihars have switched on as agricultural tenants or labours.

The terms like landowners, tenants and farm holders are used to denote the economic status of the caste.

Landowner	—one who is master of the land.
Tenant	—who cultivates land owned by some one else.
Farm labourer	—is he who is engaged in the work of cultivation on payment.

Most of the Rajputs are landowners while most of the untouchable castes are landless labourers. But there are exceptions to this generalisation. Caste, of course, is an integral and accepted part of economic, social and political life of Nepal in the rural areas as well as in the urban.

It has been realised that in the past 30 years or so due to participation in the new economic activities, a greater mobility has caused individuals and even entire castes to switch on to better occupations. It is als oa fact that to upgrade themselves they make efforts to change their last name or surname. For example a Sudi untouchable when gains wealth he converts his name for Sudi to Shah, as Shah is a high caste name in Nepal. Shahs are Chhetry Thakur of royal family. The entire caste, when it moves to another new place tries to upgrade its status. In some cases during a long span of time when such caste earns landownership or obtains wealth by economic pursuit it upgrades itself by suffixing some good titles. At the same time there are instances when individual groups have lost their caste status.

The distinction between Muslims and Hindus is that Muslims are not rigid for sub-castes. They are divided into more complex economic and social orders. Any Muslim of lower status can make his relationship with a higher status Muslim by giving good dowry.

The Muslims who are able to trace their ancestry back to Arabic, Persian or Mughal roots claim higher social status. Also those converted earlier between 800-1600 A.D. gain higher status than those who became Muslims at a later stage. There are some plain castes like Lodh, Dhami, Dusadha, Khulwat and Ragi that have no mention in the list as their traditional occupation is not known.

Plains Hindu Castes

Caste	*Status and Occupation*	*Location*	*Last name*
1	*2*	*3*	*4*
Brahmin	Highest Status. There are a variety of sub-castes and Gotras among them like, Tripathi, Dwivedi, Chaube, Shukla, Bajpai, etc. Also on region based, Kannaujia, Bengali, Maithili, Bhojpuri, big and small landowners but no labourers.	Bengali in Far-East, Maithili in Mid-East, Bhojpuri in Central Tarai, U.P. Western parts	Chatterjee, Tiwari, Banerjee, Jha, Mishra, Chaudhry, Sharma, Pandey, etc.
Bhumihar	Low status Brahmins. Do not participate in priestly functions of other Brahmins. Highly educated, economically better and sound big landowners, businessmen.	In Central and Mid-Eastern Tarai only	Thakur, Mishra, Pandey, Singh, Chaudhry etc.
Athit	Descendants of Sanyasis or holy men who gave up religious life for marriage, well educated and landowners.	Throughout Tarai	Athit, Yogi, Gosain, Dass, Sanyasi
Rajput	Second highest, Kshatriya Varna, warriors, Descendants of Royal families and Kings. Biggest landowners. Fairly educated. Active in Politics along with Brahmins.	Throughout Tarai	Singh, Chauhan, Tomar, Gaur etc.

(*Contd.*)

1	*2*	*3*	*4*
Kayastha	Generally came in Vaishya Varna, work as Patwaris, clerks, for upper castes. Highly educated, well versed in village affairs.	Throughout Tarai	Srivastava, Saksena, Verma
Marwari	Most important businessmen, shopkeepers, owners of rice mills, industries. Originally from Marwar, Rajasthan India.	Central and Eastern Tarai	Maheswari, Vohra, Jain, Dugar, Sethia
Ahirs	Ahirs are traditionally cow herders, milk and milk product sellers. In Nepal most Tenant Farmers or Landowners. A few are big landlords and Zamindars. They play important role in village and district level politics. Ahirs are the largest caste group in Tarai. Along with Kurmis they are "Yeomen" farmers of region. They are aggressive in seeking education and control of land and definitely succeeded in raising their status. They are descendants of Lord Krishna family.	All over Tarai except Far west	Yadav, Rai, Gwala, Gope etc.

(Contd.)

1	*2*	*3*	*4*
Kath, Rayniyar Agrahari and Bhatara Baniyas	Vaishya Varna, small businessmen, shop-keepers, general merchants, grain merchants, consumer goods, keep business link between Kathmandu and Tarai.	Central and Eastern Tarai Mid-west Tarai	Gupta, Baniya, Vaish, Agrahari, Bhatars etc.
Sonar	Shudra, make jewellery and utensils of gold and silver.	Throughout Tarai	
Barhai	Shudra, make wooden furniture and agriculture tools.	Throughout Tarai	
Patari	Shudra, sell religious object and ribbon, plastic toys and do hawkers job also.	Throughout Tarai	
Mali	Shudras, Gardener, grow and sell flowers.	Throughout Tarai and Far west	
Bhuja	Shudra, fry and sell rice, grams and other food grains sattu.	Eastern, Central and Mid-west Tarai only	
Gorth	- do -	- do -	
Halwai and Kanu	Make and sell sweets. Shudra.	Throughout Tarai	Shah, Sahu, Kanu.
Kairi, Morau	Shudra, grow and sell vegetables but now are tenant farmers and small landowners.	All Tarai except West	Mahto, Chaudhry
Bherihar	Shudra. Sheep herders, makers of wool goods, tenant farmers, small landowners.	East and mid-east Tarai	

(*Contd.*)

1	*2*	*3*	*4*
Gaderia	- do -	- do -	
Kumhar/ Kohar	Shudra. Making clay pots, tenant farmers.	Mid-east, Central and Mid-west	
Nai/ Hazam	Shudra. Barber, tenant farmers, laboureis.	All Tarai	Nai, Thakur
Kurmi	Shudra. Farmers, the largest Hindu caste group in Mid-west Tarai, some are big landowners and Zamindars. They are similar to the Ahirs in economic status and aspirations although their traditional caste-work includes washing dishes, therefore they are regarded lower than Ahirs who deal with cows and milk products symbol of purity.	Mid-east Central and Mid-west	Mahto, Chaudhry
Chanau	Shudra, occupation like Kurmis, tenant farmers.	Central Tarai	
Amat	Shudra. Household servants and those who carry wealthy people in wooden palki, now tenant farmers.	Central, Mid-east Tarai	
Keout	- do -	Eastern Tarai	
Kewat	Shudra. Sail fishing boats, handpoled ferries, fisherman.	Mid-west, Central Tarai	
Bhar	Shudra. Cattle herder. Tenant farmers.	Mid-west	

(Contd.)

1	2	3	4
Malha/ Gorhi	Shudra. Fisherman, tenant farmers, and part time farm labourers.	All over except Far-west	
Majhi	- do -	Far-east	
Dhanuk	Shudra. Household servants, tenant farmers and land labourers.	All Tarai except Far-west	Mandal Dhanuk
Khatwe	Shudra. Does earth work, dig ponds and irrigation canals and road work.	Central, Mid-east Tarai	
Lohar	Shudra, Blacksmiths, tenant farmers or farm labourers.	Throughout Tarai	Lohar Thakur
Kahar	Shudra. Household servants who wash pots and pans different to Kurmis who wash dishes in which people eat. Tenant farmers and labourers.	All Tarai except Far-west	Mahto
Loniya	Shudra. Sell vegetables, tenant farmers.	Mid-west Tarai	
Nuniya	Shudra. Digging of wells and earth work, tenants and farm labourers	Central Mid-east Tarai	
Lahiri	Shudra. Makers of liquor, bangles, now tenants or farm labourers.	- do -	

(Contd.)

1	2	3	4
Chai, Turaha, Tamoli, Tanter	Shudra. General Shudra occupation, now tenants or farm labourers.	Mid-west Turaha in Central	
Dhobi	Untouchable, washer-man and farm labourers.	All Tarai	
Sudi	Untouchable—caste occupation not known, businessmen, prosperous, active politician, they are the best example who have upgraded their caste.	Central, Mid-east Far-west	Sahu, Seth, Shah
Kalwar	Untouchable—caste occupation not known, businessmen, prosperous, active politician, they are the best example who have upgraded their caste.	All Tarai	- do -
Teli	Untouchable—pressers of oilseeds, now small businessmen, land owners, farmers, they are larger groups than Sudi and Kalwar.	All Tarai	Shah, Sahu, Gupta
Dhankar/ Dhaniker	Untouchable. Basket makers, farm labourers.	Mid-east Tarai	
Pasi	Untouchable. Taddy topper, prepares Tarhi.	Mid-east, Central, Mid-west	
Kalal	Untouchables—liquor distiller.	All Tarai except far-west	
Been	Untouchables—Farm-labourers.	Central and mid Tarai	

(Contd.)

1	2	3	4
Tatma	Untouchable, makes mattresses and bed covers and farm labourers.	Central and Mid-east	
Bantar	Untouchable—weavers of straw mats, semi-Hindu, Farm labourers.	Central and Mid-east	
Musshar	Untouchable—Farm labourers, menial workers, semi-nomadic, semi-Hindu.		
Arakh	Untouchable, skinners of dead animals, tanners, shoe makers, sweepers, latrine cleaners.	Mid-west Tarai	
Kori	- do -	- do -	
Chamar	Untouchable—same as above. They are largest group in Tarai among untouchables.	Central and Mid-east	
Dom	- do -	- do -	

Muslims

Caste	Status and Occupation	Location	Last name
1	2	3	4
Sayed Hashmi	High Status. They marry within their own caste, Farmers, land owners.	All Tarai	Syed first names Hashmi in last

(Contd.)

1	*2*	*3*	*4*
Sheikh	- do -	- do -	None
Pathan	- do -	- do -	Mirza, Khan, Beg etc.
Fakir/ Dewan	Higher middle status, descendants of religious leaders. Have religious knowledge, depend on offerings of villagers for food and money.	- do -	Fakir or Dewan
Ansari Jullaha	Higher middle status, marry within their own group, mainly weavers, now farmers also.	- do -	Ansari, Momin
Hazam Thakuri	Middle status, Barbers, now farming, more wealthier, marry among rich men.	All Tarai	None
Chikwa Querreshi	Middle status, butchers. Now farmers, marriage with wealthier stock.	Mid-west Central	Querreshi
Patihar Daffali	Lower middle status, small businessmen, traders, selling threads, needles, ribbons. Now farming like Hazams.	- do -	Deffali
Kawasi	Lower middle status, small businessmen, selling needles, ribbons, fruit vegetables.	All Tarai	Kewasi
Churihar Laheri	Lower middle status, glass makers, bangles, now tenant farmers.	All Tarai	None
Teli	Lower middle status, pressers of oilseeds, small landowners or tenants.	- do -	
Dhuniya	Lower middle status, carders, fluffers of cotton stuffing quilts and mattresses.	All Tarai	

(*Contd.*)

1	*2*	*3*	*4*
Darji	Lower middle status, tailors, now farmers.	- do -	
Kashgar	Lower middle status—technicians.	Mid-west Central	
Halwai	Lower middle status—sweet makers, now farming.	All Tarai	
Rangrej	Lower middle status, dyers, printers of cloth.	- do -	
Dhobi	Lower middle status, washermen, labourers.	- do -	
Gaddi	Lower middle status, cow herders, milkmen.	Mid-west, Central	
Patharkat	Low status, shoe makers, grinder, sellers of stone, recently converted, maintain semi-Hindu traditions.	All Tarai	
Dharikar	Low status—weaver of cane chairs, tables and furniture.	- do -	
Jat	Low status, tenants or farm labourers from western U.P. recently converted to Islam, retain Hindu customs.	Mid-west Tarai	Jat
Natuwa	Low status, recently converted to Islam, farm labourers. They suffer from social disabilities.	All Tarai	
Nut	Very low status, Gypsy like existence, fortune tellers, entertainers, only partly Muslimised, they are not allowed social contacts with other Muslim castes.	- do -	

From the above table it is inferred that among Hindus there are many barriers and ladders in society. Castes are compelled to be carried on and traditional occupations followed. Most of the castes have been put to the Shudra category. It is most unfortunate. Even Ahirs and Kurmis who are real earners and producers of commodities of life have been treated as Shudras in Nepal.

On the other hand Muslims have no so much hatred and they have least divisions. There are only three classes. There is no untouchable. All can dine on one table. They are allowed to change their occupation. They can marry and have good relations with highest class after improving their economical conditions. Their worship place is common. They have freedom for change of trade, occupation, craftsmanship etc.

Position of Hill Castes and Tribes

1. *Brahmins* are the highest respected people with top status. They are found throughout Tarai. Their names are common like Indian Brahmins.

2. *Hill Sanyasi—Athit* come next to Kulin Brahmins, they give names like Giri, Puri, Ban and Bharati etc. They sometimes achieve small lands also.

3. *Chhetri* : Traditional warrior class is second in the Varna ladder. They are landowners, Zamindars. Since they are addicted to liquor and bad habits, their economical condition is deteriorating. They have been rulers like Ranas and the Prime Minister. They are found throughout Tarai. Names are Shat, Shahi, Malla, Rana, Thapa, Vista, Koirala, Pandey, Dhandari etc.

   Newars : It is not possible to categorise the Newars as caste or tribe. They are Hindu and Buddhist both. They are a priest caste and a craftsman caste too. They are also farmers, traders, businessmen. As caste they are absorbed in the business class. They are found across Tarai. Names they keep are Chitrakar, Sakya, Tamrakara, Tuladhar, Manadhar, Ranjitkar.

5. *Charti* are regarded as Shudras and slave class. They are in small numbers across Tarai.

6. *Kumhale* : Shudra, clay pot makers, tenant farmers and landless labourers. Found throughout Tarai, last name—Kumhale.

7. *Majhi* : Shudra—fishermen. Only limited.

8. *Kami* : Untouchable. Blacksmiths. All Tarai.

9. *Sonar* : Untouchable. Hill Sonars have very low status. Throughout Tarai. No surname.

10. *Dansi* : Untouchable, Tailors. All Tarai.

11. *Sarki* : Untouchable, shoe maker. All Tarai.

Hill Tribes

Tribe	*Status and Occupation*	*Location*	*Last name*
1	*2*	*3*	*4*
Tharu	In 1952/54 census there were 3,59,000 Tharus in Nepal. Their ethnic origin is under dispute. They lived in Nepal much before Indo-Aryan race came, upper caste Hindus pushed them to	Throughout Tarai but large number in Far-west Tarai where they are	Tharu Chaudhry

(*Contd.*)

1	2	3	4
	jungles and more hilly terrains. They migrated to Tarai also and are now semi-Hinduised. They speak Maithili, Bhojpuri and Hindi also. Their status among Hindus living in Tarai is very low. There are many sub-divisions like Rana, Dangora Tatheriyas and Donuwars.	more than 90%	
Rajbanshi	This is one plains tribal group which maintains fairly high status. They belong to Jhapa district. They are more sophisticated. Hold grip in the politics of Jhapa district. Farmers and Tenant farmers.	Jhapa and Morang District	Rajbanshi
Sattar/ Santali	Immigrants from Santhal Pargana of Chhota Nagpur. Rice harvesters, small farmers, low status.	Far-east Tarai	Sattar
Pahan	They have also migrated from Chhota Nagpur, have similar status like Santhalis.	- do -	Pahan
Tajpuria	They hold better status and are mainly interested in education, landholders and tenant farmers.	- do -	Tajpuria
Gangai	Are less aggressive and maintain their ancestral land.	South-west corner of Jhapa Dist.	Gangai
Dhangar	Migrated from south India, tenant farmers, landless labourers—low status.	Central Mahottari and Dhanusha District	No name

Hill tribals have a tendency to live at one place. Most of them have selected places where they have concentrated like Tharus in Far-west Tarai, Rajbanshis in Jhapa District, Sattar, Pahan and Tajpuria in Far-east Tarai but at different pockets. So are the Gangais and Dhangars.

Apart from Rajbanshis who have better status, all others are on equal platform. They do not pose their superiority and are also not afraid of their low positions. All do labour, earn a rightful livelihood with honesty and labour.

Like Indian low-castes and tribesmen they have never been subjected to undue religious fanaticism of Hindus. Whether some one gives them right honour or not, is not their concern. They are also now becoming more aggressive like their tribes in India and are trying to be united to fight for the uplift of the whole tribe and other tribal people.

Conclusion

Geographically speaking, Nepal is just part of the Indian sub-continent. Nepal having its head high and facing towards south can be said to look down upon the Gangetic plain. Nepal Tarai is the southernmost region of Nepal and therefore it is the part of Nepal, most intimately associated with India. The Tarai in general is a geographical entity which lies along the southern edge of Himalaya, partly in India and partly in Nepal. It runs approximately a thousand miles from the area where Jamuna river flows and to an area along the Sikkim-Bhutan border. The eastern and central parts of Tarai form the northern edge of Gangetic plain and Eastern Tarai forms the northern edge of Brahmaputra plain.

So being the integral part of Gangetic plain of India the environments, ecological order and socio-political conditions of both countries leave much for investigation as both sides are influenced by the cultural atmosphere of each other. There were many instances and reasons when Indians had to migrate to this part of Nepal and share the socio-economic pattern and polity of Nepal. Therefore, it is imperative to study this fact in the context of India as a neighbour and Nepal as a country on reciprocal friendship.

In 1961 it was revealed by the census that Indian origin people consisted of 29% of the total population of Nepal. Hindus, Muslims, and plain tribals were still living there. Although people of Indian ethnic groups are living within the border of Nepal under the administrative control of the Nepalese Government but many of their economic and cultural ties are with India. Their general orientation is more towards India than Nepal.

Tarai is Nepal's economic backbone and it is producing 59% of the gross domestic product and contributes 76% of Government's revenue. Whatever happens in Tarai influences Indian sub-continent and what effects Indian sub-continent reflects its rays into Tarai also. Therefore, inter-relationship of both plains i.e., Tarai of Nepal and Tarai of India, are good subjects of study.

Under such unique conditions it is a well thought idea to get into the circumstances under which Indian ethnic groups are safely living in Tarai. What is their contribution in the national stream of Nepal ?

How they produce? What they produce ? What is that economic contribution ? What are their socio-political problems and cultural integrity with hill people? All these facts have been discussed in this chapter.

Indicators employed to measure the objective quality of life of Tarai people include the following factors :

(a) Economical well-being,

(b) Education,

(c) Housing,

(d) Health services,

(e) Marital status,

(f) Recreation,

(g) Residence,

(h) Occupation,

(i) Environments and the factors responsible for subjective quality of life entail measuring attitudes towards family life. Value system, preference, beliefs and goals in terms of happiness, satisfaction and a sense of well-being—all these indicators are self-rating measures to determine the general level of satisfaction and feeling of happiness.

Satisfaction depends upon the perceiving relationship between standards and attainments and the feeling of happiness upon one's tone of feeling which vary with mood, place and situation at a particular time.

All these points have been covered in this chapter. Readers will find it most interesting to assess the overall ambit of life prevailing in Tarai and on the Indian side. One can conclude his own way as to whether India-Nepal relations have been reciprocal or there seems some chillied powder between their songs.

Formation of Soils in Tarai-Nepal and Gangetic Plain

Though I have discussed this topic in more than two chapters yet a special mention is necessary here because it relates to ethnic people of Nepal Tarai and Gangetic plain both. Their life style carved due to living in similar condition and similar ecology have been influenced by not only geographical conditions but socio-economic conditions also.

From the altitudinal features of Nepal it is evident that northern edge of Tarai is established by Siwalik range, which is the outer foothill range extension of Himalaya and the last range to be created by immeasurable geological forces that thrust up the Himalaya.[1] The body of the Siwalik is borne out of the frequent earthquakes in the area and by folding action which has not yet completely stopped. This action is pushing up the level of the plains closer to Siwalik thereby creating a gradual slope to the south.

1. The Siwaliks are formed of great thickness (15,000—20,000 ft.) of Micro plestocene, sand, gravels and conglomerates. Obviously the erosion products of Himalaya itself and although not very high (rarely over 3000 ft.) heat striking witness to the extreme youth of a mountain building. From Book of O.B.K. spate, "India and Pakistan—a general regional geography, second ed., London, 1957, p. 19.

Bibliography

ADB/N, "Operational Approaches and Strategies", Agricultural Development Bank, Nepal, Kathmandu, Aug., 1988.

Abullaish, Effectiveness of Local Leadership for Change and Transformation of Rural Society, CEDA, Tribhuvan University, Kathmandu, Nepal, 1982.

Acharya Rajeshwar, *Role of Small Farmer Development Programme in Meeting Basic Human Needs*, CEDA, Tribhuvan University, Kathmandu, 1983.

Agarwal, G.R. et al., *Economic Management in Nepal Lesson of Experience*, CEDA, Tribhuvan University, Kathmandu, 1984.

Agarwal, G.R., *Decentralization for Rural Development in Nepal*, CEDA, Kathmandu, 1986.

Agarwal, G.R., *Development Perspectives for the Most Disadvantaged Groups in Nepal*, CEDA, Tribhuvan University, Kathmandu, 1986.

Agrawal, H. Narayan, *The Administrative System of Nepal: From Tradition to Modernity*, Vikas Publishing House Pvt. Ltd., New Delhi, 1976.

Agrawal, H. N., *Nepal : A Study in Constitutional Change*, Oxford & IBH Publishing Co., New Delhi, 1980.

Amatya, Udaya Bahadur, *Adoption of New Technology and its Social Impact on Rural Communities in Asia*, CEDA, Tribhuvan University, Kathmandu, 1987.

Amatya, D.B., *Nepal's Fiscal Issues*, Sterling Publishers Pvt. Ltd., New Delhi, 1986.

APROSC, *Tarai Agricultural Development Project*, Vol. I, Agricultural Projects Service Centre, Kathmandu, Aug., 1981.

APROSC, *Crop Intensification Programme—Parsa, Bara, Rautahat* (Annual Survey), APROSC, Kathmandu, Nepal, 1985.

ARTEP, *A Challenge to Nepal : Growth and Employment*, Bangkil, 1974.

Bhandari, Bishnu, "Land Ownership and Social Inequality in Nepal Tarai Area". Ph.D. thesis, The University of Wisconsin, Madison, 1985.

Bhandari, Bishnu, "Rural Poverty and the Poor in Nepal : Comparative Case Study of Hill and Tarai Village", Rural Poverty Research Paper Series No. 4, Winrock International, Food and Agricultural Sector in Nepal, Nov., 1986.

Bista, D.B., *People of Nepal*, Ratna Pustak Bhandar, Kathmandu, 1967.

Blaikie, P., et al., *Nepal in Crisis : Growth and Stagnation at the Periphery*, Oxford University Press, Delhi, 1980.

Borgstrom, Bengt-Erik, *The Patron and the Panca*, University of Stockholm, 1976.

Borgstrom, Bengt-Erik, 'The Role of Ideology in Integration and Exclusion: The Case of Sanskritization', *Asian Profile*, Vol. 5, No. 3, June, 1979.

Breman, Jan., *Of Peasants, Migrants and Paupers* (Rural Labour Circulation and Capitalist Production in West India) Oxford University Press, Delhi, 1985.

Burghart, Richard, 'The Formation of the Concept of National State in Nepal', *Journal of Asian Studies*, Vol. XLIV, No. 1, Nov., 1984.

Caplan, L., *Land and Social Change in East Nepal*, University of California Press, 1970.

Caplan, L., Administration and Polities in a Nepalese Town: The Study of a District Capital and its Environs, Oxford University Press, London, 1975.

Chapgain, D.P., *Managing Public Lands as Common Property Resource : A Village Case Study in Nepal*, Ph.D. thesis (Land Resources, University of Wisconsin, Madison, 1984).

CBS, *A Study on the Improvement of the National Sample*, Censuses of Agriculture in Nepal, CBS, Kathmandu, 1986.

CBS, Population Monograph, (Nepal), CBS, Kathmandu, 1986.

CBS, Central Bureau of Statistics, *Statistical Pocket Book of Nepal*, CBS, Kathmandu, 1986.

CBS, *Demography Sample Survey, 1985-87*, First Report, CBS, Kathmandu, 1987.

Chaudhari, K.C., *Anglo-Nepalese Relations*, Modern Book Agency Pvt. Ltd., Calcutta, 1960.

Chauhan, R.N., 'Role of Political Institutions in the Modernization of Nepal', *South Asian Studies*, Vol. 20, No. 1, South Asian Studies Centre, University of Rajasthan, Jaipur, Jan.-June, 1985.

Chhetri, Ram Bahadur, 'Migration, Adaptation and Socio-Culture Change: The Case of Thakalis in Pokhara, Nepal', *Contribution to Nepalese Studies*, CNAS, Kathmandu, Vol. 13, No., 3, August, 1986.

CEDA. *Journal of Economic Development and Administration*, CEDA, Kathmandu, 1978 and onwards.

CNAS, Contributions to Nepalese Studies, 1973 onward, CNAS, Tribhuvan University, 1978 onward.

Dahal, D. Ram, *Indian Ethnic Groups in the Nepal Tarai*, Research Centre for Nepal and Asian Studies, Tribhuvan University, Kathmandu, 1978.

Dasgupta, Jyotinindra, 'Development and Poverty Reduction in South Asia—A Review Article', *Journal of Asian,* Studies, Vol. XLII, No. 1, Nov., 1982.

Das, Lal and Arun Kumar, *Resource Mobilization Through Non-Tax Measures in Nepal,* CEDA, Tribhuvan University, Kathmandu, 1983.

Desai, A.R. (ed.) *Rural Sociology in India*, Popular Prakashan, Bombay, 1988 (Reprint).

Dhar, Asha et al., *Nepal—Lands of Gods, Goddesses and Demons*, Marwah Publications, New Delhi, 1985.

Fox, Jefferson Metz., 'Managing Public Lands in a Subsistence Economy: The Perspective from a Nepal Village', Ph. D. Thesis, University of Wisconsin, Madison, 1983.

Frank, A. Walter, 'Preliminary Report about Researches for an Ethno Demography of the Central Region in Nepal', *Asian Profile*, Vol, 6, No. 5, Oct., 1978.

Furer Hamindorf (ed.), *Caste and Kin in Nepal*, Indian and Ceylon, Asia Publishing House, London, 1966.

Gaige, F.H., Regionalism and National Unity in Nepal, Vikas Publishing House, Delhi, 1975.

Gaige, F.H., 'The Role of the Tarai in Nepal's Economic Development,' Vashudha, Vol. XI, No. 7, Ashadh 2035 (June, 1968).

Gurung, Harka, *Population Increase in Nepal, 1971-1981*, New Era Occasional Paper No. 004, Kathmandu, March, 1982.

Gurung, H.B., 'Geographic Foundations of Nepal' *Himalayan Review*, Special Issue, 1968.

Habib, I., *The Agrarian System of Mughal India*, Asia Publishing House, Bombay, 1963.

Hagen, T., "Observations on Certain Aspects of Economic and Social Development Problems in Nepal", United Nations Report , FAO/NEP/I, 1959.

Hagen, T., *Nepal, the Kingdom in the Himalayas*, Oxford and IBH Publishing, New Delhi, 1971.

Hasel, A.A., Forest Survey Plan for Nepal, U.S. Agency for International Development, Kathmandu, 1962 (Mimeographed).

Hamilton, Buchaman F., *An Account of the Kingdom of Nepal and the Territories Annexed to this Dominion by House of Gorkhe* (Reprint), Manjushree Publishing House, New Delhi, 1972.

Hitchcock, J.T., 'Some Effects of Recent Change in Rural Nepal', *Human Organization*, 22 (I), 1963, pp. 75-82.

HMG, *Madhes Jilla Jiliako Jimidar Patuwari Ka Naunka Swal*, (Regulations for Jimidars and Patwaris in the Tarai Districts), Gorakhapattra Press, Kathmandu, 2012 (1955).

Hodgson, B.H., *Essays on the Languages, Literature, and Religion of Nepal and Tibet*, Trubner and Co., London, 1874.

Husain, A., *British India's Relations with the Kingdom of Nepal (1857-1947)*, Allen and Unwin, London, 1970.

IDS, Rural Landlessness in Nepal, Integrated Development System, Kathmandu, 1987.

Iigima, S., 'Ecology, Economy and Social System in the Nepal Himalaya', *Developing Economics* 2 (I), 91-105.

Jain, G., *India meets China in Nepai*, Asia Publishing House, Bombay, 1959.

Jha, K.K., *Agricultural Finances in Nepal*, Heritage Publishers, New Delhi, 1978.

Joshi, B.L., and Rose, L.E., *Democretic Innovations in Nepal*: A Case Study of Political Acculturation, University of California Press, Berkeley, 1966.

Joshi, S.C. et al., *Nepal Himalaya-Geo—Ecological Perspectives* H.R. Publishers, Nainital, 1986.

Kanskar, V.B.S., 'History of Population Migration in Nepal', *The Himalayan Review* VI (5-6), pp. 56-68, 1973-74.

Kansakar, Vidya Bir, 'Indo-Nepal Migration : Problems and Prospects', *Journal of Economic Development and Administrative Studies*, Vol. II, No. 2, April, 1984.

Karam, Pradyumna, P. et al., Nepal : Physical and Cultural Geography, University of Kentucky Press, Lexington, 1960.

Khanal, Y.N., 'Nepal in 1985: An Uneasy Year', *Asian Survey*, Vol. XXVI, No. 2, Feb., 1986.

Kirkpatrick, Colonel, An Account of the kingdom of Nepal, William Miller, London, 1811.

London, Perceval, *Nepal*, Vol. I & II, Ratna Pustak Bhandar, 1976.

McDougall, C., *Village and Household Economy in Far Western Nepal*, Kirtipur, Nepal, 1969.

Mishra, R.P. and Tri Dung, *Third World Peasantry* : A Continuing Saga of Deprivation, Vol. II, Sterling Publishers Private Ltd., New Delhi, 1985.

Nath, Tribhuvan, *The Nepalese Dilemma 1960-74*, Sterling Publishers Pvt., Ltd., New Delhi, 1975.

New Era, *Study on the Regional Migration in Nepal*, Submitted to National Planning Commission, HMG, Nepal, October, 1981.

Oicles, Gerald, 'Contact, Conflict and Change in Nepal's Eastern Tarai Borderland: Case of Siraha District', Degree Dissertation, Deptt. of Geography, California University, Los Angeles, 1974.

Oldfield, H.A., Sketches from Nepal, 1st edn. with Allen, London, 1880, 2nd edn. Cosmo Publications, Delhi, 1974.

Pant, Y.P., 'Planning and Development in Nepal' in Rana and Malla (eds.), *Nepal in Perspective*, CEDA, Kathmandu, 1973.

Pant, Y.P. and Jain, S.C., *Agricultural Development in Nepal*, Bora & Co., Bombay, 1969.

Parmanand, 'Domestic Conflicts in South Asia: The Nepalese Political System' in Phadnis et al., (eds.) Domestic Conflicts in South Asia, Vol. 3, Asian Political Dimensions, New Delhi, 1986.

Parmanand, 'The Problem of National Integration: The Indian Community in Nepal and the Nepalese Community in India', *Asian Survey*, Vol. XXVI, No. 9, Sept., 1986.

Peritore, N. Patrick, 'Feudalism—Critique of a Model of Society and Political Economy', *Alternatives*, Vol. XII, 1987.

Phadnis, Urmila et al., *Domestic Conflicts in South Asia: Political Dimensions*, Vol.1, South Asian Publishers, New Delhi, 1986.

Poffenberger, M., Patterns of Interaction, Demography, Ecology and Society in Nepal Himalaya, Unpublished Ph.D. thesis, The University of Michigan, 1976.

Ramakant and B.C. Upreti, 'Regionalism in Nepal', in Urmila Phandnis et al., *Domestic Conflict in South Asia: Economic and Ethnic Dimensions*, Vol. 2, South Asian Publishers, New Delhi, 1986.

Rana, P.S.J.B. and Malla, K.P. (eds.), *Nepal in Perspective* CEDA, Kathmandu, 1973.

Rawat, P.C., *Indo-Nepal Economic Relations*, National Publishing House, Delhi, 1974.

Regmi, M.C., Land Tenure and Taxation in Nepal, Vol. I to IV, Institute of International Studies, Unveisity of California, (1963-1968).

Regmi, D.R., 'Ancient and Medieval Nepal', Prem Printing Press, Lucknow, 1952.

Regmi, M.C., *Readings in Nepali Economic History*, Kishore Vidya Niketan, Varanasi, 1971.

Regmi, M.C., *A Study in Nepali Economic History: 1768-1846*, Manjushree Publishing House, 1971.

Regmi, M.C., *Land Ownership in Nepal*, University of California Press, 1976.

Regmi, M.C., Thatched Huts and Stucco: Palaces, Vikas Publishing House Pvt. Ltd., Delhi, 1978.

Robert, K. Boggs, 'The Political Basis of Social Economic Development: The Case of Nepal', Ph.D. thesis, Deptt. of Sociology, University of California, Berkeley, 1982.

Rose, Leo E., Nepal's Strategy for Survival, Oxford University Press, Bombay, 1971.

Sanwal, B.D., Nepal and East India Co., Asia Publishing House, New Delhi, 1965.

Seddon, J.D., et al., *Peasants and Workers in Nepal: The Condition of the Lower Classes*, Aris and Phillips, Westminster, 1978.

Sharma Shankar, 'Growth and Development, Nepal's Economy', *Asian Survey*, Vol. XXVI, No. 8, August, 1986.

Sinha, V.N.P., *Migration*, An Interdisciplinary Approach, Seema Publications, Delhi, 1987.

Singh, Mrigendra Lal, *A Comparative Evaluation of Planned and Unplanned Resettlement in Nepal*, CEDA, Tribhuvan University, Kathmandu, 1984.

Srinivas, M.N., The Remembered Village, Oxford University Press, Delhi, 1976.

Stiller, Ludwig F., *The Rise of the House of Gorakha*, Manjushri Publishing House, New Delhi, 1973.

Stiller, Ludwig, F.S.J., *The Silent Cry : the People of Nepal*, 1816-1839, Sahyogi Prakashan, Kathmandu, 1976.

Upreti, T.P., 'Rural Settlement and Policy Processes', Ph.D. thesis, University of California, Berkeley, 1981.

Weiner, Myron, 'The Politics of Demography in Nepal', Paper presented at Seminar on Population and Development, CEDA, Tribhuvan University, Kathmandu, 1971.

Yang, C. Martin, A Chinese Village Taitou, Shantung Province, Kegan Paul, Trench., Trubner, London, 1947.

Upadhyaya, D.C. and Abueva Jose V. (eds.), *Population and Development in Nepal*, Tribhuvan University Press, Kathmandu, 1975.

Zamam, M.A.,'A Socio-Economic Case for Peasant Ownership in Nepal', Ministry of Agriculture, Kathmandu, 1972 (Mimeographed).

Zamam, M.A., Evaluation of Land Reform in Nepal, HMG, Ministry of Land Reform, Kathmandu.

Index